PETER ROEBUCK

ASHES
—TO—
ASHES

THE 1986–87 TEST SERIES

PETER ROEBUCK

ASHES
—— *TO* ——
ASHES

THE 1986–87 TEST SERIES

THE KINGSWOOD PRESS

The Kingswood Press
an imprint of William Heinemann Ltd
10 Upper Grosvenor Street, London WIX 9PA

LONDON MELBOURNE
JOHANNESBURG AUCKLAND

ISBN 0 434 98088 9

Printed and bound in Great Britain
by Richard Clay Ltd, Bungay, Suffolk

To the good people of Somerset
To friends in the box
To Greg, Jenny, Griffo, ACA, Rod, Al,
Toby, Elizabeth, Vikki,
James and a variety of
Caplices and Remonds
To John, Robin and all the lads at The Sunday Times
for making this trip possible

Contents

CONTENTS

Preface

This book has not turned out as planned. It is not a book which concentrates entirely upon the Test series. Instead it records the experiences I had in a ten-week period as I was travelling around Australia with the pen-party following the England touring team. Australia was not new to me, because I'd taught in Sydney for the previous eight winters, and had long since fallen in love with this vast, open and epic country to which, one day, I may emigrate. I like Australia and I like Australians. It's a land of hope, a land not yet formed, not yet committed in its direction, a land still finding its culture. It is not chained down by the past.

England's tour coincided with several vital issues in Australia, and I have tried to give expression to some of them. The Pope arrived for the first time in sixteen years. In Sydney the British Government was trying to prevent the publication of a book on MI5. Mr Murdoch was trying to seize a huge chunk of the Australian newspaper industry. The Aborigines were still being treated unfairly. The magnificent Tasmanian wilderness was being invaded. Botham signed for Queensland. And Australia had won the Davis Cup. I could not neglect these matters, though no doubt I have not grasped the full significance of all of them.

I hope this book is enjoyable and informative. If it is not, no fault is due to Sandy Grant or Derek Wyatt, friends at William Heinemann, who have done their best. If it is too awful, blame the hurried passing of time and the incompetence of the author.

1

Introduction

FLIES

I can think of no better way of starting the record of one man's winter following the England cricket team around Australia than by repeating Spike Milligan's favourite Australian joke:

> 'A girl becomes pregnant and suggests to her boyfriend that they should get married. "No way" says he, "I'm not the marrying kind".
>
> "In that case" responds the lass, "I'm going to jump off the harbour bridge".
>
> "That's what I like about you, Shirl" says the drunken Aussie. "You're not only a great screw but you're a good sport too".'

This is taken from Mr Milligan's foreword to *The Australian Slanguage*, Bill Hornadge's hilarious study of the Australian language. From this tome, it emerges that the Australian, who speaks without obviously opening his lips at all, does so because he is 'afraid to open his mouth for fear of flies'. So, at any rate, said Judge Sheridan in 1937.

1

In 1629 the Dutch explorer Francois Pelsaert said:

> 'We also found such multitude of flies here, which picked on our mouths and crept into our eyes, that we could not keep them off our persons.'

Australia has had a mild winter and a warm, wet spring, just the conditions for breeding flies. Our mouths will remain shut as much as possible. According to the newspapers, Brisbane suburbs are plagued by blowflies (not Mr Blofeld – though he is there too – but a particularly aggressive fly which can pinch you). Canberra is reputed to be quiet, but Melbourne is full of them, because the winds there have been hot north-westerlies, and as Dr Barton-Brown observed: 'There's an awful lot of Australia north-west of Melbourne.'

Not everyone blames the poor old flies for the habit of speaking through clenched teeth. One chap – Hector Dinning – put the blame firmly upon the weather: 'The slovenly speech of the Australians is no doubt bound up also with the physical lassitude induced by their climate.'

Australians speak with a nasal twang which is sharp and ugly. They end their sentences on the up, whereas the English would tail off. Significantly the rich speak no differently from the poor. Mr Philip Derriman has explained thus:

> 'We don't really know what a good accent ought to sound like. In Britain it is very clear what is a prestige accent and what is not. If you try to speak with a prestige accent in Australia you run the risk of being thought to be "putting on the dog".'

Putting on the dog is resented in Australia, where the anti-authoritarian streak runs deep. The President of the Victoria Football League once attended a dinner in Sydney and asked the steward for a second dob of butter. The steward said 'sorry, it's one dob of butter per person'.

'President	"Do you know who I am?"
Steward	"No."
President	"Well, I'm the President of the Victoria Football League and your guest speaker today. Do you think I could have two dobs of butter?"

Steward	"Do you know who I am?"
President	"You have me at a disadvantage there. I don't know."
Steward	"Well I'm the guy who dishes out the bloody butter."'

EARLY GAMES

Embroiled at Somerset, I did not see the first month's cricket of this tour, and pause only to record the scores in the State matches leading up to the first Test match. Somerset's meeting took place

QUEENSLAND v. ENGLAND, Brisbane
October 24, 25, 26, 27, 1986

ENGLAND

B. C. Broad	c Henschell b McDermott	7	b McDermott	18
W. N. Slack	c Anderson b Frei	1	c Henschell b Frei	0
D. I. Gower	c Ritchie b McDermott	20	(4) c Kerr b Frei	17
A. J. Lamb	b Tazelaar	1	(5) b McDermott	65
M. W. Gatting*	c Kerr b Frei	35	(6) b Henschell	13
I. T. Botham	c Border b Tazelaar	9	(7) c McDermott b Tazelaar	86
J. E. Emburey	lbw b Tazelaar	24	(8) b McDermott	0
P. A. J. DeFreitas	c Kerr b Tazelaar	5	(9) b Hill	22
B. N. French*	not out	11	(3) c Kerr b McDermott	6
N. A. Foster	c Trimble b Henschell	2	not out	74
G. C. Small	c Tazelaar b Henschell	0	c Courtice b Hill	16
Extras	(b 1, lb 6, nb 13)	20	(lb 5, w 1, nb 16)	22
TOTAL		135		339

Fall of wickets: 14, 37, 40, 44, 57, 110, 118, 129, 135, 135.
Second innings: 4, 27, 47, 50, 99, 221, 221, 231, 284, 339.

QUEENSLAND

B. A. Courtice	c Lamb b Foster	70	(2) b DeFreitas	23
R. B. Kerr	c Slack b Gatting	95	(1) c Slack b Botham	8
G. S. Trimble	c French b DeFreitas	24	hit wkt b Botham	17
A. B. Henschell	c Gatting b Botham	3	not out	38
A. R. Border*	c Foster b Small	47	(7) not out	10
P. W. Anderson†	c French b Small	20	c Small b Emburey	9
C. J. McDermott	c and b Small	18		
J. G. Hill	not out	13		
D. Tazelaar	not out	8		
G. M. Ritchie				
H. Frei			(5) not out	52
Extras	(lb 9, nb 4)	13	(lb 6, nb 1)	7
TOTAL	7 wickets (dec)	311	5 wickets	164

Fall of wickets: 154, 188, 204, 204, 251, 284, 291.
Second innings: 18, 36, 65, 139, 150.
Toss: Queensland.
Umpires: M. W. Johnson and C. D. Timmins.
QUEENSLAND WON BY FIVE WICKETS

SOUTH AUSTRALIA v. ENGLAND, Adelaide
October 31, November 1, 2, 3, 1986

SOUTH AUSTRALIA

Batsman	First innings	Runs	Second innings	Runs
A. M. J. Hilditch	c Gatting b Small	11	b Botham	7
A. S. Watson	c Athey b Dilley	9	lbw b Dilley	1
W. B. Phillips	b Emburey	116	c and b Emburey	70
G. A. Bishop	b Edmonds	67	c Edmonds b Emburey	31
D. W. Hookes*	c Whitaker b Edmonds	0	c Richards b Emburey	104
P. R. Sleep	not out	66	b Emburey	27
D. J. Kelly†	c and b Emburey	4	c Gatting b Emburey	5
A. K. Zesers	b Emburey	1	c Edmonds b Emburey	1
T. B. A. May	c Richards b Botham	15	c Athey b Botham	2
S. D. H. Parkinson	not out	11	c Gatting b Dilley	6
P. W. Gladigau			not out	1
Extras	(lb 3, nb 2)	5	(b 4, lb 3, nb 7)	14
TOTAL	8 wickets (dec)	305		269

Fall of wickets: 16, 42, 186, 186, 216, 224, 234, 283.
Second innings: 7, 9, 54, 199, 240, 256, 257, 257, 265, 269.

ENGLAND

Batsman	First innings	Runs	Second innings	Runs
B. C. Broad	lbw b Parkinson	0	c Phillips b Hookes	63
C. W. J. Athey	b Parkinson	18	c Kelly b Gladigau	0
M. W. Gatting*	c Kelly b Parkinson	8	c Kelly b Gladigau	4
A. J. Lamb	st Kelly b Sleep	105	c Sleep b Hookes	55
J. J. Whitaker	c Watson b Parkinson	108		
I. T. Botham	c Hookes b May	70	not out	19
C. J. Richards†	c Hookes b Sleep	24	(5) b Hookes	9
J. E. Emburey	st Kelly b May	4	(7) not out	10
P. H. Edmonds	c Hookes b Parkinson	27		
G. R. Dilley	c Kelly b Sleep	32		
G. C. Small	not out	0		
Extras	(b 5, lb 6)	11	(b 2, lb 2, W 4, nb 1)	9
TOTAL		407	5 wickets	169

Fall of wickets: 1, 15, 38, 210, 294, 325, 347, 407, 407.
Second innings: 7, 9, 54, 199, 240, 256, 257, 257, 265, 269.
Toss: South Australia
Umpires: A. R. Crafter and B. E. Martin.
ENGLAND WON BY FIVE WICKETS

on 8 November. Next day Brian Langford, the retiring cricket chairman, drove me to Heathrow where we were greeted by an ITN camera crew and by an interviewer asking questions about Ian Botham.

I arrived in Australia on Tuesday 11 November, the day when the first Test match was to begin, and began to write immediately. The Somerset business is scarcely referred to here. That is another story and will be told on another day.

England had played numerous matches against both country XIs and State sides. The results, from the more important State

WESTERN AUSTRALIA *v.* ENGLAND, Perth
November 7, 8, 9, 10, 1986

WESTERN AUSTRALIA

G. R. Marsh	b Botham	124	lbw b Small	63
M. R. J. Veletta	c Gatting b Botham	10	c Broad b DeFreitas	2
T. M. Moody	c Richards b DeFreitas	19	st Richards b Edmonds	45
G. M. Wood *	c Botham b DeFreitas	9	c Gatting b Edmonds	53
W. S. Andrews	b Dilley	31	b Edmonds	9
K. H. Macleay	c Richards b DeFreitas	7	run out	10
M. J. Cox †	lbw b Dilley	1	run out	8
T. G. Breman	c Edmonds b DeFreitas	4	c sub (Emburey) b Gatting	0
C. D. Matthews	c Gower b Small	56	not out	3
B. Mulder	not out	1	not out	2
B. A. Reid	b Botham	0		
Extras	(lb 10, w 3)	13	(b 1, lb 4, nb 7)	12
TOTAL		275	8 wickets (dec)	207

Fall of wickets: 30, 66, 102, 163, 176, 185, 190, 274, 275, 275.
Second innings: 18, 90, 164, 178, 186, 196, 202, 203.

ENGLAND

G. C. Small	b Matthews	3		
B. C. Broad	c Cox b Macleay	33	(1) c Macleay b Reid	25
W. N. Slack	b Reid	15	(2) c Moody b Macleay	0
D. I. Gower	b Reid	0	(3) c Wood b Macleay	0
A. J. Lamb	c Wood b Reid	0	(4) c and b Mulder	63
M. W. Gatting *	b Matthews	19	(5) c Wood b Reid	0
C. J. Richards †	c Cox b Reid	3	(6) c Cox b Mulder	17
I. T. Botham	c Reid b Breman	48	(7) not out	40
P. A. J. DeFreitas	c Cox b Matthews	20	(8) not out	3
P. H. Edmonds	b Matthews	1		
G. R. Dilley	not out	1		
Extras	(b 1, lb 1, nb 7)	9	(lb 1, w 2, nb 2)	5
TOTAL		152	6 wickets	153

Fall of wickets: 15, 56, 56, 56, 57, 69, 128, 134, 151, 152.
Second innings: 1, 5, 53, 54, 95, 134.
Toss: England.
Umpires: C. Gannon and P. J. McConnell.
MATCH DRAWN

games were hardly astonishing: a loss by five wickets (v Queens-land), a win by five wickets (v South Australia) and, (v Western Australia) a draw.

BILL O'REILLY

We had a splendid lunch at a seafood restaurant. O'Reilly the Irishman, and Hammond the Scot, whose accent has not softened after eight years in Australia, tease each other mercilessly. O'Reilly is an extraordinary man, as sharp as a buzzard, though eighty years of age. We'd met once before, briefly, in the press-box at the Sydney Cricket Ground. Hearing my name, he'd mumbled about Roebuck Bay in Perth where the first ships had landed – the ships of Captain Dampier. Dampier had landed on some blasted, red-soiled, barren wasteland on the north-west coast of Australia and had named it after his ship before leaving this appalling land, never to return. O'Reilly did not recommend a trip to Roebuck Bay, notwithstanding its distinguished name.

O'Reilly has an acute memory. He talked about Somerset where he'd played in 1938. He remembered the Crown and Sceptre pub, and talked about Wellard, Andrews and Meyer with affection and accuracy. He'd been to Bridgwater, too, to see the canals, and knew far more about the geography and history of the country than I did. Later he broadened his sweep to include the history of England, and then of Australia. He is a Catholic, with a biting wit, who writes with the same aggression with which he once bowled. His fiery catholicism got him into scrapes with the Australian cricket authorities which later used his occasional broadsides and his beer drinking to discipline him when really, he says, it was his religion to which they objected. Since these attacks, and ever since the never-to-be-forgotten omission by Bradman of his old chum Grimmett from the 1938 tour, O'Reilly has attacked officialdom, selectors and pyjama cricket with the same pungent humour.

In the Press Box he sits, wearing the collar and tie of old-fashioned journalism, studying the game, occasionally brightening the room with comments. No batsman wanted to get down Tiger's end.

O'Reilly is an Australian cricketer of the old school. One grand-father arrived in Australia from Ballyconnell in 1865, joined the police force and married a young Irish girl from County Galway who had emigrated in 1860. They lived in the Riverina, a country area of New South Wales. The other grandfather was from Adelaide, where his parents had begun fresh lives with the settlement expedition to Adelaide in 1836, under Governor Hindmarsh. (Adelaide did not evolve as a city; a site was chosen and a city built.)

O'Reilly's father was a teacher in White Cliffs, deep in the bush beyond the Darling River, a place where the crows fly backwards to keep the dust out of their eyes, or so they say. He made his own desks and benches, and had to save money to buy the textbooks (the nearest library was hundreds of miles away in Bourke). Father

O'Reilly had to go three hundred miles to Hay to sit his exams, a journey he completed on a bicycle. This was the first bike ever seen in White Cliffs, and later in life he used to describe the enthusiasm of the crowd of local inhabitants who crowded round to watch him approaching over the flat country in a cloud of dust. At first they thought the distant speck was an outsized kangaroo. On his long cycle ride he had to rely upon boreholes, sunk for the artesian water with which the drovers used to keep their stock alive when droving between Victoria and Queensland. To miss these boreholes was to die; for the sun beat remorselessly every day, and the temperature rose past 100°F.

And all this to sit an exam!

Bill O'Reilly was born in this outpost at White Cliffs and grew up in the bush, moving from White Cliffs to Marengo and then on to Wingello, twenty miles from the town of Goulburn. He had to travel to Goulburn on the train every morning, the paper train it was, and the journey took two and a half hours.

Eventually Bill attended a teacher training college, wasting his time by 'sitting at the feet of false prophets' and 'attending lectures which had no bearing on the realities of teaching life'. It was on his return to Wingello one weekend that he first encountered Bradman. He was told to grab his cricket bag and get to Bowral. O'Reilly reports that this was 'a dreadful mistake'. Early in the game he noticed a diminutive figure approaching:

'What struck me most about him was the difficulty he seemed to be having taking normal steps as he approached. His pads seemed to reach up to his navel. His bat was small and had reached the sere and yellow stage, where the yellow was turning to dark tobacco.'

Twice Bradman was dropped at slip by Selby Jeffery, a railway fettler who'd fought at Gallipoli and who (as was once the custom with country cricketers) used to light a pipe from time to time. Had he fielded anywhere else:

'There would have been a scattering of smoking preparations as he ran. He called out "sorry" after both misses, as if nothing untoward had happened. Selby's dropped catches were part and parcel of the Wingello team's programme. I was probably the only one among us who felt that he might have been able to deny himself just a little longer.'

Bradman scored 234 not out that day. O'Reilly bowled his first ball when the match resumed the following Saturday. These two men, the quiet and ambitious Bradman, the boy from Bowral, and the gregarious and aggressive O'Reilly, the Irishman from the bush, dominated Australian cricket for the next ten years. They were never close friends, any more than were Fingleton and Bradman, but O'Reilly describes the little master as the supreme genius of cricket.

O'Reilly had a talent nurtured in the bush and hardened by the rigour of life. He was left alone to work things out, away from the prying eye of surf and the distractions of the city. With television, and the decline of cricket in the country, these days fewer outstanding cricketers suddenly emerge from some forsaken outpost to shake up the world of cricket. The tradition of cricket in the bush is near its end.

2

Brisbane: First Test

Flew to Brisbane, checked in at the hotel and bumped into Mrs Edmonds. She had lost her press tag (we are issued with silly little things to hang from our belts) and didn't think anyone would take her seriously. Within an hour I'd lost mine. She is writing a book about Australia, confound her. She's spicy, tart in her comments, and doesn't have to play cricket against those she offends. She'll upset everyone because she will be truthful, unflattering and not solemn enough to satisfy the egos of the players and the hype of the promoters.

After unpacking in my comfortable room – how elegantly these journalists live! – I went to the Gabba to watch the teams practising. Both were impressive, particularly the Australians, whose practice under Bob Simpson began at 9 a.m. They looked more disciplined than any Australian team since before the Packer battle. They are not a strong team, but they appeared presentable and pleasant. England were not quite as energetic, though Stewart goaded them on. Apparently spirits had been low a few days earlier in Perth. With Stewart ill and in bed the team had turned up to the game in dribs and drabs, hardly bothering with training.

They'd played badly, nearly losing to the State team. Evidently Gatting was finding it difficult to impose his authority upon his men. He's played under two of them – Gower and Botham – and is not as intelligent nor as experienced as some of his charges. His jaunty manner irritates the more hardened pros, who suspect that underneath the bluff manner there lurks a ruthless and ambitious man. It will not be easy for Gatting to be as much the boss as he likes. The 'for England and St George' stuff is all right for novices. Wily old pros like to do their jobs and to growl. In Perth Gatting informed several newer players that they were leading too hectic a social life. He was wise to be so bold for, as has been observed, 'a good dinner isn't always followed by good cricket'.

Gatting has a certain strength about him. On a previous occasion, before he was captain, he'd raged at a senior player for losing his wicket in an irresponsible way. The player had told Gatting not to speak to him as if he were a child, whereupon Gatting told him that he'd address him as a child so long as he batted like one.

In any event there were signs this morning that Gatting had won the authority he demands. For the time being peace has been declared. If he is to last, England had better win a few games. Gatting has strong men around him, and there are not enough innocent youngsters to act as counterbalance.

David Gower has been in poor form. He bagged a pair in Perth and has apparently been wafting with that olde worlde charm born of browsing through antique shops in Canterbury. There is talk of dropping him. This is palpable nonsense. No doubt Gower, a lovable, harmless man, is more upset than he expected at losing the England captaincy. As a boy at school he'd dreamed, in his vague way, of one day leading his country's cricket team. His leadership was doomed because he did not pay homage to the leader image. Throughout he'd conducted himself in a subdued manner laced with a sardonic sense of humour. Journalists, spectators, players wanted him to be forceful, and he was flip. They wanted him to deliver orations and he preferred wry comments. And so his boyhood fantasy was snatched away from him, and in an insensitive way at that. He'd minded it more than he'd expected. Now they are saying he must be dropped altogether.

This is nonsense. Being dropped and rested is, like getting a hiding at school, the sort of thing that sounds a pretty good idea for everyone else. Gower has scored two thousand runs against

10

Australia at an average of forty-five. Gooch has one thousand runs at twenty-seven, Lamb six hundred and seventy at thirty-nine. Gower has scored five centries against the old enemy, as many as Barrington and Cowdrey. He does whiff and waft on occasions, but his record bears the closest scrutiny. If he is playing badly his problem might be technical rather than psychological. In cricket each can lead to the other, as failures heap up. Each misfortune may be the product of imprecise footwork, but each one stirs the remembrance of past failures, of past journeys to the grim reaper of cricket. Suddenly in desperation, the player, his game no longer reliable, tries something different. He tries to smite his way out of trouble. He tries to block his woes away. Neither approach works and, because both are different, comrades shake their heads at this apparent loss of nerve. They see the itching, and conclude that a failure has not been borne with fortitude. Maybe Gower needs a few quiet words of encouragement. Maybe he needs to be told to move his back foot into line. A couple of sweet strokes past point and those questions will be answered. Failure is a miserable, lonely business.

This should be an excellent series. Already Brisbane is bubbling like soup upon a cauldron. At the Gabba there were lots of cameras, dozens of reporters, and an excitement indicating that an Ashes series is about to begin and that it matters. Throughout Australia people will tune in to their radios to find out the score. In England lads will be awoken from their deep slumber by alarm clocks. They'll tune in their radios to hear about events in distant Brisbane. On cold English mornings they'll huddle under their eiderdowns and listen to Christopher Martin-Jenkins as he talks of Border and of Gatting, describing each ball as it is bowled those thousands of miles away. It should be a good series, though it is for the wooden spoon.

Australia has improved of late. Border's team played well in India a month ago, tying one Test match and drawing the other. Between them Border and Simpson have built a team spirit which might, with luck, help them to regain the Ashes. Australia's batting has improved in the eighteen months since the last battle for them. In England their batting was opened by Graeme Wood, who was a perilous runner and a fragile batsman, and by Andrew Hilditch, who was a dedicated cricketer undone by his penchant for the hook shot. A batsman is as good as his weakest stroke.

11

Now Boon and Marsh are the openers. Oddly neither opened for his State when chosen to face the new ball for his country. They've been an effective pair, averaging eighty as a partnership against New Zealand and India last year. Blindly prejudiced against rotund men who swill lots of beer, I had thought little of Boon when first he appeared. Sir Len Hutton was more perspicacious. He wrote:

> 'Boon appears to be a most contented cricketer. I can visualise him on a sheep farm in Tasmania, sipping lager on the verandah, the ideal temperament for dealing with fast bowlers.'

Boon is robust rather than rotund, and Border relies heavily on him. He's from Tasmania, and when he bats it's as if he's standing up for all the small and put-upon nations on this earth. Australians forget to include Tasmania in their map and this does not please the locals.

His partner, Geoff Marsh, doesn't like losing his wicket either though, in his case, this is because he was raised in Wandering, a tiny outpost in Western Australia where there are three hundred and sixty-four people and only three buildings (a mini-Calcutta, in fact). He learnt to bat on his father's bowling machine, and in the winter he still works as a farmhand. These things bring balance and patience. Australian outback farms are rugged places. Every year I used to spend a week on one, working with a friend to bring in the harvest: we rose with the sun and slept with the dusk, a few beers having been supped in-between. These farms are huge, and most farmers have motorbikes on which they scurry around mending fences. On this friend's farm, which was as efficient as Gower's footwork, they preferred to ride horses yet seemed to spend most of their time with their heads in engines, trying to work out why another machine had conked out.

Nor were the combine-harvesters as primitive as might be expected. One of Australia's favourite myths is the gnarled, hatted farmer toiling away under the burning sun. Even on this idiosyncratic farm the harvesters were air-conditioned and had cassette recorders in them. They harvested eighteen hours a day when the wheat was dry, with strong headlights pointing the way, but worked in shifts and did not appear to be all that heroic.

The rest of the Australian team is young, and the batting appears stronger than the bowling. Dean Jones is to bat at first wicket down. He is a combative, talented, occasionally rash player, who has a lean and hungry look and a fanatical gleam in his eye. He scored two hundred in the tied test in Madras during which innings he was giddy and sick, the after effects of a local curry. He can be heroic, though perhaps this is a weakness too, for a man may try too hard to be heroic. Border bats at four, the best player on either side, and Ritchie, a second beer-barrel of a man, another with a round body and suspicions of a lazy mind, is at five. He is a nonchalant, amiable batsman, a player of high class though not yet high achievement. Apparently he is also amusing company, and certainly Border sets great store by him.

Steve Waugh bats at six, a twenty-one year old burdened with the weight of being hailed, not least by Bill O'Reilly, as the rising star. He is talented (so is his twin brother) but at present he is more the germ of a player than the reality.

Australia's folk hero, Greg Matthews, is to bat at seven. Matthews took five wickets in that famous tied test, and he scored hundreds of runs last year at vital times. He is a gutsy, percolating cricketer who has no peculiar talent but lots of application. He too is valued by Border, for he has rescued Australia in times of trouble (and there have been plenty). Like most simple, unanalytical men, Border is deeply loyal. Whether he is wise in his judgement, time will tell. Matthews will bowl a bit too, though he is, like Waugh, a part-time bowler.

Matthews is at present milking his status as a folk hero, and this week his face peers apologetically from the front of a plush yuppy magazine. He can scarcely avoid this notoriety, but it puts a pressure upon him for which he may not be ready. Usually a cricketer is top-class before he is exposed on the commercial stage. Australia is so short of cricketing heroes that Matthews has been plucked from the pack and paraded as if he were the future. He has spiky hair, wears an earring occasionally and jumps around on the field as if he were still at last night's disco. He is an engaging, disreputable character who already has a manager, an agent and a biography. He may be gathering the accoutrements of stardom before he obliges on the field, and this is bound to add to the pressure upon him. He remains a gutsy though essentially ordinary player, and this dash for dollars will not help him if he fails.

13

The rest of the Australian team is made up of Zoehrer, a country wicket-keeper who can bat; Reid, a fastish bowler with a brutal bouncer who does not like being regarded as a strike bowler (he sees himself as a grafter); Hughes, a friendly soul who is not as fast as his bristling moustache might suggest; Chris Matthews, a novice left-armer – England is supposed to have a weakness against left-armers, an impression created because wickets in State games have been lost to left-handed bowlers (who have bowled all the overs); and Geoff Lawson, a good bowler whose fitness is in doubt.

This is not an impressive team, and was it facing formidable opposition no-one would consider its chances to be good. Yet Australia begins this Test match as favourites, at least in the eyes of the travelling reporters, who have condemned England's efforts so far on the tour. England had batted, bowled and fielded badly and had little chance in Brisbane, so they said. The team was, in theory, experienced and accomplished and included one of the greatest ever cricketers as the all-rounder, yet it has shown little form and less unity. None of the openers, Broad, Slack and Athey, have scored any runs, Gower has been laid back, Gatting has failed, and only Botham and Lamb have been reliable. So dire is England's batting that the selectors have chosen Jack Richards to keep wicket, largely on the strength of his potential with the bat. This leaves Bruce French as second wicket-keeper once again, and everyone sympathises with this patient, level-headed fellow who must have thought that, finally, his chance had come.

For England the only ray of hope has been the form of Phillip DeFreitas, a vivacious cricketer who has bowled at a rare pace in State games. He has made friends with Ian Botham, who likes to have around him people he can call lunatics, friends with a sense of fun and a willingness to be enterprising. DeFreitas admirably fits the bill. He is a good cricketer and a bold choice for this first Test match between two embattled teams, one of which will be hailed as vastly-improved as a result of winning this Ashes series.

Much will depend, as usual, on Botham. England plays differently when he is absent, sometimes well, as in India in 1984 (a side the players still remember for its camaraderie and its teamwork), sometimes badly as in the series with India and New Zealand last summer. Here in Brisbane in November, Ian Botham is steeling himself to score a century. He's only scored one Test hundred in Australia before, and is to play for Queensland here next year. No one man in cricket is more certain of scoring a hundred when his mind is set upon it, not even the great Richards. To Botham these things are acts of will-power. He has an extraordinarily strong will which, if he uses it, which he does when he's been crossed, rarely fails. For the last few years he's been hitting hundreds for losing teams, a fact that puzzles him. He is here to do well, and to win the Ashes on his last tour for three years.

In the afternoon I attended my first ever press conference. It will possibly be my last. We sat around a pool, and Gatting wisely reacted to significant questions with inane answers. A couple of cunning journos (in Australia journalists and garbage-men are abbreviated – which is intended to put the garbage-men in their place) asked questions phrased so that any answer gave them a headline:

'Do you consider dropping Gower?'

If 'Yes', we have 'Gower on the brink' or 'Gatting guns for Gower'. If he says 'No' we have 'I'm right behind Gower, says Gatting'.

He was obtuse, dull and spent his time reading a copy of *The Cricketer*. In other words, he conducted the press conference with aplomb, addressing not the brightest, most responsible reporters, but the most stupid, for fear of the headlines they could write. Gatting is not a man of books, and he treats journalists as if they, rather than their newspapers, were a chocolate short of the full box.

DAY ONE

Arrived at the ground early for the start of the Chase for the Ashes (Channel 9 likes slogans) and moved around as the day began to find its shape. In 1932, the Bodyline series, two English journalists were considered sufficient, and they didn't know anything about the game. Now, particularly in Australia, every paper and television channel is represented. It isn't quite the same in India, where one or two journalists, working under a variety of names, serve a remarkable number of masters. Since those days, Henry Blofeld, and the ubiquitous couple Rutnagur and John Thicknesse, have led more monogamic lives. One day, when a nation's papers are owned by two press barons, the press-boxes will again be empty.

The reporters arrived early to claim their places for the match (upon the same basis the Aborigines will have no trouble reclaiming their land). Throughout the day the Australian reporters hovered by their phones, popping out only to grab a cup of coffee. They have to file their reports at close of play, whereas the English reporters enjoy the rare luxury of having several hours to compose their pieces before ringing them through. The reporters on evening papers watch hard, typing at their word-processors or ringing their reports through. They are called 'bleeders' because they are committed running copy men who add paragraphs to their pieces every hour in time for the next edition as blood drops from a rubber tube.

None of the Australian writers, except Mungo MacCallum of the *Financial Review*, moved during the day. In Australia the tradition is to report the facts with a piece catching the general drift. Off-beat writing is done, not by the reporters, but by men sent specifically to write colour pieces. The English writers were different; though the tabloid men sat stoically in the box, most of the broadsheet journalists wandered around, getting the feel of the place. John Woodcock of *The Times* and Scyld Berry of *The Observer* were particularly keen to avoid the consensus in the box by finding spots from which to take a fresh view.

As the reporters met there was a sense of camaraderie. Evidently the press-box is richer in character than the team. Henry Blofeld breezed in, his booming voice calling 'good morning, my dear old things' echoing through the rafters. Blofeld is a considerable hero in Australia; once a part of the Hill was renamed by its inhabitants the 'Henry Blofeld stand'. Blofeld has milked his reputation with great effect. An incorrigible rogue, his well-spoken Old Etonian character is immensely popular. Listeners can tell that he doesn't stay at some shoddy little dive, and enjoy his sense of wealth and fun. An image persists of Henry cracking champagne bottles and entertaining blondes until the early hours, and arriving at the ground with a stinking headache. Really, of course, he snuggles up every night with a hot-water bottle, reading one of the novels of William Makepiece Thackeray.

Besides firing out articles with the alacrity of a cavalry officer leading a charge, Blofeld is also working for Mr Packer on his new radio station, which is offering a rival commentary to the more serious ABC. Packer, eager to get his pound of flesh, has told his television commentators to help Blofeld and his team and throughout the day – Greig, Benaud, Max Walker, Willis, Lawry the pigeon-fancier and Ian Chappell – climbed up the metal stairs to a loft above the press-box, where their radio station has is microphones.

Frances Edmonds turned up too, as determined to use her colourful Englishness as Blofeld. These two conform to the Australian impression of the rich landed gentry of England, and both thoroughly enjoy Australia's interest in them. Probably they feel freer to be outrageous here where people do not resent the shameless display of wealth. Men like Alan Bond, the man whose money and yacht brought the America's Cup to Perth, make no effort to hide their vast richness; rather they celebrate it as they are expected to do. In England the rich are sometimes embarrassed and embarrassing (picture the awful Sloane Rangers). In Australia the outlandish is expected of them, particularly if they are of the new rich which has fought its way up.

In a way, this is why Botham is hoping to play for Queensland. James McClelland has written that Botham:

'puts sport in its place and takes it out of the realm of being a sacrament. In his time off he does not deny himself any of the extroversions which "dedicated" sportsmen are said to eschew. But that does not prevent him from being better than all of them.

'At the risk of being jailed for treason I must say that our own great treasure, Don Bradman, was a dreary conservative, who, after amassing all those runs, settled in Adelaide as a stockbroker and amassed a great many more dollars than runs. All of his public utterances have been notably conformist.'

This is the image the Australians like: Botham as cavalier, leading a wild life in private and rising to smash them on the field notwithstanding that he's suffering from an almighty hangover. This is how Botham sees himself, a Goliath brought down by dull conservatives, whose idea of fun is to buy a pint of lager and lime.

Moreover, Australia's approach to sport will please Botham. Here it is a matter of great import. Though the sportsmen are not expected to be serious, their sports are treated with sobriety. When Border hits a hundred to save his team, responsible papers print headlines saying 'Border saves a Nation's Pride'. (The Australians used precisely this headline a fortnight later.)

In any event, Woodcock arrived – 'Good morning, Wooders old thing' said Blofeld – and so the match could proceed. Its first moments recalled the television advertisement here, in which beer is sold by men singing patriotic songs (not exactly I'm a lumberjack and I'm O.K., but pretty close) or the ones in which car salesmen scream that they have a deal waiting just down the road that is absolutely perfect for you.

I watched the toss from the far side of the ground where I was guided to a seat by a Chinese gentleman wearing a bow-tie, formal clothes and a straw hat. The captains strode out in their blazers, which was predictable from Gatting and surprising from Border. Despite the gentleman from China, Australians are not as devoted to blazers as are the English. They are not as convinced, as are certain English committees, that the world will be put to rights if everyone would only dress properly. This is not a stuffy country. In cricket clubs most people bat in the order of their arrival. In England they bat in order of seniority.

As Border and Gatting strode to the middle, they found a bright-looking chap with a microphone awaiting them. This bright-looking chap managed to remain no less eager throughout the day. His job, evidently, was to sell to the spectators the idea that something momentous was about to take place. As Border flipped the coin he followed the action rather as a patriotic commentator might follow a particularly exciting royal wedding:

> 'The call was heads ... it's fallen TAILS ... AUSTRALIA has WON the TOSS [cheers]. Captain ALLAN BORDER [cheers] has asked England to bat [hooray]. Lawson and Small are the twelfth men [puzzled pause].'

Quite what Warwick Armstrong or Douglas Jardine would have made of this we can only wonder. Not every captain would avoid thrusting this gentleman's microphone down his throat. Nor could his vibrant words conceal the fact that Border had taken two gambles. He'd left out Lawson, his only experienced bowler [one hundred and forty-five Test wickets] and preferred Hughes, Reid and Chris Matthews [nine Tests and twenty-two wickets between them]. Lawson is a man of idiosyncratic temperament, but he should not be in the twelve if he is not fit, and since he must be fit he ought to have played in the first game of a series, particularly if the captain intended to field first.

Border's second decision must have been a close thing too. England had been batting badly, and maybe this was the chance to seize an early advantage in the series. Gatting, advised by Botham and Tony Greig, intended to bat first partly because the wicket was not nearly as green as it had been the day before, and partly because Tasmania, put in by Border a fortnight earlier, had made five hundred and twenty-six. Maybe Gatting also remembered Sir Len Hutton's rueful comment after asking Australia to bat first in 1954 and seeing them score six hundred:

'Pitches are like wives, you can never tell how they're going to turn out.'

Border knew that in the previous eight Tests at the Gabba, the captain winning the toss had bowled first seven times, and on six of these occasions his team had been victorious.

As it turned out there was nothing much in the pitch, which was fresh rather than moist. Its surface greenness was misleading for grass cuttings had been rolled into a rock-hard square. It'd be a good pitch from first to last, and might be at its fastest on the second and third days.

Border's bowlers let him down. They bowled too short. A year earlier Hadlee had taken 15 for 123 on just such a pitch, though in hotter weather. He'd hardly bothered with the bumper, concentrating upon swing and movement. Hadlee has a command of the techniques of bowling, an understanding of the physics of the business. These Australians are raw, hardly out of school as bowlers, and they do not know anything of swing. (O'Reilly and Bedser argue that the spin imparted upon the ball creates a disturbance in the air, and that the spin acts as a rudder, guiding the ball in the opposite direction to that towards which it is spinning.) Modern professionals are young, and good at bowling a line in one-day games. Our game is short of expertise, particularly in bowling. These Australians raced in with gusto, bowled with their hearts rather than their brains, expressing virility rather than intelligence. Merv Hughes, all Mexican moustache, padded in over after over banging the ball short of a length at the off stump. Sometimes, searching for elusive movement, he angled the ball to leg. For the most part he allowed the batsman to play back, adjusting to whatever movement he could goad from the pitch. He never flagged and never really threatened either.

Bruce Reid, a slim, spindly man of 6′8″ had lost a lot of weight in India a month earlier. Rather like Tony Hancock in *The Blood Donor*, Reid does not have an ounce let alone a stone to spare. Last year he was introduced into Test cricket as an accurate bowler at a sharp pace who could deliver a lethal bumper. In Brisbane he had lost some of his penetration and some of his accuracy, so that he was a blunt instrument in Border's armoury. His other fast bowler, Chris Matthews, bowled a series of dangerous deliveries and mixed them with a lot of inaccurate balls. He did swing the ball and might have taken several wickets. As it was, England had lost only two wickets when rain and bad light curtailed play.

Border must have been depressed by the failure of his bowlers. This battler from Mosman stayed loyal to Australian cricket when others fled to the veldt. He did not join the World Series, survived playing under Yallop and Hughes (whose boyish face predicted those tears), and has been captain of a moderate team for the last few years, a team beaten by New Zealand, by England, by the West Indies; a team which managed to draw with India. He must have hoped that the last tour had brought a maturity to his players so that every game would not depend almost entirely upon his contribution. Border has been saving Australia for years, standing defiant behind his beard, his chiselled face chewing gum, a pugnacious democrat resisting the patrician English. For eighty-five Test matches he has fought under his green cap to protect what is left of Australian cricket.

As it was, as things began to go wrong on the field. He looked like a crest-fallen schoolmaster irritated at having to teach his charges the rudiments of mathematics. Throughout this sorry day he stood in the slips, scarcely talking to his bowlers, waiting for wickets to fall, trusting in their intelligence and their professionalism. Perhaps there was nothing much else he could do. These men were bowling for Australia. If they cannot bowl properly, if they are not versed in the craft of cricket, there is no magic wand that can be waved.

As he walked around the field, Border must have despaired of his chances of ever leading a good Australian team. As a catch was dropped he must have felt like shouting, as did one captain before him:

'Why didn't you keep your eyes open, you bloody great ostrich?'

Whether or not Border has an analytical eye for the game is another matter. Though he is so easily Australia's best cricketer he may not be able to detect weaknesses in a batsman. Yet Hadlee had painted the way. He'd studied the English batsmen, pin-pointed their faults, and probed them as incessantly as a grumpy dentist. He'd seen that Gatting was weak against inswingers, which he liked to cut and square-drive. Relentlessly Hadlee angled the ball into his body. He'd noticed that Gooch and Gower drove without moving their feet, so he offered balls to drive, at the last moment darting the ball away from the swinging bat. To Lamb he bowled off-cutters, and to Athey he tried to move the ball away, searching for an edge. Border had been in England last summer and must have watched some of the Test matches on television, yet his bowlers pitched short to Gatting, and fed Athey's penchant for leg-side strokes. Maybe Border felt that his men had to learn the hard way. Maybe he agrees with Gilbert Jessop:

> 'Don't give advice to a batsman going in. If he's inexperienced, it will only make him nervous; if he's an old hand, it is generally unnecessary. Give him credit and opportunity to use his own judgement; he he doesn't do so at first, he soon will.'

Either Border cannot analyse accurately, or he expects his bowlers to mature through their mistakes.

For England, Bill Athey played a most important innings. His colleagues have at their command an array of aggressive strokes. If the ball is softened, or if the bowlers are tired, they will score heavily. Their defences are less secure, and if Australia had taken early wickets a collapse might have begun. Athey batted throughout the day to score seventy-six runs, easily his highest score in his sixteenth Test innings. He played with a straight bat from first to last, particularly in the back defence which he was allowed to use far too often. He holds his side-on position more rigidly than any of the other English batsmen, and in his innings he combined a Boycott's dedication with a pleasant temperament. He probably didn't expect to play, not having scored any runs on tour. Had be but known it this guaranteed his place under the Wayne Larkins school of thought. His innings has had a profound effect upon the game and the series, halting the cocksure step of the Australians.

Gatting batted at first wicket down, marching to the crease

when Broad fell. He is determined to impose his authority upon the team, and this brave move will help. He's eased the burden on Gower, allowing his old comrade to step down the order, and at the same time he's shown a willingness to lead by example. After a nervous start he began to play with the chirpy arrogance he displays with Middlesex, and it was a surprise when, after feeding on the short pitches of the Australian bowlers, he was bowled off his pads.

Lamb and Athey took England safely to the close, and there was a spring in their step as they left the field. Around the ground, in the stands named after politicians (a warning sign this: in healthy States top sportsmen are honoured at the grounds they graced), spectators huddled in groups. There were only eight thousand present and, being Australians, they chose to pack together, a tribute to their tradition of mateship. In England, everyone would have kept at arms-length, frostily sipping coffee and reading their *Daily Telegraphs*.

It was sad to see the ground only half full. Apparently no tickets are available for the one-day game when the jamboree arrives in January. One day people will be sated by the induced demands of these games. At present they slog along on a wave of hype and hysteria, filling stadiums with patriotic songs. A generation of supporters is being reared to follow only one-day cricket, pop cricket. Maybe they do not any longer have the patience to watch a Test match's symphonic movements. So often the early stages of a Test are its most interesting moments, before the game fritters away and is drawn. Only cricket can build up towards an anti-climax with such seriousness. Though it is the most popular form of the game it is held in undisguised contempt by the players. It is time to step back and to consider what we are doing to our cricket. In one-day cricket you cannot, as did Charles Wright once, turn around and say 'that was a good'un – for a trial ball'!

Up in the members' stand the old stagers sat and talked about humorous and sad days. To them the Test match was a backcloth, a fascinating and aesthetic backcloth, against which old friends met. They growled at the bowlers and did not miss a ball. This is the essence of cricket, and to pretend otherwise is to harm a precious game. Today's cricket was intense, and to the connoisseur every ball was vital as the game, with its duels of character and craft, began to take its shape. Meanwhile, between overs, a voice sang

'I must say your scones are absolutely bonza.'

DAY TWO

On the way to the Gabba this morning my taxi driver said that Botham was bound to score a century. He'd seen him in the lobby and remarked upon his aura of confidence.

He was right. Upon the early dismissal of Lamb and Athey, Botham strode assuredly to the wicket, his strangely straw-coloured hair blowing behind him. For once he took the trouble to play himself in, reconnoitring his enemy when usually he sends the bombers straight in. He has a superb defensive technique when he cares to use it, and scarcely missed a ball early in his innings. He collected a few singles, unleashed an occasional thunderous drive and built his score.

Suddenly, just before lunch, as if a switch had been pressed, he began to attack, slicing Hughes over third man for six, hooking off his eyebrows for another six, pulling a four and then slicing another swashbuckling drive to the point boundary. In this mood Botham ruins a bowler's confidence by hitting him off his length so that, desperate to dismiss this fiend quickly, he searches for yorkers and bumpers, which Botham turn into half-volleys and long-hops.

He did miss one stroke in that alarming over, an appalling heave which caused the laconic Gower to admonish him, which was a bit like being ticked off for profligacy by the Emperor Bokassa. Border reacted to this assault by dropping his field back, allowing Botham to move towards his hundred with easy singles and a few spirited twos. Botham can run hard and fast, and would be a fearful sight on a rugby field. This tactic of giving away runs rarely works. It cannot be wise to concede so much in Test cricket.

Botham reached his hundred with a clout over the bowler's head, and immediately waved his bat to express his huge delight. He feels a surge of excitement when he succeeds and was thrilled with this hundred. He had batted for two hundred and seventeen minutes and had faced one hundred and fifty-six balls. It had been an innings of authority, and it ended when as England went for runs, he mishooked Waugh to long-leg. He was given a standing ovation. This is Botham at his best, massive and secure. His back foot shots were as perfect as Hammond's. He is more erratic off the front foot than is recommended in the books, but then he is also a wicket-taker and can afford these little extravagances.

This was an innings directed as much at the Somerset captain, as he walked around the ground wearing his straw hat (Papua New Guinea out of Woolworth's), as at his Australian opponents.

Gower batted beautifully too, scoring fifty-one runs before losing his wicket to a catch at mid-wicket off a hard pull. David was dropped on nought, another of those wafts, and got his first run only through a sloppy bit of fielding. Slowly his form returned, though he still shuffled about occasionally, each time looking back to the slips with the air of a child caught stealing an apple. Frances Edmonds says she feels like mothering him. Phil Edmonds says few people ever recover from his wife's attentions and has advised her to leave well alone. David is a charming man and a lovely player, and on these grounds alone must not be lost, not even in this pragmatic era. He must try to score some runs though. The appearance of beauty is not enough; he must be effective.

Incidentally, Frances appeared this morning. Willis had said on television that no-one was talking to her. I said I was. She said that was because no-one was talking to me either. She was off to see the Lady Mayor of Brisbane, and then to see an Aborigine, if she can find one still alive in Queensland.

At stumps the Australians were in disarray, undone by Athey's diligence and Botham's belligerence. After two days of a series intended to last twenty-five they are in trouble, the doubts returning after the good work in India. Already they are groggy, ready for a knock-out punch. Australians are less dangerous when they are on the defensive. They are taught to attack and to win, and so far in Brisbane they have not known how.

DAY THREE

Australia, favourites to win the match at its outset, were by the close of play following on. Dilley and Emburey took the wickets, though it was Edmonds who dismissed the mighty Border, who advanced down the pitch to slog him into Timbuktu, and edged a catch to DeFreitas at point. Edmonds annoys Border. He is regal where Border is efficient, disdainful where Border is unpretentious. Border tries to smite him occasionally, did so once in 1985, and has twice paid the price for this rare failure to play the ball on its merits. Greg Matthews resisted England's intelligent attack upon his leg-stump (a great deal more thought had gone into the English approach to the game) and nearly took Australia to safety, but ran out of partners, and left the field deeply disappointed despite his brave fifty.

Dilley was the pick of the bowlers, using his new short run, and bowling a tight line and length with occasional away-swing and variation of pace. He troubled all of the Australians with his movement, for none of them is as side-on as Athey and they prefer to hit to leg against the swing than to off with it. Dilley has had a strange career, one minute the Viking raider, the next introspective and unhappy. He has not yet etched his place in the Test match record books as a strong, aggressive fast bowler. Probably he has tried too hard to be fast and not hard enough to be good. He is not by temperament a hostile man, and his Nordic looks belie an insecure personality. His bowling action has changed several times, as the coaches at Kent have sought pace and reliability; now it is up to him to show that he is in command and ready to replace Willis as England's leading strike bowler.

Dilley did bowl well, firing the ball down the corridor of uncertainty (even bowling at the off-stump has been Americanised), troubling the resolute Marsh and returning with courage to shake up the long and incompetent Australian tail. Emburey was the other main threat, drifting the ball to his slips, never letting the batsman loose. He played on the nerves of the young Australians, who were not certain whether to attack him as a spinner or to defend stoutly in their nation's cause. Jones and Waugh, intemperate and impatient, tried to dictate and perished. Caught between the two they crumpled and shortly before 6 p.m. Marsh and Boon had to return to the crease, once more to face Dilley with the new ball.

For England this was a rare experience. They'd been embarrassed by the maturity of New Zealand and India and had been slaughtered in the Caribbean. They will enjoy the boot being on the other foot. Before each day's play they practice their fielding, and they work hard as a team. Botham is being well used too, bowling only when he's dangerous, when the force is with him. By choosing Edmonds and Emburey, and by piling on the runs, England can stay in command on the field when Dilley and DeFreitas are resting (not that they showed any shortage of stamina today). It is much more difficult, at this stage, for the Australian batsmen to make runs than it is for the Englishmen.

England were impressive in the field. Somewhere over the Nullabor they'd found their resolution, a quality absent at times this year. Presumably they were displeased to read that they couldn't bat, bowl or field: Martin Johnson the cricket correspondent of *The Independent* had uttered this immortal line that there were only three things wrong with England. To win this game they worked out a plan and so far they have stuck to it. They realised that the batsmen were uneasy in defence and Gatting asked his bowlers to bowl maidens, and not to let the batsmen off the hook. They were to put the pressure on the Australians so that they could not dominate. Ever-irreverent Edmonds has played to this plan, setting an old-fashioned defensive field and asking the batsmen to try to break out. He let the Australians get themselves out, and they obliged.

Botham did his stuff too, pitching the ball up and varying his swing rather than his length. He is helping DeFreitas, who was simply marvellous in his enthusiasm, has taken him under his wing and is showing him the way. DeFreitas has brought life to the most bloody-minded of the cricket professionals, and it is healthy for Botham to guide him. It is better for him to have a protégé than lots of bosom pals. As long as DeFreitas has the sense to plough his own furrow he can benefit from this friendship with the great all-rounder.

I rang my article through to the *Herald* (I'd been working for *The Sunday Times* yesterday). Australian papers are rather different, State papers for the most part and appealing to a wide public in order to survive. The *Sydney Morning Herald* is the best paper in Australia, with *The Age* (which it owns through a subsidiary and which makes thirty million dollars a year, largely because it has cornered the Wednesday and Saturday classified's market). Yet a story goes that when Neville Cardus rang an article through to the copy-taker he was interrupted in mid-sentence by the news that

'We don't have any semi-colons in this paper Mr Cardus.'

to which Sir Neville replied

'What to you want me to do, send you some?'

Paragraphs tend to be mere abrupt lines, following the Australian tradition of barracking and bagging. Australians do not mince words and do not want the point to be lost in long involved paragraphs. When, years ago, Mr Packer bought an evening paper, he told his editors on no account to allow a sentence of more than seven words to appear in it. He'd allow nine words in an especially complicated feature, otherwise seven was the maximum. His reporters, ever cynical, imagined the paper's coverage of the biggest story ever to appear:

'The Queen was shot yesterday. She was shot by Winston Churchill. They were making love at the time . . .'

DAY FOUR

In search of further ethnic experiences I spent the morning on he Hill, where I roasted my skin till it turned raw-steak red. Hopefully one day it will mellow into an elegant, woody brown. It probably won't: it'll probably peel and flake and remain the rotten milky colour of the English pallor. Noses are particularly vulnerable to the scorching rays of the sun. I have bought some zinc cream, a skin-toned variety because I'm vain and do not love to wander around with white cream all over my face as if I were a red and white minstrel. Our cricketers have no such scruples, and at present Dilley is more cream than Dilley.

Not that anyone on the Hill could care less. (It's a truth not universally acknowledged that Brisbane has a Hill. Sydney sniffs at it, but it is Sydney that is losing to the concrete mixers.) Between The Gabba's Hill and the cricket there is a dirt track around which greyhounds run, as they did on Thursday night, though not really fast enough to suit Mr Engel (Cricket correspondent of *The Guardian*) who recognises that gambling is the opiate of the masses but nonetheless took Sweet Nothings to win the 8.45. The Gabba Hill is remote, self-absorbed and as interested in its conversations as in the distant cricket. As the day wore on (actually, I left at lunchtime, burnt to a cinder, and rely for this information upon the young Somerset cricketer who, to his horror, bumped into his county captain wearing shorts and a straw hat in so apparently safe a haven as the Hill on the cricket ground in Woollongabba) the Hillites did feel obliged to conduct themselves in the appropriate way, whistling at the brazen Sheilas who wandered by (no-one has ever actually met an Australian girl called Sheila . . . or a man called Rolf for that matter), and yahooing the occasional eccentric who ran by with a Union Jack. There was little hostility in any of this. An image lingers of the spirit of England being typified by the 1953 holiday maker in Copenhagen who, according to *The Guardian*:

> 'Fainted in 86 degrees, was taken to hospital and found to be wearing an overcoat, jacket, trousers, woollen waistcoat, cloth waistcoat, shirt, woollen vest and long woollen underpants.'

So far I've encountered no anti-British sentiment, no genuine rivalry between the nations. England is an awfully long way away, and is noticed here only when particularly savage snowstorms are shown on the A.B.C. news and when some cuckoo of a civil servant is sent out to tell the antipodean courts to refuse to publish material which might suggest that the MI5 of Philby, Maclean, Burgess, Blunt and – who knows – is not entirely leakproof.

As the day wore on, as the dry throats demanded cold lagers, so things warmed up on the Hill. This was no more than was expected. Kids who'd been bored by the cricket returned when they'd heard that the 'can wars' had started. There was no motive, no-one was hurt, simply the Hill entertained itself in a manner now lost in Sydney, where bullishness has replaced brightness. No-one appeared to mind that the Australians were losing (maybe the reason for the plethora of patriotic advertisements on television is to encourage people to think as Australians, rather than as, say, Queenslanders) and no-one appeared to consider any of the Englishmen to be really pompous. There is no obvious, haughty villain in their team, no Jardine to aggravate the locals who have managed so well without an aristocracy. Brearley used to be booed, Edmonds says, because he was such a nancy; but maybe it was really because he was so damnably clever, and just what you'd expect of those ruddy English. Actually, Gatting's team is not obviously English at all. Only Edmonds stands apart from the crowd, and he's a left-arm spinner and so can hardly be the baddy. He is, at least, what you'd expect from the English. The rest are not upper-class but ordinary working blokes just like the Australians.

At close of play, sated with beer, dazzled by the sun, the Hillies stumbled off, leaving behind them a pile of cans, and the paper cups from which they guzzled their chips. They are no longer the earthy, knowledgeable working-class lovers of the game, celebrated by tradition. If they weren't at the match they'd be at the beach or in the pub – most of these fringe dwellers are lads – and most of them have sunburnt skin and beer bellies.

Forced to follow on, Australia had lost five wickets by the close of play, and will presumably lose their first Test match tomorrow. Wondering whether to graft or to attack (Simpson has advocated a bold approach, as people do in the dressing-room), they lost wickets slowly, mostly to Emburey, who bowled as meanly as old Farmer White. He was quick through the air, relied on curl rather than flight, which meant that the batsmen could not get down the pitch to him. Young Australians are reared to believe two things about cricket. One is that every team must have a leg-spinner (which was probably true when cricket here was played on hard-baked, shining surfaces of no use to finger spinners). The second is that batsmen must use their feet to spinners. In fact it is very difficult to do this against Emburey, more difficult than it is even against Underwood. Emburey can change his pace suddenly and unde-tectably, yorking the man who advances upon him, whereas Underwood is so accurate that batsmen can predict his line before he bowls and move their feet accordingly. These batsmen have been told to be aggressive. They'd be better advised to be as patient as Emburey, to pick up singles, to tire him out and to frustrate him. Is this not what May and Cowdrey did to Ramadin and Valentine? But few Australians are grafters. It is not in their temperament. Those who do graft, like Slasher Mackay and Bill Lawry, usually go the whole hog and slowly become national heros in the process. Grafters are usually tired men from old lands, men playing their cricket as a job in hard times.

As usual I caught a taxi from the ground at tea-time to watch the last two hours on television (the first two sessions of play are not shown in the city staging the game). Upon entering the taxi, I found several of the most respected sporting journalists in England – men who write compelling 'I was there' stuff. They too were off to write in peace.

Bill O'Reilly arrived this morning to announce that he'd 'served them up one yesterday'. He had indeed:

'The longer I think about the inexplicable captaincy of Mike Gatting on Sunday afternoon in regard to his two spinners and the introduction of the second new ball the more I realise the truth of the melancholy fact that the art of captaincy has been ransacked.

'When Gatting took the ball himself to bowl that one over which separated him from his privilege of taking the second new ball I made no attempt to stop myself from bursting into a peal of contemptuous laughter.

'Surely the England leader must have been the only man present at the Gabba who had not realised by that time that the favourable position he found his team occupying was due entirely to the magnificent effort of John Emburey, who had called the tune throughout the day.

'The new ball did not mean a thing.

'In reality, it was simply a means to diminish the stress and strain to which the Australians had been drooping throughout the day.

'Only once before in my time have I seen a captaincy incident which I classify in the same bewildering fashion as Gatting's and that was turned on by Bradman at Lord's in 1948 when the Australian lodged his claims for world-class captaincy on the strength of an unbeaten record on tour.

'In that unforgettable incident Bradman decided to take the ball away from Australia's classy left-arm spinner Ernie Toshack, who had been bowling so well that he had four wickets for 28 runs in his bag and looked like finishing with his best performance ever in England.

'Bradman's only claim to outstanding captaincy in that particular event was that he managed to get the ball away from Toshack without any sign of physical violence or any show of hostility from his talented left-hander.

'To put the lid on that little memory, which will live with me for ever, Toshack was recalled to the crease later to help finish the show for Australia after the new ball had failed to do the job.

'Back to Gatting, however.

'He might well be basking in some of the sunshine which is beaming benignly on Dilley and his five wickets, but what worries me is whether his captaincy conscience has smitten him for what he did in the heartless mismanagement of a spin attack which had comprehensively put Australia flat on its back.

'The time, I think, has come when some plain speaking is needed with which to flagellate the queer crowd which has taken control of a great game – so much so that commonsense no longer gets a hearing.

'During the next few days I demand that every one of you – man, woman and child – does a little fair dinkum thinking about the direction in which our game is going.

'Fancy, on reading your various descriptions streaming away from the Brisbane press box aimed at stupefying people right around the cricket world, imagining that hard working, honest-to-god Dilley had any really important influence on what happened to kick the stuffing out of Australia on Sunday.

'Just to help you think objectively I roll in the idea that the bloody ball should never be changed until the string starts to fray from it and the four segments of it start to come adrift just as they used to in our tenurial juvenile days when cricketers seemed to grow on trees in our country.'

Tomorrow Bill, a kindly man, will find something nice to say about Gatting. At present he was pleased to have had the chance to get stuck into 'them'. He is not actually disgruntled about cricket, but he is rarely gruntled either, and loathes the domination of un-intelligent fast bowling. This is not entirely the crankiness of old age, rather a mourning for the loss of the game's virtue.

He was a bit miffed, though, to find that one of his more colourful phrases had been replaced with the word 'tenurial', a word of which he had never heard. Unfortunately I could be of no assistance, as I didn't know what it meant either. Later I observed the old rogue reading my piece – 'What did you give 'em?' – and felt flattered.

With only five wickets left, the Australians are down and very nearly out. Only Geoff Marsh remains. His simple technique is borne of the bowling machine and his stoical attitude formed by those hours on the farm in the middle of Western Australia (into which Europe would fit). He alone seemed to have the stamina, and the frame of mind, to bat for a day to hold the rampant English at bay. Border, who did his best, fell to Emburey, who beat him with one that curled and dipped, causing him to misjudge its length. Border is happier using his feet and attacking the spinners,

31

and jabs too solidly in defence. He had appeared more confident, after his peculiar first innings which was a mixture of tentative pushes followed by one rush of blood. He hit his shots firmly, as if to tell the English that the unrecognisable Border of yesterday was gone, and it was a surprise when he lost his wicket.

At the close of play Waugh was at the crease, and he alone can give Marsh the support he needs. It is hard to see Australia escaping from this predicament. For four days they have looked younger in years, and in cricket, than the English who have transformed themselves into a cricket team in a week. Any change of course tomorrow would be a shock, not least to the local Hillites who already recognise they are in for a long hard summer.

DAY FIVE

England won the first Test match of the series with little difficulty this morning. Once Marsh was gone, beaten by Dilley, but a shade unlucky to play on, the Australian anchor had been removed, and the rest were sunk by moderate waves of English aggression. Astounding to relate, England played very well, and won its first Test match in twelve games. (Australia's record is not much more satisfactory, though it can offer the excuse of the loss of good cricketers to South Africa.) England won because the management was good, because the captaincy was good, and because Botham was good. There are those who think the first two depend upon the last.

I had arrived in Brisbane fully expecting to condemn Peter Lush as manager, Micky Stewart as coach (things have not gone well at Surrey – they rarely do these days – maybe it's something to do with the gasometers). Instead they seem to have helped Gatting to knock the team into shape. England worked hard in the field, and played as a team which, for once, did not have a false idea of its powers. The thick-headedness had gone, and so had the domination of the team by strong characters rather than by a collective will. The players appeared to have recovered their purpose. Suddenly this tour is not a bind, it is a chance to win the Ashes. And moreover, an idea has grown that this is something worth doing. Till now Edmonds has been the most obvious believer in a team of non-believers. He has been in the gully, clapping and trying to sharpen the game. He has been frustrated by the laconic, inscrutable performances of his colleagues, men for whom the idealism of playing for England had fallen rather flat after years of touring Pakistan and the West Indies. Now the team is a team of lads rather than of egocentrics. It is a cricket team rather than a loose federation of top-class cricketers, a Liverpool rather than a Manchester United. Each man, no doubt, has different reasons for this fresh purpose and of course it is futile to give the credit entirely to Lush, Stewart and Gatting. Nonetheless they'd be blamed if England had played in the old, disappointing way and they deserve some of the plaudits for this sudden, sharp improvement.

In truth our chances were never as slim as had been suggested. Too much heed was placed on early defeats in State games, defeats which are, after all, nothing new in an Australian tour. In Perth reporters saw symptoms of the West Indian debacle, and concluded that the disease had been caught and was irreversible. They saw reckless cricket and a failure of discipline and they sighed. The team was prematurely condemned, before the series had even begun.

As it was this England team, with its wealth of experience, rose to the occasion at the Gabba and the much-trumpeted Australians were outplayed.

Suddenly it is the Australians who are in trouble. On the field Border had appeared remote. They'd been so cocky at the beginning of the match, but were crestfallen by the end. That is the way with young teams. It is up to Border to lift their spirits. In Brisbane he appeared exhausted, as if he were carrying the weight of Australian cricket upon his shoulders. Today he was bad-tempered before and after the game. Temporarily forgetting that today's newspapers are tomorrow's fish and chip wrapping, temporarily forgetting that England's cricket team is the real enemy, he rose to the criticisms of the journalists.

Before play he strode up to the press-box in search of Henry Blofeld, who'd written a trenchant piece about Australia's captain. Unable to find him he rounded on an amiable A.B.C. man who wouldn't care to upset a hedgehog. Border had been upset by Blofeld's criticisms. Blofeld had said that Border did not help his bowlers and had simply stood in the slips, hands on hips, and let the game dictate to him. These observations were correct, though they were expressed harshly and without sympathy. Really it is not wise to let Blowers get under your wick.

After the game, still shocked by his team's collapse, Border was surly and did not attend the ritual interview with Tony Greig. This grumpiness was unnecessary. Newspapers do not exist to act as public relations offices for the Australian Eleven. No paper which prints solely good news has ever sold enough copies to keep a moderately avaricious proprietor in beer and nuts. Even Prince Charles is criticised from time to time. Border is not immune and if his team loses, if his tactics go wrong, he must expect to be criticised. Australia's captain must have a thick skin, particularly these days when so many international games are played. A poor team is exposed ruthlessly on an hysterical stage in front of dozens of experts whose job it is to pull the captain's strategy to pieces.

Border was not at his best in Brisbane and his critics were entitled to say so. They are not teachers writing bland school reports, but workers in an industry dependent upon good stories sharply written. It will be disappointing if, instead of fighting back like the perky warrior of old, he retreats behind the barricades, snarling at the hostility, sometimes irresponsibility, of the comments.

In Brisbane he allowed his fury to affect his leadership. This will not do. Sometimes tactics do go wrong. (As a matter of fact, they nearly always go wrong at Somerset.)

Border is not a great captain, does not have an instinctive flair for the job, but he is a doughty cricketer, easily the best in Australia, and his team looks up to him. He has lots of supporters and must not waste his energy on wordsmiths.

Of course he faces a huge task. You cannot microwave cricketers, they must bake slowly in an oven before they are ready for the likes of Emburey. Because cricket here is organised by marketing men, youngsters like Waugh and Matthews are rushed from pillar to post and get little chance to improve their games in Sheffield Shield or grade cricket, away from the hysteria of Test matches. They are not yet properly educated yet they are wearing their green baggy caps. This is what happens to the game when it is left in the hands of financiers.

England's triumph in Brisbane was due to teamwork. Now it is up to the Australians to fight back. If they have any sense they will not search for a new Messiah to bring water to a thirsty land. They will support Border and support his players.

Suddenly it is obvious that Border's team is too young for Test cricket. A good team needs a hard core of experienced cricketers around whom the novices learn their trade. Of these Australians only the captain – and maybe Marsh – is a cricketer of authority. Few of the others have anything behind them. They are still putting their toes in the water.

England's victory sent the journalists scurrying to their rooms to sit in front of their word-processors, typewriters or sheets of paper to prepare their scripts for tomorrow's papers at home. Laudatory adjectives, left in the locker for a year, had to be dusted. Some men (Lady Edmonds is the only woman in the troop) had to find phrases as tart and witty as those used in defeat. For a year snideness had been the rage, except the *The Times* in which John Woodcock, with his oracular wisdom and vast experience, had been cautious, and in the *Telegraph* in which Peter West, patriotism to the fore, had been as kind as possible. Woodcock is the doyen of the writers and the only point allowed against him by his colleagues is that he does from time to time fall asleep when dictating his piece to the copy-takers in London.

What impresses colleagues most about Woodcock is that his grandfather was alive at the time of the battle of Waterloo. This lends to his already sagacious writing the perspective of history. He's been *The Times'* man for thirty years and says he is contemplating retirement (he has a gammy leg, the result of a bout of polio in boyhood, and finds all the travelling painful). No-one thinks he's really going to retire; he'd be sorely missed because he is the only journalist who survives from the era when cricket correspondents were men of weight, and did not bother with off the field matters.

Martin Johnson of *The Independent* was in a particularly awkward position. Emburey is wearing a T-shirt with Johnson's statement on the front and 'Up Yours' on the back. Colleagues say that this cock-up has made Johnson's name. Custer's name, in the same way, was made at Little Big Horn. Apart from this *faux-pas*, he has been writing well, his wit laced with a twang more caustic than Engel's. He'd joined *The Independent* to be its rugby correspondent and finds himself writing about cricket in much the same way as Scoop found himself writing about the war in Africa.

The Guardian's Matthew Engel has avoided the pomposities of prediction and condemnation, saved by a grace and humour. He is a writer rather than a cricketer and sees absurdity in solemnity;

35

his writing is rueful rather than harsh. He could take off to his room with a smile for he had less to explain than some.

FIRST TEST, Brisbane
November 14, 15, 16, 18, 19, 1986

ENGLAND

B. C. Broad	c Zoehrer b Reid	8	not out		35
C. W. J. Athey	c Zoehrer b C. Matthews	76	c Waugh b Hughes		1
M. W. Gatting*	b Hughes	61	c G. Matthews b Hughes		12
A. J. Lamb	lbw b Hughes	40	lbw b Reid		9
D. I. Gower	c Ritchie b C. Matthews	51	not out		15
I. T. Botham	c Hughes b Waugh	138			
C. J. Richards†	b C. Matthews	0			
J. E. Emburey	c Waugh b Hughes	8			
P. A. J. DeFreitas	c C. Matthews b Waugh	40			
P. H. Edmonds	not out	9			
G. R. Dilley	c Boon b Waugh	0			
Extras	(b 3, lb 19, nb 3)	25	(b 2, nb 3)		5
TOTAL		456	(3 wkts)		77

Fall of wickets: 15, 116, 198, 198, 316, 324, 351, 443, 451.
Second innings: 6, 25, 40.
Bowling: Reid 31-4-86-1; Hughes 36-7-134-3; C. Matthews 35-10-95-3; Waugh 21-3-76-3; G. Matthews 11-2-43-0.
Second innings: C. Matthews 4-0-11-0; Hughes 5.3-0-28-2; Reid 6-1-20-1; G. Matthews 7-1-16-0.

AUSTRALIA

G. R. Marsh	c Richards b Dilley	56	(2) b DeFreitas		110
D. C. Boon	c Broad b DeFreitas	10	(1) lbw b Botham		14
T. J. Zoehrer†	lbw b Dilley	38	(8) not out		16
D. M. Jones	lbw b DeFreitas	8	(3) st Richards b Emburey		18
A. R. Border*	c DeFreitas b Edmonds	7	(4) c Lamb b Emburey		23
G. M. Ritchie	c Edmonds b Dilley	41	(5) lbw b DeFreitas		45
G. R. J. Matthews	not out	56	(6) c&b Dilley		13
S. R. Waugh	c Richards b Dilley	0	(7) b Emburey		28
C. D. Matthews	c Gatting b Botham	11	lbw b Emburey		0
M. G. Hughes	b Botham	0	b DeFreitas		0
B. A. Reid	c Richards b Dilley	3	c Broad b Emburey		2
Extras	(b 2, lb 8, w 2, nb 6)	18	(b 5, lb 6, nb 2)		13
TOTAL		248			282

Fall of wickets: 27, 97, 114, 126, 159, 198, 204, 239, 239.
Second innings: 24, 44, 92, 205, 224, 262, 266, 275.
Bowling: DeFreitas 16-5-32-2; Dilley 25.4-7-68-5; Emburey 34-11-66-0; Ddmonds 12-6-12-1; Botham 16-1-58-2; Gatting 1-0-2-0.
Second innings: Botham 12-0-34-1; Dilley 19-6-47-1; Emburey 42.5-14-80-5; DeFreitas 17-2-62-3; Edmonds 24-8-46-0; Gatting 2-0-2-0.
Toss Australia
Man of the match: I. T. Botham
Umpires: A. R. Crafter and M. W. Johnson.
ENGLAND WON BY SEVEN WICKETS.

3

Interlude I

REST DAY IN BRISBANE

On this rest day Matthew Engel and I hired a car to drive inland to see Mount Tambourine, and then to head for the sea at Surfer's Paradise. The car cost us sixty dollars for the day. Engel said he'd drive as he was used to driving in foreign lands. He'd hired a car in America and had been presented with a vehicle substantially bigger than his flat in London. He would remember to drive on the left, though he warned, he had no instinctive sense of right and left. This was odd, from a *Guardian* journalist. It had always been thought they had no instinctive sense of right and wrong.

Engel is without doubt the worst driver I have ever encountered, worse even than Vic Marks, who once stopped at traffic lights behind a line of parked cars. Engel never dared to approach within fifty yards of another car, and braked hard whenever anything in the least surprising occurred. Moreover his sense of direction was undistinguished and, although we found Mount Tambourine, we did not, to our satisfaction, find its peak.

We did walk for miles through an area of rain forest for which the mountain is justly celebrated, walking through trees from which at any moment Tarzan might spring, and walking past Lace

Goannas (long lizard-like reptiles which are about five feet long, live in timbered country, and are remarkably adept at climbing trees).

Despite Engel's best endeavours we did not get lost, although we chatted on as if we were lost in the wild, as if Brisbane and Somerset were never to be seen again. Australia is a big land and people can disappear in it. Lots of Australians prefer the solitude and empty space of the outback, with its burning heat and its flat lands, to the noise and squalor of the city. After all, lots of the Aborigines chose to stay in the bush, taking their living from the land; till the area was denuded of life and then moved on. With the bush and the rain forest the idea of a unity with nature endures in many Australian hearts.

Most private schools send their children into the bush every year to live close to the natives. I accompanied one party a few years ago, abandoning my bed and my radio. It had seemed a good idea at the time. Our trip coincided with the worst months of the drought which ravaged the bush area of Australia during the summer of 1982. In some areas it hadn't rained for years and occasionally, to the heartbreak of the farmers, dark clouds built up, approached their property and veered off at the last moment towards a neighbouring farm. Everything was dusty and dry (except, of course, for the bowling greens), and on the farms the animals were boney, skin clinging to their ribs. The creeks had dried into festering pools, and only the stolid gum trees, with their soldierly stance, survived in the shimmering aridity of thirsty outback Australia.

A total fire ban was in effect, for the land was tinder-dry. Smoking was an offence and fires could not be lit to warm the water for the billies. Many farmers had moved their herds to the pasture lands nearer to the coast. Some of them, we heard later, were swindled by unscrupulous businessmen who pretended these arrivals had died when in fact they'd been sold. The bulls used to be fattened on a mixture of cotton and oats, and now even these crops had failed, so that the arrivals had neither water nor food to sustain them beneath the unsympathetic glare of the sun. Hardly anything, not even plants, had any greenness to indicate life and hope.

We stayed for ten days, and as we queued for seconds of food we'd never deign to eat in Sydney, we began to bear a weary resemblance to the children in *Lord of the Flies*. In a way this experience did purify us, temporarily, and we retired fitter and harder – though deeply appreciative of the creature comforts available in the city.

From Tambourine Mountain we drove east to see Surfer's Paradise, reputed to be one of the most beautiful shore lines in Australia. This paradise was disappointing, its beauty spoilt by skyscrapers which stood up over the beaches like gigantic fingers. Their domination of this once-lovely coastline spoke of corruption and exploitation.

We had to move across the beach to avoid the shadows cast by these monstrosities. We fled to its far side, because the best area was ruined by noise from the local pop station, which took upon itself the duty of blasting tinny sound into the eardrums of the bathers and sun-worshippers.

Engel lay down on the sand, sleeping under a dressing-gown, his body curled up. He'd never really wanted to be a cricket writer, just wanted to write. He said this was Botham land, not Roebuck land. I'd been happy in the forest and was bound to feel contempt for this shameless hedonism. Botham and Queensland were made for each other – big, brassy, noisy and aggressively masculine. This is the land of Sir Joh Bjelke-Petersen, who has arranged democracy in Queensland so well that he can rule with only thirty-two per cent of the popular vote. It is, in fact, recorded that Queensland has not won the Sheffield Shield during Sir Joh's tenure. Presumably he has not been able to arrange things so that Queensland does not have to score as many runs as its opponents. His wife is a Federal Senator. She makes scones and says the hour cannot be changed because the curtains would fade. Queensland is a private enclave in Alabama-down-under, a State living under an outdated, right-wing regime. Demonstrations are not allowed and protestors are treated with contempt. In this paradise the worshippers belched and gambled, enjoying loud chauvinsim in the male and boldness in the female. Brisbane had appeared to be a pleasant city, and no doubt out in the west there are lots of hard-working farmers, yet there is a streak of corruption, racism, nihilism and violence in Queensland society which is only partly hidden. A year or so ago Sir Joh passed a law making it illegal for publicans to serve gays, lesbians, weirdos, drug takers and other assorted folk.

And as we drive across Queensland on the rest day we passed one park called Lamington and another called Russ Hinze. It is not every State which names parks after a cake and a minister for local government, main roads and racing. It is not every State which *has* a minister for local government, main roads and racing.

S U R F I N G

'When you're driving hard and fast down the wall, with the surf curling behind yer, or doing the backside turn on a big one about to tube, it's just this feeling. Yer know, it leaves yer feeling stoked.'
A surfie quoted by Hugh Atkinson in *Quadrant*.

One man, we were told, hailed from the east coast of California. Another was called the Raging Bull. His rival was dubbed the Surfing Messiah by some, and Cannonball by others. Prizes were presented by the managing director of the civic board of B.H.P. Steel (rod and bar division). Manufacturers of coca-cola, coal, steel and television sets supported the event. A middle of the road radio station sponsored the Long Board competition, won by the legendary Nat Young and competed for by all manner of veterans of the waves. A rock station promoted the ladies as they paraded their talents on the board. Everywhere driving rock music blared through the speakers, stealing contemplation, guiding thought. . . . 'I want to be free'. Mostly there were trashy Australian songs; the Beach Boys were not heard. We were fed chips, coca-cola, pies, ice-cream and chilli rolls. We were on Newcastle beach, thousand upon thousand of us, wearing billabong shorts and covered with pink zinc.

We gazed at the sea, mouths open, in eternal smile as we absorbed its movements. Surfing is the Walkman of sports, a private trip, almost a trance, utterly self-absorbed. In Australia it has its own culture, a sub-culture really, and its own language. Youths sat huddled in groups, smoking cigarettes, chatting forlornly about their schools. Kids stared at the breaking water of the ocean and spoke of waves building up out the back and of surfers being munched. On Saturday, after the storms, the swell had been 'humungous', ten feet and more, and even the top board riders had not mastered it.

During the rides (in the semi-finals each competitor had seventy minutes into which he could fit ten rides, the best five to count) the crowd did not cheer or clap, simply watched the dreary, distant dance of the surfers on their boards. Occasionally the commentator tried to persuade the spectators to shout for one man or another, usually with little effect for this was an experience shared between friends, not a violent struggle between adversaries. Surfers (apart from those riding) did not appear to be 'into' competition.

Through the speakers the disc jockeys used their jargon, chatting on, using pop and wave as if they were one. We were told that a particular surfer 'just loves these Newcastle barrels' and that another had caught 'a great little left-hander'. For ages nothing seemed to happen, less even than at the cricket, and then, somewhere in the distance, we'd see a tiny figure climb on to a board and begin to move. When Freda Zamba caught a wave we were told, and could see, that she was 'up and riding as smooth as silk – check the cutback!'

Suddenly we had 'a big nose dip from Westpac'. We scanned the horizon to study Mr Westpac's remarkable manoeuvre, only to realise that our genial hosts were pointing us towards a sponsored helicopter. Everything was sponsored, except the sand and the sea.

Freda won the women's championship, beating a blonde bombshell called Pam Burridge and as they left the water in their wetsuits the autograph hunters surged towards them. Freda, we were informed, had a trainer, mentor, manager and friend all rolled into the character of her fiancé. They were 'a great combo'.

Throughout Sunday, when the surf was rising majestically, like a pregnant belly, the surfers and their followers were bold, brash and brazen. Later, as skins burned or tanned, Tom Curren, a calm neat rider, met Mark Occhilupo in the final. Occhilupo is a wild, hysterical man who tears into the waves as if he were disembowelling a maiden in Oslo. He rode two clean waves before the southerly winds arrived to spoil the water. Curren cut into his waves, swivelling on his board, bumping up and down near the shore as the wave died, draining it of its energy and its power, 'hanging in there for the white water'. He was poised, and then exciting, as he climbed onto his board to slide across the crest of a wave.

41

Occhilupo, in contrast, was savage, a brute in the water, a broadsword against an épée. These duellists fought out a tactical battle, dashing to the surf to get first choice of wave. With his luck holding, Occhilupo the romantic defeated Curren the classic, and screamed with delight as he took his prize.

A few miles away the cricketers of England and New South Wales finished their match. At first, in the wonder of the surf, under the sun and admiring the dolphin movements of the surfers, it appeared that cricket had been rendered redundant. These pastimes are as different as Hawaii and Leeds. The surfing was great for a day, yet its culture seemed indulgent. Beauty on the waves was surrounded by incoherence off it, a sport packaged as a symbol of protest.

M I 5

Caught a taxi and went to the law courts in Macquarie Street, Sydney. Took a lift up to the eighth floor, and, following instructions, wandered into court 8D of the New South Wales Supreme Court. Bowed to the judge and sat in a comfortable chair, ignoring a piece of paper marked 'Legal'.

In the dock there sat a man, a poor deserted lonely man, with a mouth which curved downwards and a jaw which jutted out. Sir Robert Armstrong, Cabinet Secretary, had been thrown into this brash court and into the harsh light in an effort to prevent the publication of a book called *Spycatchers*, written by Peter Wright, a former agent of MI5. He was not a happy man, rather a servant doing his duty. He was a grey eminence representing a crusty, obsessively secretive establishment and was hacked to pieces by a rude barrister. 'No' he hadn't read Chapman Pincher's book, he said, and he hadn't watched a *Panorama* programme on the issue. 'No' he could not confirm that MI5 followed people. Did he deny the existence of G.C.H.Q.? 'It's a bit late for that' smiled Sir Robert, implying that he'd deny his own existence if he could. This puzzled the Australians, who could not see the advantage in failing to acknowledge facts that everyone knew. The truth of the matter was that none of it, in Sir Robert's opinion, was anyone else's business but his Government's. This book was a breach of confidentiality; it was a breach of the Official Secrets Act. This was a serious matter. It was irrelevant that the book didn't say much new. True, his Government had not objected to the publication of books by Chapman Pincher or by Nigel West containing similar material, but this was because they were journalists. He did not know if Pincher had worked as a double agent for MI5, nor did he think that Pincher had been chosen to release material on Philby, Burgess, Maclean and Blunt because he was a conservative. Really it was no-one's damn business anyhow. This is what happens when an honourable, decent institution like the British civil service allows itself to appear in a colonial court.

Star of the show was Malcolm Turnbull, the advocate representing Heinemann, the publisher, and Wright; his voice full of derision, his face full of contempt, he'd stare at his audience, rarely at his victim. Between each question he'd pause, contemplating his next shaft. At the end of each question he'd barked 'is it?' or 'does it?', demanding specific replies which Sir Robert was never prepared to give. He'd rephrase his question so that, emboldened by qualifications, Sir Robert could dare an answer. It was an intellectual duel, a game of cat and mouse designed to make the British civil service appear as pompous and as stuffy as possible, a none-too difficult task. Turnbull relished his role as grand inquisitor, revealing a cunning, devious intelligence. He was appalled that the British Government was, so late in the day, objecting to the production of certain documents. Shuffling in his seat, coughing occasionally, his face draining of life during the day, Sir Robert paused and defended, giving as little away as he could. From time to time spectators chuckled as Turnbull, loud and waspish, gazed around the room like one of Bertie Wooster's aunts after some outstandingly cautious answer. Once Armstrong refused to react to a question without knowing where Turnbull was leading:

'You want to know where I'm leading? O.K. I have no secrets from you, Sir Robert.'

To which Armstrong, dry and heavily ironic, replied:

'I wish I could say the same.'

And so the laborious script continued, with Sir Robert doing an accurate impersonation of Sir Humphrey Appleby. He reacted to sharp questions as an old maid might do to a proposition from a leather-jacketed bike rider. In a distant land, where they didn't understand the need for secrecy, he was being dissected as if he were a locust in a laboratory. His adversary, only thirty-two years of age what's more, had been asking these perfectly awful questions for five days. A few yards away the judge, with his recording angels sitting below and in front of him, wondered why Sir Robert had bothered to come to Australia at all. He agreed with Turnbull that it might be necessary to subpoena the MI5 file on Chapman Pincher to see if he had ever been an agent (if so, it would destroy the Government argument that it objected to this book rather than to previous books because Wright was an 'insider'). He agreed with Turnbull (to shudders of horror on the plaintiff bench) that it might be necessary to subpoena the Attorney General, Sir Michael Havers because there were so many matters upon which Sir Robert could not speak.

And so the trial continued, Turnbull presenting his case massively. We had a coffee break at 11.30 and lunch at 1 p.m. In these breaks Sir Robert and his lawyer, pained expressions on their faces, hurried into a conference room while Turnbull winked at his colleagues and went to the café to buy a white coffee with two sugars.

People walked in and out of the court throughout the day, listened to the dramatic trial and then wandered off for lunch. In court they followed the slow unwinding of a great drama, performed in front of an amused, quietly-spoken judge in a small modern court-room in a high-rise building.

Sir Robert's own counsellors were, unlike Turnbull and his youthful assistants, bewigged and aged. Several times his Q.C. rose to object to a line of questions or to confirm that the Government was admitting nothing.

'I find myself placed in an intolerable situation. I am quite unable to know from one day to the next what is the attitude of the plaintiff in this case. The defendants are being placed in an intolerable situation and one in which I fear they will be subjected to grave injustice. Tactics of the British Government were either a *danse macabre* or an exercise in futility.'

Peter Wright has arrived in Sydney and was pictured wandering through Hyde Park carrying a walking stick, wearing an Australian hat, his wife on his arm, scarcely a man to topple the Empire. Outside the court he bumped into Sir Robert. They shook hands and Sir Robert said:

'Hello Peter, nice to see you again. It's been a long time.'

Wright said:

'Yes.'

Armstrong added:

'You live in a nice country.'

To which Wright, who'd lived in Tasmania since 1976, replied:

'Yes, for eleven years now.'

Interviewed in a newspaper, Wright said:

'If Hollis was a spy, and I am ninety-nine per cent sure he was, you'll have to rewrite the whole history of what Russia has done in the West. That includes the Cuban missile crisis and Salt I and Salt II.'

Wright had been the man who debriefed Sir Anthony Blunt, upon which task he amassed more than two hundred hours of taped conversations. The trial goes on.

4

Newcastle: England v. New South Wales

DAY ONE

Newcastle is a city of coal and steel, an industrial city which lies on the coast and yet has the feel of a country town in the mid-west. It is much more like rural Dubbo than sophisticated Sydney. At the game today there were lots of odd people and country hicks. The ground was dark and miserable and the weather unseasonably chilly. A few days earlier they'd had the hottest day for this time of year since 1948, and yesterday had been the coldest November day since 1930. It was dreadfully cold at the ground, and each time we left the windshield of the decrepit main stand we felt like an antarctic explorer leaving his tent. Though this was a day for coffee the enduring memory is of John Woodcock sitting under layers of clothes, clutching a can of Toohey's beer. Meanwhile Peter West was smoking his pipe and contemplating his *Daily Telegraph*, a picture of contentment. In every report back to England the Pope was blamed, for he is at the Sydney Cricket Ground. After today there is little chance of any English cricket reporter being received into the Catholic Church.

The cricket itself was desultory. It had an alka-seltzer feel about it, as if the team was still hung-over from the euphoria of

Brisbane. For those not involved in Queensland this was a vital match, and despite the wretched conditions they tried their best. The stars, on the other hand, are more confident that they can peak in the big games, and treat these State matches as if they were racing drivers on their warm-up laps. England's cricket was a bizarre mixture of solemnity and frivolity. Botham was in one of his clout and stroke moods, smiting the ball to the deep and then heavily walking a single. He can do this and still play well, and does not understand how difficult it is for the other players to do the same.

Sadly England did not bat well. Athey was trapped LBW by Lawson, who was cheered by the shivering local supporters in recognition of his disappointment in Brisbane. Lawson did not bowl with any pace, and appeared reluctant to let himself go, lest his body fall apart. Gower fell cheaply, lifting a catch to cover. He has scored only one century in forty-six innings in this calendar year, and that in a Test match. He has lost the Leicestershire captaincy and must wonder why he bothers. Today's shot was a poor one, to these eyes at least. Gower, like so many outstanding players, has a defence mechanism which rejects blame. To him the shot was just another shot. He hits drives like a fellow putting up umbrellas in the rain. It is a casual matter and sometimes it goes wrong. Whitaker failed too. He is finding it hard to bat only once every second week, and appeared to be losing confidence in himself. Nets are a poor substitute for runs in the middle. Maybe he, like Foster, thrives on work. Foster and French scored some late runs to give England's total a measure of respectability. These are the two unfortunates of the tour; men who are forever chosen by England and nearly always left out. Now they have been by-passed by Richards, DeFreitas and perhaps Small. It cannot be easy for French and a long tour looms ahead. He'll have to find some mountains to climb (he nearly turned up to his first Test match in his climbing trousers, till Chris Broad gently pointed out that blazers were expected) and he'll have to listen to more of his John Martyn tapes. He is a sane, pleasant man in a brittle world. It cannot help that everyone regards him as the best 'keeper in England.

Really the only cheerful part of the day was to see Bruce Holland in action. This ageing leg-spinner, who first played against England in 1985, still moves with the dainty tread of a scullery maid in a vicarage (and Broad still walks like Groucho Marx). He took five wickets, which helped to rescue a miserable day. He hardly ever bowls a googly (only bowled a couple in the entire tour of England in 1985), is a bowler who depends on flight rather than spin. He is not one of Australia's great leg-spinners, simply an honest and charming leggie, who plies his trade with experience and enthusiasm.

New South Wales had lost two wickets to Emburey's off-spin by the close of play, as the wind lashed the waves outside our hotel.

DAY TWO

Spent the morning and afternoon pottering around the cricket ground, wondering what to offer *Sunday Times* readers by way of informed description. It had been a quiet day. Reporters sat in the sunshine chatting to each other. Then, just before tea, things began to happen.

At 3.22 Chris Broad was beaten by Gilbert and adjudged to be leg before, a shade unlucky perhaps, for the ball appeared to pitch outside his leg stump. At 3.27 Athey missed an inswinger and he too departed LBW for a duck. At 3.40 tea was taken. At 4.21 Whitaker edged Whitney's cutter and was caught by the wicket-keeper (an old chum of mine). At 4.24 Gower indiscreetly pulled his second ball to mid-on and pottered off. Later, in the pavilion, he disagreed that his shot had been indiscreet:

'I saw it. It was there. I hit it. A bloke caught it.'

David is an advocate of freedom at the crease.

When Slack was bowled between bat and pad the scoreboard apologetically recorded the score as 5/25. The clock stood at 4.36 as Bruce French did not see a full-toss and was trapped in front. There followed a tense partnership of thirteen runs in fully thirty-seven minutes between Botham and his acting captain, that wily old bird Emburey, which ended when Botham, head in the air, missed a full-blooded drive and was bowled. Emburey, ever as crooked and as fidgety as a cockroach, lasted for sixty-eight perilous minutes till, at 5.45, he snicked an unremarkable delivery to the 'keeper. At 5.59 Foster was bowled as he tried to pull a ball from Holland which was not as short as he imagined. Foster's back foot strokes are less effective than his front foot drives. Finally, at 6.09, we all went home with England's score standing at 9/66.

Five batsmen made ducks, three batsmen scored six, Wilf Slack scored eighteen, the combined total of his dismissed comrades. There were thirteen extras, Edmonds remained unbeaten on fourteen, and Gladstone Small held his wicket intact, ready to do battle tomorrow morning with three already against his name. It was so nearly 10 for 66 and all that.

These are the bare bones of a bizarre day, which we described as best we could in our various papers. Readers in England must have imagined that the pitch had played up, or that England's team had not yet shrugged off the champagne of Brisbane. Neither is the case. Damp on Friday after unseasonable rain, the pitch had as it dried developed a crusty top, upon which the ball might spin, if the spinners got on. Holland took one wicket and Matthews did not bowl in this innings. Earlier, on the same pitch, England had taken ninety-four overs to bowl out New South Wales.

Certainly the pitch had patches of thick grass upon it, offering the seamers hope, but there was little evidence of uneven bounce or awkward movement. Wickets were lost through incompetence. Several New South Welshmen had been bowled cutting at spinners, and in the evening several Englishmen were beaten by mild swing, in the air not off the pitch. Few, as they left the field, stared with recrimination at the grass prepared for them to bat upon. It was one of those collapses which happen from time to time, though rather less often in teams which include in their ranks one of the masters of defence: Barrington, Boycott, Cowdrey, Edrich. Peter Robinson, Somerset coach, says he once took 7/11 at Trent Bridge on a wicket that did absolutely nothing. Cricket is an intriguing game. New South Wales did bowl well, a lot better than Australia had in Brisbane, which is not surprising since Gilbert, Lawson and Whitney are twice as experienced as Reid, Hughes and Matthews. No unplayable balls were bowled, instead the bowlers pitched the ball up and allowed it to swing as the batsmen groped. If Australia had bowled this well at Brisbane we'd still be alarmed about England's top order batting, and there'd be none of this nonsense about Border resigning.

Whitney was the best of the bowlers, dipping the ball onto the pads and occasionally cutting it away, to take 5/27 in fourteen intelligent overs. He's a twenty-seven year old quickie who played two Test matches in England in 1981 when Lawson was injured. He disappeared for a few years after that, no doubt recovering from Botham's hundreds and Hughes' captaincy – a potent brew – and spent his time upon his other love, riding the waves. England's batsmen must wish he'd joined the great board riders who have congregated in Newcastle, just outside our hotel, to compete in the B.H.P. Steel Championship on Nobby's Beach. Until he bowled so well Whitney too might rather have been out catching the waves, for the swell was up though rather choppy. We are only in Newcastle because the Pope is to arrive in Sydney on Tuesday, to speak to the young on Thursday evening at the Sydney Cricket Ground. Thousands will be there to hear him. Thousands were at the beach today. Now, if they can arrange for the Pope to surf on one of these beaches it'd be the most enormous fillip for Catholicism in Australia.

With this abject collapse England undid the good work of the morning. Two things stand out from the more prosaic proceedings before tea. Steve Waugh batted for sixty-nine minutes and under-lined his immense potential. Leaning onto the back foot he smashed Botham through the covers and directly afterwards clouted a re-spectable delivery from Edmonds over deep mid-wicket for six. In his green baggy cap (actually it was blue this afternoon) and his preference for robust back foot play Waugh has the appearance of an old-fashioned Australian. He was beginning to get the measure of Emburey when he fell to the second new ball.

Over on the Hill – even Newcastle, a town of coal and steel has its Hill – Greg Matthews walked out to see his girlfriend; like some modern Pied Piper, he was followed by two hundred and fifty kids. He lined them up and signed autographs for everyone. He even signed for the old man who passed the day wandering around holding a palm branch with which, from time to time, he swatted the flies which gathered on his, as on everyone else's back.

By the way, Bill O'Reilly informed everyone that flies were indigenous. We had not brought them with us two centuries ago, as we brought sparrows, rabbits, work, disease and cricket.

Oh yes, one more thing. I made it into the *Sydney Morning Herald* quotes of the week!

'One-day cricket thrives upon fervour. It creates climaxes, whereas Test cricket is a slow, unwinding of duels between cricketers. In Tests, the players dictate the course of the game: in one-day cricket, the game is the boss.'

Peter Roebuck, cricketer and author.

DAY THREE

England lost the State match by eight wickets, the second defeat of the tour. The pitch had dried and New South Wales made the runs easily enough, with Mark Taylor, a tall left-hander, and Dirk Wellham doing most of the work. Wellham is a worker, a grafter who collects runs here and there. At the crease he resembles a good English player, on the front foot and pushing. He scores lots of runs, is also easily the best captain in State cricket, and unless my sources have misled me has no chance whatsoever of being chosen again to play for Australia. A story goes that Border sat his team down a year ago and told them that it was up to them to lead Australian cricket back to the light after the renegades had taken the Krugerrands. His team listened and agreed. They'd lead the fight back. Four of them – Wood, Bennett, Phillips and Wellham – had apparently already signed contracts to go to South Africa, contracts from which Bruce Francis later released them. Border apparently detected a certain hypocrisy in this conduct and will have nothing to do with this quartet, who did go to England and who were also paid extra money because of the South African business.

Wellham is ambitious and intends to contest a seat at the next election as a Liberal (Australian word for ultra-conservative). He will probably not be chosen to represent the Prime Minister's XI next month either.

Sadly this match ended in controversy. The teams had promised to play an extra twenty-five over match if the game ended before 2.30, an offer intended to bring people to the ground in the morning. England evidently did not fancy working overtime. On the field they adopted every manoeuvre to delay the dreaded moment of defeat so that New South Wales did not pass England's score until 2.40. It was infuriating. Nor did the local players make any effort to hit off the runs so that the crowd could get its money's worth. They had been lured to the ground under false pretences and should have been given their money back. An apology should also have been made for these deplorably selfish tactics (which, no doubt, we have adopted at Somerset from time to time). As the players left the field some people in the crowd booed. Very few clapped New South Wales for its great victory and everyone felt that the match had been spoilt. It told Lush and Gatting that they'd lost a lot of friends this day, and they nodded. It was foolish to make such a promise and then deliberately to see that it could not be fulfilled. Professional cricketers understand the absurdity of a twenty-five over game, children and spectators do not. And the ground was full of children and cricket-lovers for whom this was the day of the year.

In the press-box Henry Blofeld alone of my colleagues was horrified by this episode. Others chose to be discreet, wrongly so in my judgement. Cricket sometimes does itself a disservice, and this was one such occasion.

Meanwhile the *Sydney Morning Herald* has published an editorial attacking Border's captaincy, and Bill O'Reilly has written that the selectors must

'take the bit between their aching teeth and drop Allan Border from the team to play England in the second Test to start in Perth next Friday.'

Bill said that this was a 'crisis of great magnitude' because Australia is being led by a man who considers some of his team to

'belong to a band of no-hopers who could not win an argument in a shuttle alley.'

He named Boon, who has Border's faults without his great batting powers, as his successor.

I take a different view. Since the 1985 Ashes series Australia has played thirteen games, winning one tying one, losing four and drawing seven (the other great cricket nation – England – has played twelve, won one, lost eight and drawn three in the same period). Border does have a bad record as captain (played twenty-two, won three, lost eight, drawn ten, tied one) yet in his seven hundred days as leader he has been given by his selectors, of which he is not one, thirty-one different cricketers. He has never had a decent bowling team and his side is inexperienced. In Brisbane he led a team which had, between them, played one hundred and ninety-four Test matches (Border has played eighty-five of these).

Between them Gatting and his men, including two debutantes, had played three hundred and eighty-nine games.

Border is not a good captain, as has been noted earlier, but seventy-six days ago he saved a Test match in Bombay with an innings of skill and tenacity. On 22 September he was praised for his bold declaration which led to cricket's second-ever Test match tie. He is a man of vigour and quality who has never let Australia down, despite so many disappointments, despite the conduct of some of his former colleagues. In his team he has no senior professional to help him (Alderman, the obvious candidate, is in Johannesburg). He is on his own and in charge of a desperately young team which nearly to a man is still taking tentative first steps in Test cricket.

Australia's team is scarcely representative of great cricketing nation. Cricket may be in decline, even if it is still being played in the bush, as Australia is gradually filling its empty land with people who have never heard of this mysterious game. Moreover such players as it has are divided between South Africa, an official list of outcasts (Wellham and friends) and Border's young side. Cricket is not so strong here that two good teams can be run. At its best an Australian team might include Wessels, Marsh, Hughes, Border, Ritchie, Phillips, Matthews, Hughes, Rackemann, Alderman and Reid. Notwithstanding the advanced age of some of these gentlemen this is still a formidable side, one which would trouble England.

It is Border's destiny to lead Australia in hard times. His faults are obvious, but there is not a man to beat him in Australian cricket. Who else has stood so resolute on the bridge? Mistakes were made in 1977, and Australian cricket is still suffering from them. The administrators were foolish, and they deserved Packer. In their foolishness, they appointed Yallop, a weak and silly man though a fine batsman, to succeed Simpson. If they had chosen Inverarity, a senior and respected cricketer ready to guide the youngsters, the disasters caused by Yallop might have been avoided. With Inverarity in charge Australia might have beaten Brearley's tourists instead of losing five : one (opportunities presented themselves in nearly every game), in which case World Series Cricket, which had endured one vastly expensive and failed experiment the year before, might never have caught on. As it was, with England crushing the establishment Australian eleven, eyes turned to Chappell and his team.

Not satisfied with this dreadful and costly mistake, the authorities then proceeded to appoint Hughes to replace Yallop. Hughes had never won the respect of his team in Western Australia, and his immaturity was displayed on his innocent, boyish face. Had Rod Marsh, well-loved and proudly Australian, been appointed in his place the disastrous South African business might have been avoided. Australia, and Border, are paying for those mistakes now.

They can do better, with wise selection. Whitney bowled very well in Newcastle, and appeared to be the best new-ball bowler in Australia. It is hard to believe the selectors will chose so poor a team again.

NEW SOUTH WALES v. ENGLAND, Newcastle
November 21, 22, 23, 1986

ENGLAND

C. B. Broad	lbw b Whitney	31	lbw b Gilbert	0
C. W. J. Athey	lbw b Lawson	3	lbw b Whitney	0
W. N. Slack	b Whitney	16	b Gilbert	18
D. I. Gower	c Wellham b Matthews	16	(5) c Holland b Whitney	0
J. J. Whitaker	c and b Matthews	4	(4) c Waugh b Whitney	6
J. E. Emburey*	c Waugh b Holland	10	(8) c Dyer b Whitney	6
I. T. Botham	c Taylor b Holland	14	(6) b Gilbert	6
P. H. Edmonds	b Matthews	6	(9) not out	17
B. N. French †	not out	38	(7) lbw b Whitney	0
N. A. Foster	c and b Lawson	25	b Holland	0
G. C. Small	b Holland	26	lbw b Gilbert	14
Extras	(b 3, lb 2, nb 3)	8	(lb 10, nb 5)	15
TOTAL		197		82

Fall of wickets: 16, 51, 61, 74, 75, 97, 106, 106, 142, 197.
Second innings: 0, 0, 22, 22, 24, 25, 37, 53, 57, 82.

NEW SOUTH WALES

S. M. Small	c Edmonds b Emburey	8	c Edmonds b Foster	9
M. A. Taylor	st French b Emburey	4	c Slack b Edmonds	31
R. G. Holland	c French b Edmonds	36		
D. M. Wellham*	lbw b Foster	18	(3) not out	29
M. D. O'Neill	b Foster	0	(4) not out	13
G. R. J. Matthews	b Emburey	25		
S. R. Waugh	c French b Small	47		
G. C. Dyer †	b Edmonds	4		
G. F. Lawson	c French b Small	26		
D. R. Gilbert	not out	10		
M. R. Whitney	c French b Foster	1		
Extras	(lb 1, nb 1)	2	(b 12, lb 3, nb 2)	17
TOTAL		181	2 wickets	99

Fall of wickets: 12, 15, 43, 43, 86, 110, 118, 165, 170, 181.
Second innings: 23, 57.
Toss: New South Wales.
Umpires: R. A. French and A. G. Marshall.
NEW SOUTH WALES WON BY EIGHT WICKETS.

5

Interlude II

THE POPE

'If you want peace, work for justice; if you want peace, defend life; if you want peace, proclaim truth; if you want peace, always treat others as you would like them to treat you.

If you want peace, you must love; you must love the Lord your God with all your heart, with all your soul, with all your mind, and with all your strength; you must love your neighbour as yourself.'

For the first time for sixteen years the Pope has arrived in Australia. Naturally he went straight to the Sydney Cricket Ground, where thirty-thousand young Catholics had gathered. They provided an extraordinary spectacle, like a series of concentric circles. Then five hundred youngsters dressed in white and carrying yellow streamers ran on to the pitch to unfurl a huge banner upon which was written the word Peace.

In the midst of this the Pope arrived in his Popemobile, driving around the ground to acknowledge the spectators. His speech was emotional and poignant, a reaction to the stirring spirit of the occasion. Later he *danced* with the youngsters during an astonishing and moving finale. Throughout the evening, six thousand young

55

Catholics performed an array of numbers, which rivalled the brilliant opening to the Brisbane Commonwealth Games. Dramas, songs, dances and videos were shown to the thousands of children in the stands to mark the occasion.

The Pope is here for two more days, and will be giving open-air masses at Randwick race course at 6.00 p.m. tomorrow.

Father Karol Wojtyla is a remarkable man. His father was a poor professional soldier, and his mother died when he was three. In 1938 he studied Polish literature at the University in Krakau while still following his interests in soccer (he was a goal-keeper), poetry, skiing, swimming, canoeing and theatre. In the war he worked in a quarry and later in a chemical factory. His theatre company was forced underground. Wojtyla joined an underground theological seminary in 1941 and, after studying for his exams in the Palace of the Cardinal Archbishop of Krakau, he went to Rome and returned in 1948 as a curate. In 1952 his beloved Poland became a communist country under the heel of atheist Russia. He rose rapidly through the Polish Church and was made Archbishop at the age of forty-three.

Pope Paul VI, the conservative Pope whose Humane Vitae encyclical told Catholics living in a desperately overpopulated world not to use contraception, died in 1978. In his place, after the usual Vatican intrigues, a cheerful and unassuming cardinal, Albiro Luciani (sixty-five) Patriarch of Venice was elected to widespread surprise (Ladbrokes had not quoted odds for him).

Taking the name of John Paul I (familiarly Gianpaoulo) this Pope planned to remove two prelates – the Bishop who was head of the Vatican Bank and a Cardinal whose financial and sexual activities had become a scandal. Before he could take these actions Gianpaoulo died (according to Jasper Carrott, Birmingham City became the first football team not to score a goal during the life of a Pope). Documents from his room and details of his death have been suppressed. Many Catholics believe that Gianpaoulo was poisoned. An autopsy was not considered by the Cardinals to be necessary.

And so the Cardinals returned to Rome to decide between two rival Italian prelates. Wojtyla, who had won only five of the one hundred and nine votes in round one, only nine of the one hundred and eight votes in the second ballot, nine of one hundred and nine in the third ballot, twenty-four of the one hundred and seven in the fourth ballot, only emerged as a compromise candidate in a straight contest with Berelli of Florence. To win, one man requires two thirds of the vote; the votes were cast as follows:

Fifth ballot	Berelli 70 Wojtyla 40
Sixth ballot	Berelli 59 Wojtyla 52
Seventh ballot	Berelli 38 Wojtyla 73
Eighth ballot	Berelli — Wojtyla 97

This Pope, the first under the age of sixty since Pius IX (elected in 1946) was also the first non-Italian pope since the Dutchman Adrian VI (died 1523).

He has been, so far, rigidly conservative. He did not dismiss the allegedly crooked Bishop or the allegedly corrupt Cardinal, even promoting the Bishop (Marcinkus) and allowing him to hide in the Vatican when Italian officials sought to interrogate him for banking irregularities. (It's said that these two provided Solidarity with money.) And it's alleged that the Pope's dearest and most trusted political advisor has been the C.I.A., and that in 1980 he received information that Moscow intended to invade Poland, whereupon he sent a message to Brezhnev to say that if they did so, he, the Pope, would leave Rome and join his fellow Poles at the barricades. There are those who believe that this is why the K.G.B. is widely believed to have organised the attempt on his life in 1981.

Perhaps he has been too conservative. Certainly the Dutch and the Americans – radical branches of the Catholic Church – believe so. Certainly those in favour of a more modern attitude towards divorce, fertility control, censorship and the ordination of women think so. The Church has criticised the progressive Catholic leaders in Central America and the Philippines (where Father Gore, whom I met last year in Australia, worked with the poor and against the murderous Marcos regime, for which service he was criticised by his Church and imprisoned on a trumped-up murder charge by his Government). The Pope, of whom so much was expected, has been unhelpful towards those brave prelates who take an active role in resisting the oppression of the poor. Of course the Pope must be cautious. His Church is a worldwide Church and embraces different cultures. Changes must be made with care. Still it is not helpful to speak of peace, to identify with the young, and yet to do so little about the oppressed and the poor. It is surely foolish, too, to expect Catholics to obey the encyclical on contraception.

Pope John Paul II is evidently a man of deep humanity and great courage. He's leading a church which speaks to six hundred and twenty-nine million people (nearly four million in Australia – many of them of Irish and Italian descent). Yet he's in danger, as he drives around in his Popemobile on this trip sponsored by a beer company, of becoming a Pope of the people, a public relations Pope, rather than a Pope who lives for the people. He has done little so far, apart from these journeys, to join together the faithful and to uplift the young, to make fellow Catholics mourn less the tragic death of Pope John Paul I. At present many Catholics, particularly those in the first world, like the singer but not the song. Still three hundred thousand people are expected at Randwick racecourse to attend the Pope's mass. In Australia the Catholic Church is, by tradition, conservative, and John Paul II will not suffer during his visit here the protests he found in Europe and America.

I am a Catholic by upbringing. It was interesting to see the Head of the Church, *the head of the faith*, arriving here in Sydney; and to watch the way in which he endeavoured to spread the word.

MR HENRY BLOFELD

We'd flown to Newcastle in a wobbly Fokker aircraft. Blofeld was on the plane, bouncing away. Whether or not he any longer recognises that he is laying it on with a trowel is a matter for considerable speculation amongst his colleagues. Some take the view that he has a twinkle in his Old Etonian ('my old school') eye. Others argue that he has become the being he created to amuse himself and to pay the substantial bills which result from his somewhat exotic lifestyle. At these State games he sits by a 'phone and on the hour he rings a series of radio stations, switches on and reports on the previous period of play, his foot tapping as he speaks. After the call he puts down the 'phone, says 'my dear old thing' and wonders where a bottle of Chardonnay might be found. Not everything he says, not every word he writes has been analysed with great care but the world would be duller without him. With his cravat and his somewhat experienced expression he is like a cheerful Mister Kurtz.

Blofeld was in splendid form at dinner.

Apparently a child was struck by lightning just outside the hotel, a few days ago. According to our taxi-driver he died four times before being revived. He is conscious now, and has asked for a coca-cola. Henry Blofeld, riding in that same taxi, rather suspected he might ask for something stiffer than a coke if he had died four times and lived to tell the tale.

He told two stories about Bradman which bear repetition. During Percy Chapman's tour of Australia, Jack Fingleton, one of the many Catholics in the team, was out of form. He'd played badly in the first two Test matches, both of which England had won. He journeyed to see a Bishop to be blessed, and to have his bat anointed. Despite these precautions he lost his wicket cheaply in Adelaide. Bradman, next man in, waited till Fingleton had reached the dressing-room, to say that he'd 'see what he could do with a dry bat' before scoring a double hundred.

Another time Bradman had twice been dismissed for low scores by New South Wales, who'd adopted the tactic of putting on a bad off-spin bowler to bowl wide of the off-stump. Twice Bradman, frustrated at the tactic had thrown his bat at the ball and lost his wicket. He travelled up to Queensland, where his old chum Bill Brown adopted the same tactic. Bradman studied this bowler for a few minutes and then called Brown over to talk to him. 'Here Bill' he squeaked, 'I was going to get a hundred and then give it away, but now I'm going to get two hundred and fifty.' He scored two hundred and eighty-three not out.

Cricketers can now experience the phenomenon of Bradman again. Usually, watching old newsreels, modern players are cynical about the heroes of yesteryear. No cricketer I've met has been less then staggered by Bradman's genius, however briefly they have seen it on film. How did he strike those good-length balls between mid-on and mid-wicket? His off-drive is extraordinary for its precision and power. He'd slaughter any attack in 1986, defeat any tactics.

6

Perth: Second Test

PREVIEW

Tomorrow the second Test match begins, and Australia is fighting
to level the series. They have added Peter Sleep, the South Australia
leg-spinner and batsman (with ten first-class centuries) to their
twelve at Brisbane, and omitted Merv Hughes, who is neither as
fast nor as ferocious as his demeanour indicates. England will,
perhaps, pick the same team.

Both teams practised at the W.A.C.A., where the nets are good
but rather dead. At the Australian net, Border lay on the ground
with a video machine, watching film of his batting. He appeared
more at ease than in Brisbane, ready to return to his best.
Strangely, for his Test average is fifty, people still have reservations
about Border's status as a cricketer. He is, as Woodcock has
observed, a pragmatic cricketer. Nothing in his game provokes
gasps; he is a run-maker, an efficient batsman who does not add
to the aesthetics of the game as does Gower. It is no wonder he is
chums with Botham, another simple man who hates the pomp,
the ceremony and the style.

Botham took a rare risk at practice. The local papers have
been full of the Ashes and Botham's influence upon the series, and

the critics are saying that the Australians fear him, believe they can do nothing about his genius (he is, beyond doubt, a cricketing genius – that is the problem really, a genius that found itself in the body of an ordinary, troublesome lad from unremarkable Yeovil). He stood in front of the Australian net, in the midst of the bowlers as if he'd been reading the papers and believed the psychological influence he is supposed to have upon these presumably sloppy Australians. He is, I think, misunderstanding himself. If he has any effect, it is because he does not give a damn, or at least appears not to. He stands in the net, thrashing and guffawing. He so obviously fancies his chances. This is what rocks the Australians, not standing and staring at them. His outrageousness, his unique mixture of undisciplined spirit and sense of occasion, is his strength. These little theatricalities would be better left to Brearley. All Botham is doing is adding to the pressure upon himself.

As far as can be told, the pitch is good. It was relaid two years ago, and was hardly ready when New Zealand and Australia met here last year. The outfield was long and slow, and the pitch lifeless. John Mailey, the groundsman who built Packer's greenhouse pitches which were taken from the hothouse and set down on sporting ovals to be ready for the great cricketers at W.S.C., says that he had to relay the pitch because the roots of the dead common 'couch' grass were, by some mysterious process, slowing it down. He wanted to produce a traditional hard, fast and bouncy Perth pitch, one upon which the ball would fly through. Perth is by reputation the second fastest pitch in the world, after Barbados (where the groundsman is a friend of Joel Garner). Mailey said the speed would not return for a year at least.

The pitch was as white as usual, and had cracks running across it. These cracks are firm, do not wobble and probably will not be a threat. Wickets are lost when pitches are damp, helping the fast bowler to dig the seam into the grass and to move the ball; or when they are dusty, which helps the spinner to get grip and purchase. Cracks can appear frightening and do very little. If the edges were brittle it would be different, for then the ball might dig at the edges, shaking the soil at every impact until holes were formed. Batting might not be so much fun then.

Down the road at Freemantle the yachts are racing. Next door to the West Australian Cricket Association the horses and chariots are chasing around the arena (horse racing, like football, has a variety of forms here). Tomorrow the cricket begins, as these two ordinary teams resume the battle for the Ashes.

DAY ONE

Australia's bowling has been breathtakingly incompetent and for the seventh time in the last eight Test matches England is heading for a score of over four-hundred and fifty in its first innings. Australia renewed its chore this morning when the pitch was fresh. For an hour scarcely a ball was bowled at the stumps behind which Zoehrer flung himself around to collect the new ball wasted by the bowler.

Chris Matthews, retained after Brisbane yet still so raw that he has neither a regular run nor a grooved action, was the worst offender. He is untutored yet to be the hope of the nation. Reid bowled with purpose and was never taken lightly, but he is still only a fair bowler and took only two wickets in a long day. Lawson was disappointing, the slowest of the friendly trio. He was a shadow of the man who took thirty-two wickets in the 1982–3 series and may be near the end of his career. Maybe he has simply bowled too much and his lean body has rebelled. He had very little pace here and did not bowl accurately. He appears unlikely to be able to change from being a fast bowler into being a skilful fast-medium pacer as Roberts, Hadlee and Lillee have done so well. His action is not good enough, and his command of swing and cut less advanced than that of those illustrious gentlemen.

In the stands Walker, Lillee, Meckiff, Malone, Massie and Bragshaw sat and said little. Around them critics wondered if they might not have used the pitch and the breeze to greater effect.

Nor did the support bowlers offer much. Steve Waugh is military medium, and appears surprised whenever he is asked to bowl. He does not consider himself to be a bowler, and a look in his eye indicates that he wouldn't mind facing his own bowling. Greg Matthews dragged his off-spinners too wide of the stumps to be effective. He is at present scarcely a State bowler (so says his personal and Australia's collective manager, Bob Simpson). He is bowling poorly. Waugh and Matthews are really batsmen. They hardly ever bowl even for New South Wales, yet here they were toiling away as if someone seriously thought they might be able to bowl out the English.

Really this is scarcely a county attack, let alone a Test one. None of the bowlers presented any problems once the shine was gone. They rushed in, banged the ball down in the general direction of the stumps and hoped for the best. They had no mastery over the ball, no subtleties, no deceits or riddles to be unravelled. They were plodding and pedestrian.

Not that this is really an Australian attack at all, simply an inferior version of an English one. Four seamers and a finger spinner were chosen, as if this were a damp pitch in Derby. On these rock-hard surfaces batsmen must be beaten in the air, with swing or flight, or off the pitch by bowlers who cut the ball by ripping their fingers across it, or spin it by snapping their wrist. These Australians relied too much on swing, and once this had failed so had their prospects.

Without pace or wrist-spinners to threaten them a moderate batting team would score runs on such a pitch. Yet, on the morning of the match, with a white pitch and with a hot sun, the selectors left out their leg-spinner, Peter Sleep. There are leg-spinners on the selection panel, and Bob Simpson is an old leggie.

Australian teams used to include two fast bowlers, a leg-spinner and a left-arm spinner. Men who merely hit the seam were regarded as cannon-fodder. Despite this, Border was given a modest attack from which the one bowler capable of surprise was omitted. Macbeth murdered sleep; maybe they feared Gatting might do the same.

Until Border is given a proper Australian attack it is hard to imagine that he can lead his team to victory. Until an Australian team is chosen to play Australian cricket it is hard to see any hope for the home team.

This is not to belittle the efforts of Athey and Broad. Athey was not at his best. He was dropped three times and twice was perilously close to LBW. Australian umpires are notoriously conservative in the application of the LBW rule, particularly if the batsman is even half forward, a tribute to the years when a ball might be expected to bounce high over the stumps.

Athey's hooking was sketchy too, and if he is to be solid in defence he must cut out these forays into the unknown. He is still not entirely convincing as an opening batsman, being determined rather than gritty and stubborn. He has some of the Yorkshireman in him, and a little of the gifted youth too.

How odd it is that England's opening batsmen both left counties to further their careers. Broad, confident and ambitious, left the amiable atmosphere at Bristol, where men followed their careers without truly pushing themselves hard, to go to Trent Bridge. Athey left Yorkshire, where his career had risen and fallen, and where he'd appeared to be dogged by Boycott's domination of Yorkshire cricket, and lo and behold went to Bristol, where David Graveney was wondering how to build a tougher attitude.

Broad did play well, tucking the ball to leg and punching it smoothly off the back foot past point. He is the only one of England's opening batsmen (the others being Athey and Slack) whom I'd have picked for this tour. He is steady and unflappable, at his best on hard pitches where the ball comes on to the bat. He did not attempt anything too exotic apart from a couple of square cuts – cross-bat shots from a straight-batted player – and simply waited for the right ball to arrive before playing one of his fluent, well-tried strokes which sent the ball skimming to the boundary.

Athey fell to a yorker – W. G. Grace said he'd never been bowled a yorker, only full-tosses and half-volleys – and Allan Lamb fell for a duck. His highest score in an overseas Test match is sixty, and he has not scored a century in twenty-three Test matches. He's appeared listless, as if exhausted at the number of Tests he has been expected to play. Moreover his game relies on eye, as he punches at the ball with his right hand without much footwork, and now that he is thirty-one his eye may be beginning to fail him. He is a terrific fieldsman, a funny man, and very much part of the set-up. He is, though, in urgent need of a good Test score.

DAY TWO

With his score on one hundred and fourteen Jack Richards received a full-toss from Chris Matthews and hit it to the boundary. A spectator called out 'hey, that's friendly Chris, real friendly'.

So it was throughout the day. So it has been since Friday morning. Rarely can any team, even in India, have batted for two days with such little trouble.

This is the same England team that left Heathrow on 9 October. Jack Richards is the fellow who keeps wicket for Surrey. They are not suddenly supermen. They are encountering some woeful Australian bowling.

Jack Richards can bat a bit. He scored a thousand runs for Surrey last year and has a cunning way of crashing the ball through gully. He is a good professional who has never aspired to be or regarded himself as a batsman of high calibre. In Perth today he could scarcely believe his luck, as he belted the ball around the field as if he were Viv, not Jack. He reached his hundred in one hundred and ninety-five minutes off one hundred and sixty-eight balls, very few of which troubled him. He did not offer a sniff of a chance, not even when he improvised as Gatting prepared to declare. He batted well, but when Richards is able to treat a Nation's bowling in this way it is time to go back to the drawing-board. Eventually he was caught in the deep, to end an intrepid innings which was a revelation to his friends and a scourge to the Australians.

No-one in the press-box had thought to see the day when Australian cricket would be treated with the disdain bordering on contempt displayed by Richards. Australia did not take a wicket for two hundred and fifteen minutes, in which time Gower and Richards added two hundred and sixteen runs with the utmost ease.

Gower is, of course, an accomplished player. He was at his best in this innings, reaching his hundred off one hundred and twenty-five balls. At the crease he drifted back (Gower never moves, he drifts) to persuade the ball to the off. He punctuated his innings with graceful drives which brought gasps from the crowd. Watching Gower bat is one of life's pleasures, like sipping a gin and tonic as the sun slips over the horizon. Occasionally he was imprecise in the execution of his strokes, but for the most part he was elegant and effective, using his wrists to glide the ball to the fence. He was batting as if he were driving a Porsche through the countryside, a blonde in the passenger seat and champagne on ice in the back. Few batsmen in the history of the game have been given the ability to delight through movement.

He scored many of his runs with pulls and off-drives. A fortnight ago, his place in the team was in doubt. Now he's batting with courtesy and beauty, a gift from the gods.

It is hard to see why we worried so much about him. He cannot be as fragile as he appears. He's scored six thousand runs in Test cricket, lots of them against Australia, and has never once denied his gifts nor played an ugly shot (not that he is capable of such a deed).

By the time Gower was out lobbing a catch, the Australians

were in a daze, undone this time not by brutality but by kindness. Broad and Gatting had lost their wickets early in the piece, and at 12.16 Botham fell for a duck. Maybe his psyching of the Australians had had an effect. He appeared heavy-footed and the waters did not part as he walked out to bat, swinging his arm hugely.

Australia's Prime Minister, Mr Bob Hawke, was in the press-box to announce his team for the Prime Minister's XI in Canberra next month, when Botham took guard. He stood surrounded by officials and journalists and yelled 'got him' when the catch was taken, followed by 'you beauty, well done Reidy. There's your story fellows: Prime Minister Dismisses Botham'.

It was Australia's only bright moment of the day. Gatting declared before the close, and Dilley dismissed Boon, whose foot-work is betraying him. Border sent in Waugh to act as a night-watchman, a bold move and one which gives Waugh the chance to build an innings tomorrow. Like so many of the Australians he is at present 'midway between the gift and the act'.

DAY THREE

At the end of the third day's play the Australians, with their captain at the helm, were batting hard to avoid following-on for the second Test match in a row. If they can avoid this ignominy they ought to save the game, because the wicket is still honest.

Border left the field with his wicket still intact and his score on eighty-one. Rarely can any cricketer, let alone any captain, have saved his team so often. Border did nothing remarkable, just went out and battled away as usual. He is certainly an off-side player, cracking the ball through extra-cover and cutting with a swing of the arms when the chance presents itself. Against spinners he jabs forward, and if the ball is near leg-stump he sweeps energetically. It is rare for him to hit the ball between the umpire and square leg. England set a field for the sweep, a deep square leg and a short fine leg, but Border did not hit one in the air. He did once lose his wicket sweeping in England's last tour, trapped by Vic Marks' slower loop. Emburey is a faster bowler, wanting to rattle the ball at the bat, and top edges are less likely off him.

Emburey bowled too short, well below his best after his triumph in Brisbane. His arm was low, which made it more difficult to bowl stump to stump as he prefers to do, and too often he drifted to leg and too often he dropped short, allowing Border to cut. Border left the field unruffled and determined, ready to begin again next morning.

Australia's other main scorers were Waugh and Matthews, the two men from New South Wales, who, critics from other States say owe their selection to the preponderant influence of the Sydney newspapers. Waugh is an old fashioned back foot player. He bats like one imagines men batted one hundred years ago, his green baggy cap pulled over his head, his manner silent and resolute, and his footwork moving towards the stumps, eager for the hook and cut. For a while England fed his strength, defining their aggression by banging the ball into the middle of the pitch. Waugh, his place in doubt, hooked a six and hit his back shot past point with regularity.

At lunch Waugh was set as if in concrete, yet to the first ball after lunch Emburey got one to go with the arm and Waugh was taken at slip. Later Emburey said that this ball had been a fluke, a swinger when an ordinary spinner had been intended. In the press-box (which is still being constructed) it looked like a beautifully conceived arm-ball. Waugh had played with crisp pace and now we wait for his raw talent to emerge.

Greg Matthews batted well for the second time, working hard to save the team. He lost his wicket near the close of play to Dilley, whose later spells were better than his short bowling with the first new ball. Matthews was furious at his dismissal, but he had batted grittily, working hard at the crease. Curiously he is a hero and Border is not. Presumably Border is too rugged, too conventional. Matthews jumps around a lot, hams it up on the field, focuses the cameras on himself. It is not entirely showmanship designed to draw attention to himself; Matthews is the real thing, half crackpot, half dedicated cricketer. He bats with Border's determination and footwork, and allows his character to intrude upon the play. He might get on the nerves of stoical types in a team, for he is forever a jack-in-the-box, forever saying things and calling to the lads to seize their game. Not every cricketer enjoys such electricity from team-mates.

Despite bowling badly in the morning, and despite Emburey's loss of confidence (he can be surprisingly brittle for so distinguished a bowler), England had a good day in the field. The moved with an arrogance brought by success and with a confidence and cohesion absent in English cricket for years. Men chased and fielded as if possessed by a desire to hold the Ashes, as if at last they realised that they could not expect to succeed without hard work.

DeFreitas fielded with particular brilliance. He threw like a West Indian, which isn't altogether surprising since he was born in Dominica, and he lifts England's cricket.

Also those regular morning field practices are paying dividends. Between them Mickey Stewart and Mike Gatting, bubbly coaches, are doing a good job of returning to English cricket those values many cricketers believe to be important, values which have been lost at times in the hurly-burly of international cricket.

Till Dilley's late improvement, Edmonds was the pick of the bowlers. In Brisbane he'd bowled to a simple field, with a ring of fieldsmen in the covers. He, too, has his doubts. For a time a few years ago he lost his bowling, bowling head-hunters and double-bouncers. In India he once lost his run-up, stuttering sometimes as many as forty-one times before releasing the ball. He ended up bowling off one pace, as he can do because his shoulders are so strong. He'd never admit to insecurity, might be unaware of it, but his career points unerringly to it as part of Edmonds' temperament.

This will probably be his last tour and evidently he has decided to bowl line and length, to abandon his flights of fancy which have irritated captains intent upon pressing batsmen. Whatever the appearance, however taut his manner, he's simply a good bowler, a steady bowler not a master of flight or guile. He is a much better cricketer for adopting professional attitudes rather than playing his cricket as a protest against them.

DAY FOUR

Upon stepping onto the back foot and cracking Emburey to the boundary past point Allan Border jumped for joy and punched the air. He is not an emotional man, batting with a matter of fact air, and this was a rare release of his self-discipline. In triumph Botham holds his bat high above his head, his arm straight, saluting the applause and saluting himself. His ego is boosted by success, as once again he defeats those who doubted him. Border is not fuelled by this need for an enemy, does not rely upon adversity or by a tempting of the fates. He finds his team in difficulty and he saves them in a way designed not to bring attention upon himself but to deflect it. Botham is an anti-hero. Border is a reluctant saviour.

It was, again, an innings of great courage. He's scored over six thousand runs at a Test average of fifty-two. For him, it was just another day at the office.

England had whittled away at his partners and had been held up mainly by Geoff Lawson, who combines a terror of fast bowling with an ability to play terrific drives. He cobbled twenty-odd runs before losing his wicket. When Border played that vital cut his partner was the tall Bruce Reid, a man who bats below Mervyn Hughes, a natural number eleven. As Reid walks out to bat so the groundsman starts up the engine upon his roller. This time Reid, to the huge cheers of his local crowd, played sound, short forward defensive shots as his partner collected the runs required to save the follow-on, and, in all probability, the game.

With a big lead, England tried to force the pace and did not do so convincingly. Wickets fell in a rush at the end, many to the persevering Steve Waugh (his haul will probably guarantee him a bowl in Adelaide, so for England every cloud has a silver lining). Lawson was expensive, and short; after his first spell he limped forlornly from the field and probably left the Test match arena for good. Reid was again the best of the faster bowlers, proving hard to attack with his steep lift and ability to dart a sudden, wicked bouncer at the batsman.

A clutch of wickets fell as England chased runs, batsmen throwing away their wickets as cricketers are rarely asked to do in Test cricket. Gatting's innings was curious. His fifty in Brisbane is still his highest score of the tour, and here he set about building an innings and restoring his form. Only as stumps drew near did he biff and bang. The Australians did bowl accurately as the day wore on, and they fielded well too, their spirits raised by the un-expected saving of the follow-on. Nevertheless England's captain might have impressed with more daring. He is a powerful, simple striker of the ball who, like Botham, does not regard spinners as serious bowlers. Gatting does not think much of Edmonds and Emburey, let alone Greg Matthews, and in the field he wonders why batsmen allow them to bowl such rubbish. Australia scarcely delivered an over of spin (Border's opinion of Matthews may be not dissimilar to Gatting's), but forced England's captain to hit runs off nagging medium-pacers who bowled at the stumps, denying him the width he requires to belt the ball through he covers.

Gatting, like Border and Botham, does not hit the ball so well between mid-on and square-leg. He can loft spinners to the deep, but the on-drive, a mark of the great, is not his strongest shot. His body does not easily move into position to play this difficult stroke, as mastered by Greg Chappell, Viv Richards, Gavaskar, Crowe and a few others. His head rests on the off-side of his body, rather than on the left shoulder, which makes it difficult to lead it into position over the ball on leg-stump.

England led by three hundred and ninety at the close. Gatting could have declared at three hundred and fifty, to give his bowlers twenty minutes at Boon and Marsh. Australia could hardly have won, for they have only one outstanding batsman. Had England batted with a little more flair an hour earlier they could have led by three hundred and seventy at 5.30, an impregnable position. Boon had lost his wicket in just such a period two days earlier.

Gatting might have got his declaration wrong in the match. I was not certain about his decision to close the innings at five hundred and ninety-two on Saturday, notwithstanding the loss of Boon. England had been sailing along and another fifty runs or so could have been useful in forcing Australia to follow-on. In failing to close tonight he has improved Australia's chance of saving the game. Probably after the pounding England has been given in the last twelve months Gatting and his team are loath to rush anything. It is understandable; Test match cricket is for keeps.

The only other event which disturbed the tranquility of sitting in the sunshine and watching the English batsmen reach five hundred and ninety-two for the loss of eight wickets was an article which appeared in *The Australian* quoting the memoirs of King George V's doctor Lord Dawson who, it was revealed, had hastened the death of the king so that

'the death received its first announcement in the morning papers rather than in the less appropriate field of the evening journalist.'

John Thicknesse, the ubiquitous representative of the *Evening Standard*, was not amused by this slight.

DAY FIVE

Despite losing Boon to the first ball of the day Australia easily saved the second Test match. England took only five wickets on a slow pitch which offered occasional turn. In the end the cracks did widen but the ball only turned a couple of times, and then shot wastefully to slip. Marsh and Jones resisted stoically, with Jones using his feet well and Marsh trotting mildly along, a farmer bringing in the eggs. Border fell for twenty-eight which left Ritchie and Matthews to secure the draw for Australia.

England plodded through the day, apart from Dilley who swung the ball away from the bat. As Ellison showed in 1985, the out-swinger is the wicket-taking ball in Test cricket, because the out-swing bowler has slips waiting for a catch, whereas the in-swinger is allowed only two men short and square on the leg-side. If the authorities in 1933 had chosen to rule against the length of bodyline bowling rather than the line, in-swing bowling might have survived. If they'd drawn a line across the pitch and said that anything pitched short of it was intimidating and illegal, and left captains free to field men in a ring on the leg-side, the tradition of in-swing bowling might not have been lost.

England has the only out-swing bowler in either team, Dilley. But Botham and DeFreitas try to swing it away, as for that matter do Small and Foster. Most of the Australians are straight up and down merchants, or left-handers who try to bring the ball back after aiming it at the slips. Only Alderman of the Australians appears able to entice an appeal for an edge of a full, rising ball. And he is in South Africa.

Dilley is a good bowler now that he has absorbed the lesson taught by Hadlee last year. Hadlee runs in a straight line, veering neither to the right nor to the left, and at the bowling crease his arm swings through 270° without ever leaving the straight line between stump and stump. Gladstone Small has copied him too, cutting down his run and concentrating upon technique. In contrast Greg Thomas is still erratic in his movements, and is off balance at the moment of delivery.

As Australia propped and cocked and the game drifted by, Gatting had one plan: that Edmonds and Emburey would trap the batsmen with bat/pad catchers. Once this did not work he appeared to abandon hope of winning, did not strain muscle and brain in an effort to secure a second victory. In any event nothing much happened for hours as the game faded away.

Brian Close was not pleased. In fact he was in great form. He'd arranged for a fortnight's holiday in Perth last June because his wife deserved a break and it'd be fun to get away. He said you could have knocked him down with a feather when he found that his holiday coincided with the Test match. 'Yes,' I said. His wife had been a bit miffed. He was off home in a few days' time, just as well really because he couldn't stand another couple of days watching this lot. Imagination had gone out of the game. Gatting was doing it all by the book. A captain had to fiddle batsmen out in these conditions. He'd have tried a few things and if a bowler hadn't taken a wicket in a few overs he'd be off. A captain cannot let the game wander, he must take charge of it. Don Wilson and Raymond Illingworth would have soon had them out on this pitch if he was leading them. They were bowling at the wrong ends and the field placing was rotten, any fool could see it.

Later I talked to Jack Birkenshaw, and we too discussed the use of the spinners on this final day, and their place in English cricket in general. Here, after all, was the ideal opportunity for spinners to win a game, playing with runs on the board, a hot sun and a fifth day pitch. Yet they failed. He echoed some of Close's sentiments. He observed that Allan Lamb and Bill Athey had contrived to walk twenty metres or so up and down the pitch to resume their position on the edges of the wicket, ready to fling themselves forward at the hint of a catch. Nothing fell their way and yet nothing different was tried as the match fell to sleep. Athey and Lamb never moved from short leg and silly point; like doomed explorers they paddled along their dusty trail, forever waiting for the drinks to arrive, though when they did they sipped not artesian water but lemonade. Birkinshaw and Close were puzzled, wondering if England's tactics, which may reflect the tactics universally used by today's spinners, were wise. Could not more have been done to take wickets than just to bowl tightly and to ask Athey and Lamb to crowd on the edge of the set. Was a spinner's repertoire now so limited?

In the last twenty years or so the techniques of spin bowlers have changed. Whereas spinners used to place men at short leg and close point only when the ball was turning sharply, now it is customary. Birkinshaw and Close advanced a pile of reasons for this gradual change. Fieldsmen wear helmets and so crouch closer to the bat, without peril. Suddenly inside edges onto the pad are not moral victories for the bowlers, they are chances. Any edged defensive shot which does not snick off dead bats can carry. Other parts of the game have changed too. Tail-enders do not slog their wicket away any more, do not lift their heads at the sight of a flighted delivery; moreover there are fewer incompetent batsmen down the order. Also this is an age of percentage cricket, as players scramble for runs and obey the laws of probability in their choice of shots.

Despite these matters, both these new fielding positions and the decline in the attacking art of spin bowling are caused as much as anything by the heavy bats currently in vogue. Close and Birkinshaw both agreed that this is a factor in forcing Edmonds and Emburey, and those who follow, to fire the ball into the pitch, rather than into the air.

Older spinners grew up believing their job was to encourage the drive and to beat it. They'd place men at slip and gully and try to entice an outside edge. Batsmen could play their strokes freely. If they did not get to the pitch of the ball, they might edge it to slip. Batsmen could be expected to work for singles and to stroke the ball into gaps, rather like Larry Gomes. Few players bat so delicately these days. Most either blast the ball or defend it. In reaction to this spinners place their men close and deep, the old ring of fielders in the covers does not last long and a single clout over the top is enough to send fieldsmen to the boundary.

Years ago a spinner wanted a batsman to go for a big hit, because he might beat him in the air and take his wicket. A bowler who used the air had a chance. Now the odds have changed. Batsmen like Pollock, Richards, Gooch and Botham began to use bats like railway sleepers. They found they could carry the boundary regularly, and that even edges drifted over fieldsmen's heads. Spinners stopped playing the game, learned to bowl with flatter trajectories to stifle strokes, relying upon pressure for wickets. They began to search for inside edges in the hope that the ball might plop off the pad into the hands of the intrepid men hard by. They began to defend with the ball and attack with their fieldsmen. Inside edges are the product of strangled strokes, outside edges are the result of free shots, the bat swinging without the body intruding.

73

With men so close to the bat spinners could not, in any case, risk flighting the ball for fear of endangering the shins of team-mates. Their captains preferred these tactics because it helped them to keep the pressure upon the batsmen in the war of attrition upon the field. It is a trend that has restricted the mastery of flight and the development of young spinners, who find themselves expected to bowl to thunderous batsmen holding prodigious implements, with fellow professionals a yard from the bat. Unsurprisingly there are very few promising youngsters in Australia, England or the West Indies who express their talents by spinning the ball.

Nor has the spread of one-day cricket helped, as bowlers learn to defend rather than to attack, and get used to public batterings. At present the most important art for a young spinner is to be able to bowl, as flat as possible, at a batsman's toes.

And so England drew the second Test match, a draw that will lift the hopes of the Australians. Border continues to be the backbone of nearly every Australian innings. Here he did nothing flash – he never does. His greatness lies in the frequency with which he makes vital runs for his team. His Test record is superb, and hard earned. The teams will go to Adelaide with England one up. Usually the Adelaide pitch is a friendly host for the batsmen, and a draw can be expected there. After that we go to Melbourne, where the seamers will have their say, and then on to Sydney, where the spinners can be expected to dominate the match. By the end of the series these two teams will have been stretched and tested in every direction, which is as it should be.

Gatting has only one worry at present. In mid-afternoon Botham left the field, clutching his ribs. He is rarely forced from the field when playing for England, and this injury may be serious. He is prodigiously strong and very brave, and would not have walked off without due cause. If he is unfit to play in Adelaide, with which two men can England replace him?

SECOND TEST, Perth
November 28, 29, 30, December 2, 3, 1986

ENGLAND

B. C. Broad	c Zoehrer b Reid	162	lbw b Waugh	16
C. W. J. Athey	b Reid	96	c Border b Reid	6
A. J. Lamb	c Zoehrer b Reid	0	(4) lbw b Reid	2
M. W. Gatting*	c Waugh b C. Matthews	14	(3) b Waugh	70
D. I. Gower	c Waugh b C. Matthews	136	c Zoehrer b Waugh	48
I. T. Botham	c Border b Reid	0	c G. Matthews b Reid	6
C. J. Richards†	c Waugh b C. Matthews	133	c Lawson b Waugh	15
P. A. J. DeFreitas	lbw b C. Matthews	11	b Waugh	15
J. E. Emburey	not out	5	not out	4
P. H. Edmonds	did not bat			
G. R. Dilley	did not bat			
Extras	(b 4, lb 15, w 3, nb 13)	35	(b 4, lb 9, nb 4)	17
TOTAL	(8 wkts dec)	592	(8 wkts dec)	199

Fall of wickets: 223, 227, 275, 333, 339, 546, 585, 592.
Second innings: 8, 47, 50, 123, 140, 172, 190, 199.
Bowling: Lawson 41-8-126-0; C. Matthews 29.1-4-112-3; Reid 40-8-115-4; Waugh 24-4-90-0; G. Matthews 34-3-124-1; Border 2-0-6-0.
Second innings: Reid 21-3-58-3; Lawson 9-1-44-0; Waugh 21.3-4-69-5; C. Matthews 2-0-15-0.

AUSTRALIA

G. R. Marsh	c Broad b Botham	15	(2) lbw b Emburey	49
D. C. Boon	b Dilley	2	(1) c Botham b Dilley	9
S. R. Waugh	c Bothan b Emburey	71	(3) run out	69
D. M. Jones	c Athey b Edmonds	27	(4) c Lamb b Edmongs	16
A. R. Border*	c Richards b Dilley	125	(5) not out	24
G. M. Ritchie	c Botham b Edmonds	33	(6) not out	14
G. R. J. Matthews	c Botham b Dilley	45		
T. J. Zoehrer†	lbw b Dilley	29		
G. F. Lawson	b DeFreitas	13		
C. D. Matthews	c Broad b Emburey	10		
B. A. Reid	not out	2		
Extras	(b 9, lb 9, nb 11)	29	(b 9, lb 6, nb 10)	25
TOTAL		401	(4 wkts)	197

Fall of wickets 4, 64, 114, 128, 198, 279, 334, 360, 385.
Second innings: 0, 126, 142, 152.
Bowling: Botham 22-4-72-1; Dilley 24-4-79-4; Emburey 43-9-110-2; DeFreitas 24-4-67-1; Edmonds 21-4-55-2.
Second innings: Dilley 15-1-53-1; Botham 7.2-4-13-0; DeFreitas 13.4-2-47-0; Emburey 28-11-41-1; Edmonds 27-13-25-1; Gatting 5-3-3-0; Lamb 1-1-0-0.
Toss: England.
Umpires: P. J. McConnell and R. A. French.
Man of the match: B. C. Broad.
MATCH DRAWN.

7

Interlude III

THE PRIME MINISTER TURNS UP

Mr Hawke was immensely impressive. He is Labour's second Prime Minister since the war, his predecessor being the charismatic Gough Whitlam, whose Government was dismissed in disgraceful circumstances by Sir John Kerr, the Governor-General of Australia, the Queen's Representative and an old friend of Whitlam's; a man with an ambitious wife, a taste for alcohol, and a keen sense of disappointment in himself. In 1975 Kerr invoked powers, widely regarded as moribund, to oust the Whitlam Government elected in 1972 and re-elected in 1974. Whitlam, a man of ideas, had revived the arts, helped the Aborigines, and taken his soldiers out of Vietnam. He'd brought a fresh spirit to Australia, a spirit contrary to the philistine tradition of the Liberal Governments before him. Writers had returned to their homeland, Aborigines had been given hope, and the dispossessed felt at last that they had a chance. Unfortunately Whitlam governed at the time of the oil crisis and unfortunately some of his ministers, for so long in opposition, had hurried too much to give substance to their ideas. The Labour Government appeared to be accident-prone, and slowly it was undone by the right-wing forces behind the scenes, who rather

76

than waiting a year for an election, caused Whitlam and his party to be dismissed from office. Even Rupert Murdoch who had twice supported Whitlam in elections, (his string of newspapers advocating his cause) worked hard to undermine his cause. This business left a sour taste, for a left-wing Government had been brought down by a philistine, prudish force of the right and apparently by one of its own men. Worst of all, because of its inefficiency, because of its indiscretions, the Labour party had given its enemies the rope for the hanging.

Whitlam and Hawke have in common a belief that they are born to rule, a belief which in Whitlam found expression in ideas, arrogance and humour (unlike Hawke, who is not a man to cross, Whitlam could see the funny side) and in Hawke in driving ruthlessly to the top. Hawke was elected leader of the Labour party within two years of leaving his job as leader of the Australian trade union movement, and taking a seat. He was determined to present his party as capable of efficient management of the economy, as a pragmatic party of government, rather than as a radical party of ideas. He has won two general elections and might very well win the next. He is fighting to be allowed to rule by the forces of business and of the right, fighting to win them over. He has not helped Mr Lange to keep American nuclear bombs out of the area, and he has not helped the underprivileged as much as might be expected of a Labour leader.

I found Hawke, in this brief encounter, to be a man of enormous strength. He has a sharp voice which embraces a rasping Australian twang surprising in a Rhodes Scholar, and less surprising in a populist Prime Minister. He has greying hair, brown and slightly gnarled skin and sharp features, like something out of *Wind in the Willows*. He has a way about him, which suggests that though he is meeting the Pope tomorrow, he'd really rather be on the Hill with the boys.

Hawke sees himself as a man to unite Australia, and he wants to be loved; a characteristic, with his ambition, which has been the driving force in his life. He talks of consensus, and is forever knocking together the heads of businessmen and trade union leaders as if politics were not a battle of opposites, as if conflicts were not the order of things. Whenever Australia triumphs at anything there is Hawke, pleased as punch, celebrating though not drinking (in his earlier days someone said of him that when he was drinking nothing was possible, and when he was off the drink anything was possible. Hawke is now teetotal).

This was a brilliant performance by an intriguing man, lasting a few minutes. He stalked off, security advisors and officials fore and aft, to meet the Channel 9 commentators and to add his wisdom to theirs. Thereafter he dashed off, a schedule to keep, hands to shake, and a curious shyness to protect. That brashness is typical of Australia. Hawke's democratic, pragmatic and matey approach, which has won him the fame, the love and the power for which he yearns, seems to hide an essentially insecure and shy character. Hawke, like so many apparent extroverts, seems to need the blessings of love and success.

Reporters did, as he suggested, record his sharp as a shark's teeth reaction to Botham's dismissal. Really he had not been in the press-box for twenty seconds when Bothan fell for a duck. His reaction: 'Got him you beauty, well done Reidy. There's your story fellows: Prime Minister dismisses Botham', was instantaneous. He was pleased, genuinely pleased for Australia and the Australian team, and a second later he milked the occasion for all it was worth.

PATRICK EAGAR TAKES SOME PHOTOGRAPHS

Spent an afternoon with Patrick Eagar and Adrian Murrell, cricket court photographers. We chatted in spurts, between bowls. As the bowler ran in they'd stare into their view-finders, on edge in case a wicket fell, or a vivid stroke was played. Occasionally, a fraction of a second after the ball had been bowled, there'd be a click. They studied the batman's movement, searching for hints of vulnerability or vigour. Then the moment passed, and they'd resume their conversation till the bowler turned once again.

Unlike the reporters lingering over their wine and cheese, Eagar and Murrell did not miss a single ball. Murrell had been caught out the day before. Trapped in conversation by a journalist, he'd missed the first ball after lunch and Waugh had lost his wicket to it.

Throughout the afternoon Eagar and Murrell chatted away, clicking occasionally, watching the clouds, ready to change their exposures. It was a particularly cloudy day, and if the sun was hidden as the bowler ran in, they'd adjust their cameras, gambling on predicting the light accurately. Nothing could be worse than a picture showing half light and half shade. They'd rather the skies were clear, or the cloud cover total. Every ball they worried about the bands of light and dark shooting across the ground. They'd chosen their position high in the stand, over mid-off, because they expected wickets to fall. Also the background was clear, nothing to distract the eye. Backgrounds were the most important thing. Choose the wrong angle and the whole thing was ruined, because irrelevant things would catch the eye. This position, they said, was not so effective for batting shots, being too far away and too high up to catch the drama. Maybe if the batsmen settled they might move to ground level, nearer to the action. It was hard to tell, whether to expect wickets or runs; they had to guess this too. Border was a nuisance. At this angle, if a left-hander played a drive, the shadow from his arms might hide his face. It depended what shot he played really. Hooks and cuts were fine, but those moves down the pitch to drive were no use. Trouble is, you'd click them by instinct, wasting a shot.

Eagar takes about two hundred photos a day at a Test match, though this varies depending upon the cricket. At home he has a library of a quarter of a million photographs, stored mainly as negatives and transparencies, as precious as a cellar of wine. He's been a sports' photographer since 1965, and has concentrated upon cricket because he likes the game and because few other photographers are prepared to sit through the thirty hours of a Test match in the hope of a handful of excellent prints. He wasn't allowed to work at Test matches in England until 1972, because till then they were the exclusive domain of the photographic agencies. He used to trot around all the counties seeking photographs of possible England players. It was even worse with the tourists, because some of them might not play in particular games and rain might fall when their turn came. Since 1972 he has been able to photograph Test matches, though at Lord's he cannot go in the pavilion to do so, and must therefore work at an angle not always of his choosing.

Patrick is sending photographs to *The Sunday Times* to accompany my reports. Usually he sends his film home to be printed two or three months later, when he has time. With *The Sunday Times* though, he rushes off to develop the film at the close of play, having noted the position on the rolls of possible photographs. In whatever darkroom he has been able to locate he studies the negatives, dries them and chooses one. It must be the right shape, for *The Sunday Times*, unlike other papers, gives him a specific hole to fill, so it isn't a matter of sending his best photo, but one which will fill the hole. A picture of someone edging to gully is no use if he has a long, thin space available.

He'd choose one, print and enlarge it, and put it on the machine which sent it to London. Something to do with a beam of light, he said, and was not asked to expand. On Saturday, he'd been in place every ball, and had moved his cameras only during intervals. Moving was quite a business, because his equipment was heavy. He was amused at Adrian's interest in off-beat photographs of players chatting or spectators fighting. That wasn't really his scene. He did think, though, that the reporters had it pretty easy, enjoying their lunch, living on expenses, faxing (handwritten articles can now be 'faxed' across by one of those beam of light things) or ringing or using word-processors to get their copy through. Reporters were looked after, photographers were not. It was fun, though, except in Pakistan or the West Indies where the facilities were poor and he'd experienced obstruction and frustration in getting his work back to England. Still, the sporting photographic fraternity around the world was very friendly, and someone usually lent a hand.

Eagar is an artist and a craftsman in his own right, and throughout the afternoon he worked with meticulous love, playing his part in the vast empire of international cricket.

8

Melbourne:
England v. Victoria

DAY ONE

On the Saturday of Test matches England batsmen score centuries on flat pitches. Botham scored a hundred in Brisbane, Richards and Gower reached three figures in Perth. On the Saturdays of State games wickets fall, in the words of the estimable Blofeld, like ninepins. In Newcastle seventeen wickets were taken, and in Melbourne today sixteen were lost.

In part today's collapse was due to a fresh pitch which had a hint of green about it. Though the ball did not seam (according to the bowler) it did so after uneven bounce (according to the batsmen). Whitaker and Athey were particularly unfortunate to encounter deliveries which bounced at their chests. But really there was no devil in the pitch and wickets should not have fallen so easily.

Mike Gatting had an extraordinary day. He first appeared on the field at 10.50, rather later than expected. Apparently this was due to an alarm clock that failed to do its presumably awesome duty. He continued with an erratic spell of bowling during the course of which one wag called 'get 'em on the pitch, fatso' (which did not please England's captain) and three batsmen hooked bumpers to long-leg. His day ended with a back foot swish which was taken by Whatmore in the slips.

Sleeping in is the sort of thing a chap does from time to time, and it is a good idea to take wickets by way of recompense; it is not such a good idea to lose your own wicket to an undisciplined slash when your team is in trouble.

England, fielding two wicket-keepers, three bowlers, a belated captain and a sick Lamb, did remarkably well in the morning. Foster trapped Frazer in front to end thirty-one minutes of sullen resistance, Jones was caught at slip, for once failing to leave alone a wide delivery, and poking at an out-swinger, while Whatmore's top-edge off Small dropped into French's gloves. The forgotten men, those who will do to change a scene or two, had rather a good morning. At this point England's third seamer, the rotund Gatting, was asked by Gower (who did not immediately surrender the power which had so precipitously been invested in him) to replace Small. Gatting bowled his out-swingers at a more belligerent pace than usual, and was able to lift the ball over the batsmen's head, which tried the patience of French (which appears to be infinite) and persuaded the batsmen to hook to long-leg where Foster, who brought a helmet out with him after lunch in case the barrage continued, held three catches. Dodemaide, Siddons and O'Donnell fell in this way as Victoria's collapse continued. In the stand, Ian Redpath, who knew when to sway, was aghast at their incompetence. Only the sprightly Dimattina, a typical wicket-keeper, offered a correct defence. Once Hibbert had flashed at Foster the innings was near its end, though Hughes' edge was productive for a few minutes.

Foster bowled well, and Small was not far behind. England may find themselves without a batsman and bowler in Adelaide (both called Botham). If they decide to play a batsman in his place it might be wise to leave out Edmonds or DeFreitas, and to let Foster help Dilley. He has bowled splendidly throughout and is desperately unlucky to find his colleagues in such good form.

Having surprised themselves, not to mention the three thousand three hundred and sixty spectators (the other one hundred and thirty-five thousand six hundred seats in this cavernous ground were empty) by dismissing Victoria for one hundred and one England began losing wickets with the accustomed Saturday rapidity. Slack, hauled from the nets, hooked to long leg which will make him more lugubrious still. Whitaker was caught and had to walk back to the pavilion (which is a bit like walking from Taunton to Bridgewater) without a run to his name. It is hard for those who bat only twice a month. Gower, in pleasing form, snicked one and Richards found the going rather tougher than in Perth. After Gatting's fall, Athey and French settled in for an hour, feeding off a spate of short pitched deliveries from bowlers excited at seeing a ball lift in Melbourne, and the sixth wicket did not fall till the last over, Athey being caught at short leg after one hundred and sixty eight minutes at the crease. It's just as well he lasted so long. Lamb was still sick and Edmonds was prostrate in the dressing-room wondering how, with all his subtlety, he had taken four wickets less than Gatting.

By the close Victoria was back in the match. Apart from Hughes, the Sancho Panza of the these parts, most of the bowling was done by Dodemaide and O'Donnell, two sturdy lads who pick their bats up high and who bowl out-swingers at fast-medium. They are products of their time, and might play in the one-day series. At gully the ageing Bright watched the strange proceedings draw to a close. He is long in the tooth and not even cricket's most curious days catch him by surprise.

DAY TWO

England took a substantial lead, with Foster and Lamb batting effectively. Lamb, in better health, hit the ball hard. A pebble of a man with a harsh voice which has lost none of its South African edge, he is fighting to hold his place. It can be harder to get into the England team than to get out of it. Once a man is accepted into the inner-ring he needs only to hit a fifty every fourth inning or so and his omission is not countenanced. Loyalty is a word used by men of quality and strength. Lamb, like DeFreitas and Dilley, has won his place in the inner-ring because of his character and his attitude to cricket. He has served the side well in the past and Gatting would be reluctant to disturb the subtle balance of character in his team by losing him.

Inner-rings are splendid for those within them. To outsiders they can be infuriating and destructive. Nothing is more perplexing, more disturbing, than to fail to be accepted within a cabinet. Codes, messages, collective opinions are misunderstood, and the distance between the group and the individual exaggerated. In these circumstances the outsider can either crumple and disappear, or fight against the insiders. Edmonds fought Brearley in 1978–9, and the more he pricked the bigger grew the barrier against him. The England team led by Willis, like the team led by Ian Chappell, like the one led by Clive Lloyd, had a sense of unity which was intolerant of intruders and sceptics, a mood which forces away outsiders like Edmonds. It can happen in county cricket too. At Somerset, Jeremy Lloyds felt that he was never really accepted, that his face never quite fitted. He was right, in a way. He had an air of might and style which angered some of those in charge at the time, which in turn made his failings more obvious, and made it more difficult for him to succeed.

Foster hit well, swinging the bat hard and straight. He hit Ray Bright back over his head several times, and displayed some tremendous off-drives. He ought really to bat up the order for Essex and to turn himself into an all-rounder. He is a man who needs regular cricket to be at his best, yet there are times when, somehow or other, he appears to be the perennial twelfth man. He misses the work upon which he relies to be at his best. He bowled well yesterday, considering this characteristic, and batted well today. He must wonder what DeFreitas has done to enjoy his eminence.

Botham's relationship with DeFreitas continues to be intriguing. They are inseparable. Towards the end of his days with Somerset Ian did not have a following among the young players. I do not know why. Richard Ollis was a good friend but he did not make it, and none of the others lasted the pace with him, however dazzled they were at first. Ian had sensed this distancing between himself and the youngsters in his years as captain, and had been unable to do anything about it. He clung to his friendships among the older players, and had to be content with that. Probably the youngsters were not of the same spirit as Ian, were not men to live their lives in the same way. They were either too young or too strong-minded. Towards the end Ian, a man who is desperate to be surrounded by friends and by fellow-travellers, was nearly alone.

With DeFreitas in his wake he is happy again, a mate and a follower to accompany him. He will give to DeFreitas the full force of his remarkable character, with its streak of generosity and fellow feeling. If DeFreitas is strong enough to understand this mateyness from the lad from Yeovil it will bring him fun and advancement.

Victoria fought back at the close of play, and finished the day eighty runs or so behind England, with all their second innings' wickets intact.

DAY THREE

These State games are degenerating into farce. Today's cricket was played in front of a disappointing crowd, enlivened only by hordes of schoolboys who were there, presumably, by way of punishment. In the press-box everyone sat glumly, hoping for rain, watching Hibbert grind his way to seventy-one not out in five hours.

It'd help if people at the Melbourne Cricket Ground were a friendly lot. Melbournians have a reputation for surliness. Though the streets are wide to accommodate the trams which still breeze through it, though the city itself appears to be interesting, the people are reputed to be pale, wasted and dreary. Experiences so far support this traditional view of Melbourne.

Since the authorities had not considered it a part of their duty to provide refreshments for the press we repaired to the pie-shops to queue with the kids. Mr Hornadge says that Australia is a nation of pie-eaters. One Miss Wong Lai Sin, interviewed by an airport reporter, said that she

'had long wanted to visit Australia and eat a meat pie and see a kangaroo.'

In the outback in the old days pies could be filled with crocodile's rump, bandicoot's brains and catfish, or so the ballad-mongers say. According to Bill Haden's *Cook Book*:

'In those early days, possums were caught, cleaned and cut up, put into a hollowed-out pumpkin which was then roasted until the meat was cooked; a very tasty pie it was, too.'

Around the ground, pies were guzzled and beer sipped as the game slowly slid towards a cold and showery close of play. A game played on the edge of the square, a game for which neither side had shown any particular enthusiasm (for which neglect England can largely be blamed) will die tomorrow and no-one will mourn it.

It'd be far better if these games were played in some small country town where the match would be an occasion. It'd help, too, if prize money were put up to goad the players to play their best. This might not be necessary in a better world, but at present these fixtures played between Test matches are dreadful.

Victoria is fighting on and might save the game, not that anyone appears to care much. England will need quick wickets in the morning if a second State victory is to be recorded. If England does win it will be by accident, despite the application shown by Athey, Foster and Small (who bowled very well today, much more accurately than Foster who has lost his line). For Victoria the most stubborn batsman was Paul Hibbert, an angular left-hander, who was one of the many men who represented Australia during the revolution in 1977 to have returned to obscurity, and the most dashing batsman was Simon O'Donnell, who has the good looks, long hair and simple approach to cricket of a lesser Botham. His bowling is ordinary but he is a gifted if inflexible striker of the ball. Botham, of course, is flexible and imaginative. He is not as dull-witted as some of those who follow him, and has a shrewd psychological feel for the game.

In the press-box Gatting's late arrival on Saturday morning has turned into a *cause célèbre*. Henry Blofeld has written an ill-advised article in a local paper describing Gatting as a 'little Hitler' and condemning him as cliché-ridden (which wasn't bad from Blowers!). Presumably he was no less forthright in *The Sunday Express*. No doubt this was a piece Henry jotted on the back of an envelope, and of course, he must respect the Australian loathing for English circumlocution but even so it was a bit strong. Henry is the most terrific media ham, but these words are in print and indelibly stamped on Gatting's mind. Understandably he is offended.

Gatting was, perhaps, a trifle indiscreet. Still it was hard for most of us to take the matter seriously, and it would have been forgotten had not a couple of tabloids, as desperate for a hard news' story as an alcoholic in a desert for a beer, seized upon it. One or two reporters rushed around, whereupon the others had to do the same for fear of being blamed by their editors for missing a scoop.

England's management team made the mistake of creating a smokescreen around the matter and soon headlines blazed, sating the appetite even of editors, and from a tiny misdemeanour came a raging crisis.

The England team with the Australian Prime Minister Bob
Hawke just before their game against his side. Canberra,
December 23, 1986.

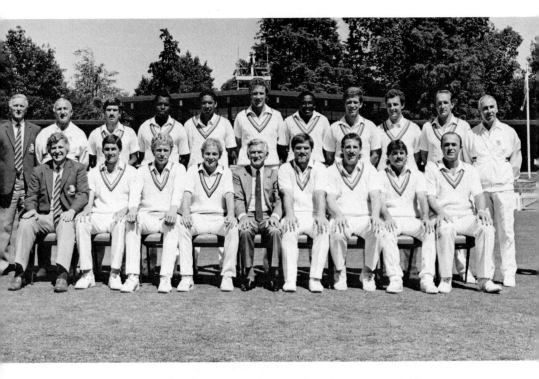

England completed a unique hat-trick. They retained The
Ashes 2–1, they won the 'Perth Challenge' Quadrangular
series and a 'World Series' Triangular one-day series
involving Australia and the West Indies.

(a) The way in which Australian cricket was sold on Kerry Packer's Channel 9 came in for much criticism. It is a moot point as to whether these 'fill-in' entertainments could really be justified.

(b) Second Test at the WACA, Perth 1986: entertaining the crowd during the lunch interval.

(a) Chris Broad's success was warmly appreciated by players and spectators alike. He was confident when coming to the wicket and the Australians were glad to see the back of him. Aside from his three centuries, he topped the batting averages and was made Man-of-the-Series.

(b) Mike Gatting established himself as England's captain for some time to come. No-one, not even Brearley, handled Botham better.

(a) The England dressing room was awash with champagne . . .

(b) . . . and the odd intruder, after England won the fourth Test in Melbourne – and retained the Ashes.

(a) Allan Border was the target of the Australian media for much of this series. Australians could win the Davis Cup while Freemantle was the centre of the world's sport stage with the America's Cup, yet what they wanted most was cricket success, and cricket success against the Poms.

(b) Fortunately, Border was not the only one to come in for some good humoured criticism, though the selectors had the last laugh when they selected spin-bowler Peter Taylor from grade cricket for the fifth Test.

(a) Peter Taylor is congratulated after another wicket. In his Test debut, he took 8 for 162 and scored 53 runs.

(b) Meanwhile, Greg Matthews had become a folk-hero of sorts. It may just be premature, but the Australian public badly wants a Botham-like home-grown success story.

(a) *Left:* Jack Richards was another inspired selection. Few would have gambled on him making the Test side and no-one would have bet on him making a century before the second Test in Perth.

(b) *Right:* Philip DeFreitas was an enthusiastic, energetic and ebullient member of the team. The players' fancy-dress Christmas party (a tour highlight) saw him as a poor man's James I, or a very happy hooker.

(c) *Left:* James Whitaker, ever waiting in the wings, has immense talent and in the end talent wins out.

(d) *Right:* England's unsung hero was undoubtedly tour manager, Peter Lush; his quiet diplomacy and sensibility ensured that there could be no repeat of last year's tour to the West Indies.

Cricket photographers, Patrick Eagar (glasses) and Adrian
Murrell (non-cricketing tie), outside the Grace Gates at
Lord's. It makes a change to see them without cameras,
zoom lenses and tripods.

Goaded by the newspapers into an appearance of resolve, Mr Lush had issued a statement, the contents of which were slipped under my door in the dead of night. Peter Lush, they revealed, confirmed that Mike Gatting had been severely reprimanded for over-sleeping. To any sensible reader the idiocy of this statement would have been apparent. Even third formers are ticked off, rather than severely reprimanded, for over-sleeping. The document also solemnly informed reporters that

'Mike has been severely criticised for what has happened, and quite rightly so.'

Presumably this is a public relations exercise. Blofeld blew his top and a couple of others, scenting a story, found some indignant objections. Determined not to appear faint-hearted Mr Lush and his advisors adopted what could be described as a firm position – the smack of firm government to convince critics that they are tough. The power of the press had been allowed to provoke an over-reaction, or at least the appearance of one. It was a silly affair.

As a sidelight to the supposed story it is worthy of remark that scarcely any of the English journalists were present when Gatting finally took to the field. Our bodies were not convinced that the time had changed by three hours between Perth and Melbourne, whatever the clocks said. Presumably, too, one or two had drowned their travelling blues in time-honoured fashion. Moreover few of us realised that the game was due to start at 10.30, at which time a roll-call of the press-corps would have been interesting.

Of course, the Australian reporters found the whole thing hilarious. Their papers, less impressed by gestures of authority, less desperate for a story, simply let the matter rest. English reporters, apparently, used to be able to draw the veil over such things too. The Australian tabloids are not more literary than their English brethren, but they are a good deal more responsible.

To take our minds off such idle matters, and to remind readers of the Australian ambivalence towards words like ambivalence, I came across the rewriting of a suitable tale in Mr Hornadge's *The Australian Slanguage* (which is proving an even more constant source of delight than Frances Edmonds, Engel and *Yes, Prime Minister*). It's the miracle of the loaves and fishes:

'G'day 'Ave you 'eard about the day Jesus and His mother had been working flat out with this big mob, curing warts and leprosy and all that?

'After a while the Apostles said "It's time to tie on the feed bag – but there's not enough tucker for this mob".

'Andrew said "There's a kid with five loaves of bread and two fishes". So Jesus said, "Righto, bring me the bread and the bream". He blesses it, breaks it into bits and the Apostles take it around.

'Jesus said "Collect what's left over, or we'll be in strife for littering".

'They found there were twelve baskets of food left over. Jesus had fed five thousand blokes – that's not counting all the sheilas and lads.'

This was an extract from the Catholic communications centre, which had tried to render into Ocker, that which was once well writ. The kiss of death to this idea was given by Molnar's cartoon in the *Sydney Morning Herald* which had an Ocker clergyman addressing his congregation from the pulpit, on which rested a can of beer, with the words 'Dearly beloved mates and sheilas'.

DAY FOUR

England did win the match, with Foster bowling out the tail and then Slack, Whitaker, Lamb and Gower hitting off the runs. Gatting was bowled by a shooter to complete an unhappy match. Slack's innings cheered everyone up (it is rare for a cricketer to be able to do this – usually at least a couple of colleagues are dubious about the joy of another's return to form). He'd lashed one down long-leg's throat in the first innings, an untypically rash stroke, the sort of thing a player does who is out of form and short of match practice. Here he played his shots, hitting his drives crisply before losing his wicket to a questionable decision. He could feel, at last, that he has contributed something concrete to the tour, and will feel less miserable in the weeks ahead.

He'd played with a sore shoulder earlier in the season and had been unable to hit the ball properly. Some Australian reporters had spoken witheringly about him, remarking in the comfort of the press-box that he was playing more shots in the knock-up

VICTORIA v. ENGLAND, Melbourne
December 6, 7, 8, 9.

VICTORIA

D. F. Whatmore	c French b Small	4	c and b Small	43
I. D. Frazer	lbw b Foster	0	(7) c Richards b Small	10
D. M. Jones	c Lamb b Foster	4	c Richards b Small	29
P. A. Hibbert	c French b Foster	25	c Gower b Edmonds	91
J. D. Siddons	c Foster b Gatting	7	c sub (P. A. J. DeFreitas) b Small	3
S. P. O'Donnell	c Foster b Gatting	4	st Richards b Edmonds	77
A. I. C. Dodemaide	c Foster b Gatting	6	(2) lbw b Small	24
M. G. D. Dimattina†	not out	19	c Lamb b Foster	20
M. G. Hughes	c Gower b Gatting	17	b Foster	20
R. J. Bright*	c French b Small	0	lbw b Foster	1
S. P. Davis	b Small	2	not out	0
Extras	(b 1, lb 3, w 1, nb 8)	13	(b 9, lb 8, nb 10)	27
TOTAL		101		345

Fall of wickets: 7, 7, 16, 33, 37, 55, 63, 91, 92, 101.
Second innings: 60, 106, 107, 112, 239, 263, 308, 342, 344, 345.

ENGLAND

W. N. Slack	c sub (G. L. Jordan) b Hughes	10	c Dimattina b O'Donnell	35
C. W. J. Athey	c Hibbert b Hughes	58	c Dimattina b Dodemaide	10
J. J. Whitaker	c Frazer b Hughes	0	c Whatmore b Bright	48
D. I. Gower	c Dimattina b O'Donnell	23	(5) not out	28
C. J. Richards	c Dodemaide b O'Donnell	0	(7) not out	0
M. W. Gatting*	c Whatmore b Dodemaide	1	(6) b Dodemaide	17
B. N. French †	c Whatmore b Dodemaide	58		
A. J. Lamb	c sub (G. J. Jordan) b Dodemaide	46	(4) c Jones b Bright	36
P. H. Edmonds	c Dimattina b Dodemaide	0		
N. A. Foster	not out	46		
G. C. Small	c Dodemaide b Bright	3		
Extras	(b 10, lb 6, w 1, nb 1)	18	(lb 1, w 8, nb 1)	10
TOTAL		263	5 wickets	184

Fall of wickets: 28, 30, 58, 78, 83, 128, 193, 199, 238, 263.
Second innings: 14, 88, 112, 140, 180.
2nd innings C. J. Richards kept wickets from 0/56 to 6/269.
Toss: Victoria.
Umpires: R. C. Bailhache and D. W. Holt.
ENGLAND WON BY FIVE WICKETS

than he'd managed in the entire tour so far. This innings will help to bring to Slack the respect he deserves.

Whitaker played well too, striding out to bat as a man who means business, despite his first innings' duck. He hit the ball hard, punishing the short delivery and driving straight back past the bowler as the opportunity presented. He might play on Friday in Adelaide if Botham is still unfit.

Really there is nothing much else to write about this game,

except that it ended in victory and we were in time to catch the early evening flight to Adelaide for the third Test match.

As we took off the captain of the airplane asked us all to talk quietly as Mike Gatting was trying to sleep.

9

Interlude IV

INTERVIEW WITH JOHN EMBUREY

Shivering under a sweater as play continued on the M.C.G. (Melbourne Cricket Ground) John Emburey, England's thirty-four year old off-spinner, contemplated his fifth visit to Australia.

He liked bowling here, he said, because the wickets were harder and bounced more. He wasn't, he remarked, a big spinner of the ball so it didn't matter if the pitches were rock hard and the ball did not grip and bite. Tony Lock never turned a ball in his life, they say, and he took hundreds of wickets for Western Australia. Bounce matters to Emburey, because if the ball bounces the edges will carry. Nothing is more aggravating than those slow English wickets where edges fall in front of slip.

He hadn't bowled well in Perth. He'd been thrown off because of the wind. He'd told Gatting that he didn't feel right into the wind, but Gatt had said have a go, so he did. This ruddy great gale blowing up from long leg stopped him attacking. He'd lost command of the ball, dropped his arm to compensate and then lost the lot. He'd been bloody awful, really dreadful. Once his arm goes down, the bounce is gone, and he relies on bounce and pressure. He couldn't lean forward into the wind, had lost his action and given runs away. He doesn't like doing that, it goes against the grain. Edmonds is a more generous bowler, buying wickets. Mind you, even he is more defensive these days, knuckles down now, line and length the same as everyone else. Sir Robert might be economical with the truth – spinners have got to be economical with the ball. Emburey said he likes to bowl down the wind really, but has little chance of that with faster men bowling in the team. Edmonds likes bowling down the wind too, because it stops them hitting the ball back over his head. Batsmen don't like lofting into the wind. John doesn't mind being hit though, because this gives him a chance. It is just that the wind stops his aggression. A week later he was still furious about his bowling in Perth, furious that his standard had dropped.

Brisbane had been O.K. He'd hit a nice rhythm right away, hadn't varied it too much. As usual, in his first few overs, he'd tried a bit of this and a bit of that, found the right pace and then nagged at the batsman like a drunkard's missus, till he had an old heave-ho.

Stretching his arms back on the seat he began to consider his opponents. He said he didn't enjoy bowling to Greg Ritchie, because he couldn't work him out, didn't know where he'd be. Ritchie plays back all the time, forcing the bowler to pitch it up, whereupon he'd jump down the wicket and hit the ball into the third row of the stand. Emburey had been thinking about it since Perth. He'd drop a man back straight away in Adelaide, force him to work for his runs. That's what Test cricket is about, pressure and work. A bowler must be patient, can't expect a wicket every ball, not on these pitches.

It'd help if his captain would give him an extra-cover instead of a man at point. Gatting hits the ball square when he bats, so he puts a man there in the field, too, but it's wrong because it makes Emburey bowl short. They'd have to compromise about that.

He'd bowl over the wickets to Border. He went round in 1985 and Border kept moving down the pitch and smashing through extra-cover. This gave him confidence, so he'd tried over the wicket to tighten him up. Border can sweep and get a single if he pitches on leg, but he hasn't been so commanding since they'd adopted this tactic. Emburey thinks Border's defence is suspect too, because he jabs at the ball and might give a catch in close.

He doesn't really like too many fieldsmen in close, says it makes him bowl short to avoid being driven. He could see no point spinning the ball and then dropping short, even though a spinner can get away with it here because the pitches are quicker and the bounce slower so that short balls hurry on and cramp the batsman. A spinner can vary his length more in Australia.

He'd found bowling in Australia different from his work in England. Lads here are taught to move back and across, in behind the ball, and then they whip you to leg. He aims further outside the off-stump to stop them doing this. He'd found, too, that he cannot deliver his 'swinger' so well because the ball cuts up in the footholds early in the innings and won't swerve by the time he gets hold of it. He relies for variation upon small movements of the wrist. He bowls his 'drifter' by undercutting the ball, causing it to curl away from the bat. He'd beaten Waugh with a beauty in Perth. Emburey smiled and said it was a good one. Must've hit a crack. Sitting on the bench, not shivering so much, he demonstrated with his fingers as he talked.

He's near his peak now, he thinks. He probably bowled more consistently in 1982–3 in Sri Lanka and South Africa, but rarely better than in Brisbane. Funnily enough he didn't take many wickets last year, only thirty-nine all told. People had criticised him for that. He'd hardly bowled at all, in fact, and it'd taken him seventeen overs per wicket rather than nine, which had been the average in previous years. He didn't think he was in decline though and might have two or three more years in Test cricket. He might play for Middlesex until he was forty. In any case who else was there? There is no-one else.

He agreed that bats had made a difference, and the field placings, agreed with what I'd written in Perth. He'd been made to bowl to that sort of field by Brearley. He'd started in Middlesex's second XI as a bowler who could deliver all sorts of balls, full of flight and guile. He'd been told to forget all that when he began as a professional, and had to learn his trade from scratch. Brearley had made him bowl with a silly point and a short leg and as he ran in he could see these two friends on the edge of the wicket and it had made him bowl down a tunnel. Brearley had turned him into a hard, miserly bowler, on to the batsmen all the time. He was a more effective bowler, but something had been lost. He'd never, since, gone into the unknown.

Emburey isn't a man for frilly bits. He's a battler, a cockney who recognises the main chance.

As the cricketers drifted from the field Emburey continued to analyse his craft, continued to discuss the Australian batsmen. He'd bowl to their weaknesses in Adelaide, never to their strengths. He hoped it wouldn't be windy in Adelaide, hoped Gatting didn't bowl him in long spells to let the batsmen get used to his ways. It had turned in Adelaide, a month ago, and he'd taken nine wickets in the match. The pitch had been dry and devoid of grass. Now they'd had a storm there, hadn't they? Emburey, ever the pessimist, ever an intelligent and yet caring professional, thought this would mean the pitch would help the seamers.

And so he chatted on, a man fascinated by his craft and forever trying to improve his mastery of it. He is a mean bowler, has learnt to be so in the way of the cockney, adaptable, chirpy and street-wise. We'd have been there till dusk if the cricket hadn't stopped and if it hadn't been so cold.

EXPERIENCES WITH ENGEL

Engel, mourning the loss of the traditional rest day and the tra-ditional rest day trip to the wilderness on the Yarra, suggested we go to Mount Lofty, which looms sombre and impressive over the Adelaide Oval. It seemed a good idea, at the time.

Our first misfortune was to find, in Adelaide's train station, the Adelaide casino, which has been open for a year. Engel didn't want to go in, fearing he'd catch the bug. We did go in and he did catch the bug, disappearing from my sight as we con-templated the roulette tables. He reappeared ten minutes later, (by which time I was engrossed in the two-up school), in a fury and to say that we were leaving immediately. He added, with spirit, that it had not been his idea to go into the place from the start. Moreover the cards had been bad. Slowly it emerged from his growls that he'd found himself at a blackjack table from which he'd been unable to extract himself, before losing every cent on his person when he entered the casino. It emerged, further, that this was my fault. By way of recompense I had to buy the train tickets. He'd return to the casino at a more ap-propriate hour to recoup his losses. He realised, now, that any man who entered such a place on a sunny afternoon deserved his fate.

We caught our train to Mount Lofty which, we quickly realised, was a surprising distance hence. We stopped twenty or so times, once or twice in national parks, which looked interesting, before finally leaving the decrepit old chuffer on a dirty and empty station somewhere north of Adelaide. We checked the timetable for the time of our train back to the city and encountered our second problem, for there were two timetables. A train, one said, would arrive at 6.48. The other was of a different persuasion, predicting a train arriving at 7.43. We chose the 6.48 and went off up the road.

We didn't find Mount Lofty, never saw head nor hair of it. Mountains were slipping through our grasp at quite a rate. Tambourine Mountain in Queensland had proved no less elusive.

We walked around a pleasantly leafy suburb, up hills and down dales, seeing hardly a soul, apart from the drivers in the cars that rushed by. Finding neither mountain nor bush we trudged back to the train station where we spent some time wondering whether we were right to stand on the same side as that on to which we had descended. Would not the trains bump into each other? Finally we saw an old lady who said they didn't bump, just turned around up the top somewhere and came back. We did not, however, see any trains. Nor is the station a hospitable place. Locked doors and cold alley-ways predominated. The weather had turned rugged, damp and chilly, for which turn I was wholly unprepared. 6.48 passed with Engel and me pacing up and down the platform seeing not another soul. Engel contemplated pinching one of those trucks they use in the silent comedies to scuttle down the track but there was not one to be seen. He lay on the track to listen for the sound of a train approaching, but no sound came. We began to wonder where is this place we might find a bed for the night, or at least a cafe. It was, by now cold. Finally at 8.17 a train chugged towards us and we hopped on, to find warmth and, in Adelaide, a cup of cheer. I am beginning to have doubts about Engel and his voyages. He wants to be described here as a reckless libertine (thinks it will be good for his image as a *Guardian* journalist), but I can only describe the events and leave the reader to wonder whether Engel was wise not to try his hand at something more practical than writing about cricket matches and attending the press conferences of Mr Michael Gatting.

ENGLAND'S NEW CAP

The selectors have picked James Whitaker, the twenty-four year old Leicestershire middle-order batsman to replace Botham for the third Test match. Partly by chance, partly in anticipation of this, I had lunch with Whitaker yesterday. He's interested me ever since his first game against Somerset, in 1984 (it was not quite his first county game, though it was his first game of that year). He'd taken guard with Botham on a hat-trick and with a slip area full of wily old pros, and scored a hundred and sixty-six. Vic Marks said that Whitaker had been brilliant on the off-side, whereas I remember his leg-side shots. We concluded that we'd have some trouble with this fellow. Some of our team took a dim view of his character, because he strutted a bit, but everyone recognised at once that he had talent and conviction.

He was interesting at lunch, only partly obeying the usual sportsman's law of apparent humility. He did mutter the traditional platitudes 'the lads have been great . . . team spirit is terrific' until he got started with 'it will be worthwhile even if I'm never chosen again'. To which, after a pause, he added 'which I will be'. He said he strutted because he wanted to feel ten feet tall as he walked in, didn't want to appear timid or apologetic. If this irritated bowlers, then so be it. He said he was really shy and nervous, which drew a gasp from Phil Edmonds on the next table. He said that his stately air was a projection not a reality. Slowly drawing back the curtains, he revealed that this not entirely bright-eyed young man was a mixture of northern steel and southern style. Born in Yorkshire (and so this Test team's second refugee) he was not raised in a grimy industrial town but in a pleasant village six miles from Skipton. He did not live in a red brick council semi-detached but in a well-to-do country house. His dad was not a stoker on a train, but a manufacturer of chocolates. He was educated not at the local comprehensive but at effete Uppingham, where his father had gone before him. Whitaker's bowling is captured by the old rhyme, suitably adjusted by Engel:

> There once was an Uppingham Rover
> who bowled ten wides in one over
> which had never been done
> by a chocolate-maker's son
> on a Friday in April in Dover.

His character has a resilient northern quality and his manner a hint of turkish delight. He admires David Gower for his ability to relax at the game – apparently he falls asleep sometimes before he goes in – and he means to enjoy his life as a cricketer as much as does Gower, who is rather taken by champagne at the moment. He admires ease and poise and adds to it a grit and ambition.

Whitaker does not resemble Gower at the crease. Gower is a flower, blossoming from time to time. Whitaker is a rock. He stands still, waits for the ball and from a short backlift hits hard and straight. Early in his innings he takes risks, particularly against spinners, because he likes to dominate. Gower does not think in these aggressive terms. Things happen to him. Whitaker likes to make them happen.

He had dedicated the previous year of his life to being picked for this tour, and deserves his chance. He didn't return to Glenelg (a palindromic grade club in Adelaide) last winter and instead stayed in England working as a distributor of photocopiers, running five miles in the sleet and the rain every night so that he could be fresh when the new season began. Every time he batted last year he recalled those long runs. It hadn't been merely a matter of fitness (though he is not a natural athlete) but of hardening his will. He'd set a goal, a brave thing to do, and he meant to keep it. His other target was to score sixteen hundred runs in the season and he'd made that too.

He broke two fingers during the season, facing Malcolm Marshall. Ken Higgs, his coach at Leicestershire, had told him that he'd lost his chance of being chosen to tour. Whitaker replied that there'd be fixtures left when his bones had mended and he'd score runs in them. On his return his team was bowled out for two hundred and twenty-three, to which he contributed an unbeaten century.

He'd watched England play Australia in Adelaide four years ago and, as he sat around the boundary, promised himself that he'd be playing for England by the time they returned to South Australia. This is a young man with a single-minded approach to the game which, in the world of Gatting, Gooch, Gower, Lamb and Botham is unfashionable. He will not settle for second best and it'll be a surprise if he does not impose himself on international cricket in the next few years.

97

10

Adelaide: Third Test

PREVIEW

In its hour of need, Australia has recalled the honest Ray Bright, Victoria's captain, gully fieldsman and stout-hearted cricketer. Bright has taken eight wickets at sixty-eight point six two in his six home Test matches spread over fifteen years, and fifty-three wickets at forty-one point one nine in the twenty-five Test matches which have been the highlight of his career. If he has been chosen as a match-winner the selectors are taking a long-shot. Maybe he has been picked to act as twelfth man, and to add his maturity to this fresh, inexperienced team under Border's command. He will be a senior professional in a struggling team, and might neverthe-less be left in the dressing-room. It says much about the current state of Australian cricket that the timeless qualities represented by Bright are needed by Border. It is uncertain that his team more needs a father figure than a strike bowler. As it is it has been given a bit of each.

If Bright is left out, Australia will take the field with two proper bowlers, Merv Hughes (who has been recalled for no obvious reason except that Lawson and Chris Matthews were so hopeless in Perth, and no other candidate has presented his credentials in the meantime), and Bruce Reid. In addition, Border can use Sleep, Waugh and Matthews, ordinary State bowlers at best. The pitch is good. It is hard to see Australia winning.

Frankly England does not appear to be the likely victor either. Botham is unfit, and will return to the team in Melbourne on Boxing Day, and may not be able to bowl flat out even then. The pitch is not as bare as Emburey had hoped (maybe it was the storm, or maybe Mr Hookes has been instructing his groundsmen to prepare things for Sleep and Tim May) and it will not be easy to take wickets. England have chosen two spinners, to be helped by Dilley and DeFreitas with Mike Gatting in support. This is not an adventurous choice either.

Still, two new men will be playing and good luck to them. It is easy to sit in these plush hotels and to regard this as just another game of cricket, just another Test match. To Sleep and Whitaker it will be a great occasion, the time their names are put into the cricketing history books, never to be removed. To county professionals, whether or not a man plays for England becomes, to a degree, a matter of chance. A player follows his career and, when he is not outstanding, forgets about his youthful illusions of fame and fortune. Occasionally such a man is plucked from his peers – Steele, Radley and Slack are examples – and forever more is an England cricketer. To youngsters though, to fellows still on the rise, it is an honour, the pinnacle of a brilliant youthful career rather than a surprising and delightful interruption in a long and dignified one. Whitaker and Sleep will have butterflies tonight, realising that they have made it, and wondering just what it is they have made.

DAY ONE

Today's cricket can have reminded the twelve thousand two hundred and twenty-two spectators of nothing so much as Leeds and Arsenal playing a football match, both under the impression that a goalless draw is a good result.

Australia finished the day on 2/207, slow-going against a friendly attack on a good pitch. Border demanded that Bright be left out before play began, and entered the match with two proper bowlers and a batting list with Dyer at number nine (Zoehrer is injured) and Sleep at eight. Dyer's first-class average is forty-one and Sleep has hit ten centuries in State cricket. Border could have played an extra spinner, or another fast bowler. A goalless draw is not a good result for him.

England's caution was at least understandable. Botham is injured and England is not used to leading in a series and once in front, does not mean to be caught. To pack the side with batting was the work of the whispering voice of caution, but it was at least rational. It might have been wise, though, to choose Small in front of DeFreitas, who was given the new ball on this showery morning. He is not ready yet to open the bowling in Test cricket, besides which he has appeared tired this month, missing the last two State games. He is not used to regular travel or life on the road and in hotels. He's played only one season in county cricket, and his body and mind have not been hardened by its demands.

DeFreitas did not bowl well, dropping short to Boon, and feeding his favourite leg clip. He might have taken Boon's wicket early on, a plumb LBW being denied him because he had over-stepped the front crease. As it was Boon escaped, and played some punchy shots as he returned to form. He has hit three Test centuries and, as a curiosity, umpire Steve Randell, his mate from Tasmania, has been standing on all three occasions. Boon is not a convincing opening batsman at present, and despite his scores against India and New Zealand, his position is in peril. Like several of the other Australians he does not move his feet correctly against swing bowling. He reached his hundred today because, for the first time in the series, the Englishmen could not swing the ball away from the bat. Boon still played and missed frequently (Ken Barrington used to be angry if he made one mistake in a session of Test cricket) and even at the end of his innings had not solved his technical problems. Maybe he is simply too stout to move his feet properly.

Boon lost his wicket near the end of a day in which the English bowlers contained the Australians without difficulty or challenge. After a tame opening from DeFreitas and Dilley (who was not in good humour, once diving warily to stop a drive, staying on the ground in the hope that someone else might give chase, and then rising to run after the ball as the batsman added five to the total), England bowled accurately. Gatting only bowled a few overs, though he did bowl with control if not threat. For the most part the Englishmen glided around the field, recognising the deadness of the pitch, prepared to bow to its variety.

Marsh lost his wicket sweeping to Edmonds, who bowled with subtle variations of flight. He took only one wicket but was easily the best of the bowlers, kidding the batsmen with tantalising glimpses of a half-volley, and using his shoulder to hang the ball in the air, denying the batsmen runs. Upon Marsh playing on, off his arm, Edmonds signalled that he'd been lucky to dismiss a man in such a way. I did not agree. He was tossing the ball up, giving the batsman time to think and to err. Slow spin bowlers sometimes take wickets with their worst deliveries. Maybe one of the reasons Edmonds and Emburey have taken their wickets so slowly in Test cricket is that they are not willing to risk a bad ball, not interested in taking wickets any old how, preferring to beat batsmen rather than to seek their help.

Boon threw his wicket away near the close, whereupon Border strode to the crease with a positive energy which found its first expression in a lofted sweep over mid-wicket off Emburey. Maybe Border had read Emburey's comment about bowling over the wicket to him, had heard about Emburey's belief that Border had not been so much in command, and set about shattering this illusion. No great cricketer is prepared to admit that a rival has the last wood on them. In any event, after sweeping Emburey he leaned back to cut him past point, whereupon Emburey returned to his old tactic of round the wicket line and length. It had taken Border to bring the spirit of challenge back onto the field.

This was a disappointing day's cricket, with neither side pressing for the initiative. The crowd sat quietly, which is unusual for Adelaide, because most spectators sit square of the wicket, where they can barrack about no-balls and can grouse about LBW and caught behind decisions without the benefit of accurate information. It was here that the trouble began in the Bodyline series. Bill O'Reilly, sitting in the press-box, poised over his pen as ever, a glistening eye like a snake ready to strike, recalled the crowd of fifty-five thousand, recalled that the ground had hardly changed since and observed that Adelaide is the hottest and dryest of the Australian cricketing cities because of the prevailing wind is northerly from the Nullabor plain and the Simpson desert. He said this explained the troubles and the reputation Adelaide has as a staid city of churches which is also a home of wife-swapping parties and unorthodox murders.

As stumps were drawn Robin Marlar (who has arrived) was

vastly amused to hear that I worked for Fairfax as well as Murdoch, a feat he considered to be unique in this time of media war between the two giant corporations. He pointed to a man a few seats away, a Mr Ron Brierly who, it emerged, had just sold his shares in the *Herald* and *Weekly Times* to Mr Murdoch at a profit of $A100 million. Not a bad day's work.

Australia 2/207.

DAY TWO

From the time Gatting failed to declare on the fourth evening in Perth England have adopted the tactic of conserving the lead gained in Brisbane. The Australians began this game defensively too and for a day and a half both teams played carefully. In the last couple of hours of today's cricket the Australians began to open their eyes and to see the English caution and to conclude that it is founded upon fear. Late in the day Matthews and Waugh seized the initiative and plundered the English attack.

In trying to preserve a rare lead England have been unduly timid. They had a chance, here and in Perth, to deliver a knock-out punch to a tottering opponent and instead they choose to go for a victory on points. If the world is for the bold then England may pay for these conservative tactics. A weak Australian team, outplayed for the first eight days of this series, has been running hard between the wickets and thumping bowlers who previously intimidated them. With only Dilley and DeFreitas to relieve them (Gatting bowled four point eight balls an hour and can be discounted) the spinners had bowled in long spells which allowed them no respite when first Jones and Border, and later Matthews and Waugh, collared them. Emburey didn't bowl badly and Edmonds flighted the ball cunningly, yet between them these two took three wickets for two hundred and fifty-one runs in ninety-eight overs. A pair usually so economical with runs had to place four men on the fence as young Australians ran them ragged. England might pay for this when they play on a turner in Sydney.

Border's strategy of not dropping a batsman was based upon a reluctance to break the spirit he has built in lean times. When Boon, who had been in the doldrums, reached fifty on Friday, every man in the Australian dressing-room stood to clap. This sort of thing goes on in other dressing-rooms; the difference is that these fellows meant it. Every time a player reached a landmark he turned to salute his colleagues. Matthews kissed his bat too. Englishmen take a different view; they shake their fists at the press-box. They don't kiss cricket bats either. They don't even kiss their wives.

Boon, Marsh, Jones and Ritchie have each played their part in building this camaraderie and Border does not want to lose them. Nor is he prepared to sacrifice Matthews or Waugh (who gave evidence this evening of his vast and as yet untapped potential). He cannot keep them all if he intends to win the Ashes. After Christmas it will be up to the Australians to attack, and two specialist bowlers will not be enough.

Most of the Australians scored runs. Jones used his feet to drive, his face hungry, his eyes narrowed. Border was as effective as ever. So many of his shots go to the boundary. He is not more aggressive than anyone else, he is simply more efficient. Ritchie was amiable and full of benign strokeplay until, with his partner Matthews scoring too slowly, he lofted DeFreitas to mid-on. He does not yet work hard enough at the crease to realise his talent. Matthews beavered away, and Waugh moved on to the back foot to drive through point, and occasionally lifted a tiring spinner to the deep. He has the silent strength of the bush man, this Waugh. In the press-box Ashley Mallett predicted, as so many old hands have done before him, that Waugh will be greater than Greg Chappell.

It will be a hard label for a young man to carry. Australia has had several young Bradmans – Peter Toohey was the most recent example – and none has been up to it. Toohey did not have the ambition to drive to the top, to be the latest boy from the bush. He was a gentle fellow with a talent for batting, whereas Bradman was single-minded, cold and ambitious. Waugh has hardly made his mark in State cricket, has hardly learned to play four-day cricket, and suddenly he is supposed to be the hope of the nation. Upon reflection his twin brother might be the luckier of the pair, learning his trade and experiencing tough times before being chosen to play Test cricket. He is not being thrown into the cauldron of Test cricket, a boy among the men.

If Waugh is lacking anything it is education. Since P.B.L. marketing took charge of cricket in Australia the old route to the top, years in grade cricket as a boy, a grounding in shield cricket and finally, triumphantly, an invitation to represent Australia, has been forsaken. Waugh has played some grade cricket because he went to a State school and was free on Saturday afternoons. McDermott had played only four club matches before being chosen by Australia. He knew nothing about the game, had never had his boyishness knocked out of him, and when things began to go wrong had nothing upon which to fall back.

This is why Bob Simpson has been appointed to manage the Australian team, and why Bright was brought to Adelaide. The lines between grade (in which Test players used to play regularly), Shield and Test cricket have been broken. Youngsters are rising to the sixth form before they have passed their 'O' levels, and it is scarcely surprising that they are performing below their potential. PBL, by creating so many internationals (this Adelaide Test match used to be played in late January and has been moved forward to allow time for the various one-day series) has taken the top cricketers away from their roots. Before their trunks have thickened they are put into the hothouse. Shield and grade cricket has been degraded because of the absence of top players (Western Australia will not play between 19 January and 12 February). Also they have been undervalued as the education of young Australians (there are some pretty tough men in grade cricket). Until the balance is restored it is hard to see how Australia can expect to field a mature team, able to consider the game intelligently, aware of its lessons and its requirements.

Broad and Athey took England to the close after Border's declaration. The pitch still looks full of runs. So do the Australian bowlers and so do the English batsmen.

DAY THREE

Every morning we stroll to the ground across the gigantic straight roads which criss-cross this town, past the stone houses with their wrought-iron railings supporting a balcony on the first floor. This wrought-iron was brought as ballast on the convict ships and is less common in Adelaide than in Sydney because it was not founded as a convict city, and as such wasn't built on blood. Every morning we arrive at the ground, sit in our seats square of the wicket, sip the coffee and munch the pasties brought by the media lady, and watch as batsmen pile up the runs.

104

England batted throughout the day, and reached 5/369 by the close. Broad hit his second century of the series in his fourth innings and, again, it was an innings of patience, judgement and humility, an innings without frill or fancy containing very few mistakes. Australian bowlers are appearing less than venomous, partly because Broad so often takes the sting out of them. He is not giving them the chance of a crack at England's middle-order batsmen while they are fresh. It is astounding, watching him so composed, that he has not played for England since being dropped for scoring a slow eighty against Sri Lanka in 1984.

Mike Gatting hit a century too, taking England to safety after Athey had chopped a ball onto his stumps. He was particularly severe on Greg Matthews, marching down the pitch to smash him over mid-on, and then between long-on and deep mid-wicket. This may have been a pre-determined attack, to show England's already scarcely disguised contempt for Matthews' bowling, or a simple expression of Gatting's general disdain of spinners. He cut Matthews too, leaning back to thrash the ball to the point boundary. Matthews' off-spin was found wanting, though he did not give in. Between overs he practised his action, and after every ball he still jumped as if a wicket was in his grasp. At the close of play he slipped off to seek the help of Ashley Mallett, and they arranged to meet in the nets tomorrow morning for a good, hard session.

It was good to see Gatting do well. He had lived in the shadow of Botham till 1984 when, with Botham resting, he was picked to tour India and at last produced cricket to match his ability. He was only chosen, in fact, at Gower's insistence for he was not beloved of the selectors, nor of the old guard in English cricket.

He'd risen with Botham in 1977, and they'd gone to New Zealand as the great white hopes of English cricket. Gatting had been eclipsed by Botham, who'd hit a century, taken wickets and run out Boycott, a string of recommendations which cemented his place in the Test team. Gatting began to flit in and out of the side, and for the next seven years seemed to freeze whenever he was called up by England. In the 1984 series against the West Indies he lost his wicket several times padding up, the most frustrating and inane way to be out, particularly for an aggressive batsman. In the middle-age of his career he still appeared ill at ease, as if he did not really belong in Test cricket. He is used to being the boss, and there he was an invader, and one treated with suspicion.

Finally, in India with Botham away, he began to play in Test cricket as he had for years in the county game. In the last decade England has bred fast-hitting batsmen because county bowling is of a low standard, ripe for the plucking by an abrasive player. Gatting, Lamb, Gooch and Botham are not merely England's fastest hitters, they are also England's class players, or supposedly so. Cricketers like Barrington, Edrich and Boycott, great defensive batsmen, are less necessary because a batsman's defences are less severely tested in the era of dry pitches and unskilled one-day bowling. Gatting is not a master of defence. Fieldsmen do not stand at slip and admire his flawless technique. They fear his striking power, as they fear Gooch's, Botham's and Lamb's. These are men who murder ordinary bowling, of which they encounter plenty, and score runs against good bowling too, though not in the old way of technique, graft and collect.

Now Gatting is not the servant but the master. His period as an outcast has hardened him, and he is breathing a fresh spirit into English cricket. He owes nothing to the old guard and is free to demand pride from his men without reference to the past. Good men have been found to help him, cricketers not yet tired from the ludicrous tours arranged for them. Small, Broad, French and Slack in particular have brought an honesty to this team. They are mature and impressive, hungry to play for England; and they do not share the attitude of the old guard. A year ago, cricket followers mistook England's A and B touring teams because the B team was so much more organised and dedicated. No such mistake could be made on this trip, and most of the credit is due to Gatting. This hundred will help him in his gradual rise in stature as a man and as a captain.

England hit runs towards the close, but suddenly lost the way, with Gatting pulling a long hop to mid-wicket, Broad hooking too indiscreetly at Waugh, Gower losing his wicket to a cutter from Reid and Lamb lobbing a catch to mid-off without moving his feet. Till this late flurry of wickets England had a chance of reaching seven hundred and attacking the Australians on the final day. Gatting was angered at this wastefulness, because he felt England could have won, despite Australia's big first innings score. And if he'd brought it off, it would have been a coup not only for virtually ensuring the Ashes would stay in England, but against those of us in the press-box where cricket is so different a game, who believe that with a little more aggressive approach England could have won this match.

Whitaker was unbeaten on four at stumps, and Emburey had come in as night watchman, protecting his young partner as a mother hen protects her chicks.

DAY FOUR

England subsided to four hundred and fifty-five all out, not a paltry score by any means but not a match-winning score on this pitch either. In the last nine Test matches against Australia, England's first innings scores have been 533: 290: 456: 7/487: 5/595: 464: 456: 8/592 and now 455. Australia won the second game and has not been in a position to win any of the others. Apart from Reid now, and McDermott briefly during 1985, Border has not had any good bowlers at his command. Hogg, Rackemann and Alderman would probably all be in his team at present if the wretched split had not occurred.

Whitaker lost his wicket to a disappointing stroke, lifting a pull to mid-off after being dropped at slip by Border off the previous ball (Australia has few reliable slip-catchers at present; Border and Boon have dropped too many). Emburey hung on bravely, collecting forty-nine urgently needed runs, once falling on his backside as he pulled Sleep to the leg boundary. He'd be a good treasurer, this off-spinner from Middlesex because he will not go beyond his budget. With Edmonds you'd either be a millionaire or a bankrupt within the year.

None of the others scored many as the sun blazed down upon the pitch, though Jack Richards again looked the part of a Test cricketer. He kept well on Friday, and is rising in confidence as the tour wears on. He probably felt like an imposter until that hundred in Perth, now he must feel like a player of class. He was only in the team at first because of the rotten form of the top batsmen, and he has taken his chance well. It is vital for a 'keeper to be able to bat in these days of one-day cricket because it gives depth of batting to a team, a vital ingredient in a run-chase.

By the close Australia had lost three wickets, and if Border is to attack tomorrow he must be careful to do so intelligently.

To be frank I did not stay till the close of play, but strolled home for a sauna and a spa bath. On the walk through the park a young Vietnamese lad wandered by wearing a T-shirt upon which was written, beside a drawing of a youth:

'We beat 'em,
fair dinkum.'

Australia is a most culturally diverse society. Adelaide, like Melbourne and Sydney, is full of Greeks reading *Ta Nea* and Italians sipping capuccino and discussing football. Despite the media militancy this is a remarkably tolerant country, apart from the treatment of the Aborigines and even that is improving (and there have been faults on both sides). John Pilger says only Israel is more diverse. According to a government survey more than half the Asian-born immigrants had Australian neighbours whom they regarded as friends. In groups and in communities there is rarely any trouble. John Pilger says that he attended a ceremony in a Sydney town hall at which twenty-one nationalities were naturalised. 'A female barbershop group sang *'We want you to be our mate'* and a Mrs Chong made one of the most stirring speeches I have heard. Mayor Len Harrass's gold chain broke and was rescued, with style, by a paper clip. 'G'day congratulations' was about as formal as anybody got.'

As long as people are fair dinkum blokes they will be accepted. If they go around wearing America Cup T-shirts, don't appear stuffy, don't talk high falutin' poppycock and don't look down their noses at anyone they will be treated with warmth. An Australian friend popped into a Chelsea pub a month or two ago. He asked the barmaid for 'a couple of pints, luv' which he assumed to be ordinarily friendly. A toffee-nosed twit, told him not to call her luv 'as she is only a servant'. At first this friend laughed, assuming the comment to be an obscure joke. When he realised it was no such thing, he nearly thumped the idiot. Those who find Australians rather too forcefully lowbrow might one day care to visit Sloane Square and decide for themselves whether the openness of the Australians is not to be preferred to the snobbishness that still exists in parts of England.

DAY FIVE

A game always destined for a draw duly petered out and, at 5.30, the umpires lifted the bails and declared the honours to be even. Australia had hinted at aggression in the morning, and rumour had it that Border was considering giving England a target to chase. Unfortunately rain fell and a draw was agreed after that. Nevertheless Border marched to another century, his twenty-third in Test cricket, playing exactly the same shots as he plays in every other innings. I have never seen a player vary less than Australia's captain. He wears a cap, dips his body as the ball is released, and then plays the appropriate stroke as if it had been chosen automatically. Border must have acute judgement, for he rarely plays the wrong stroke, rarely has cause to change his mind. For this reason he has fewer bad patches than any other batsman of the era.

After the game he waved his century aside, arguing that it was meaningless because Australia did not win the game. One day he'd score a hundred and they'd take the match. Till then he wasn't interested in his performance. Not every cricketer could offer these opinions with sincerity. Border can, as his career shows.

His partner and chum, Ritchie, batted carefully, trying to secure his position which is suddenly under threat – because his fielding is weak (as is that of the other plump cricketer, Boon) and because it has dawned upon the selectors that they must pick at least one more bowler in Melbourne. He has worked hard, but needs to find a meaner, greedier streak if he is to justify his talent. He is the second best batsman in the Australian team and the bowlers, particularly Emburey, would be delighted if he were dropped.

As the game slid to a close, not with a bang but a whimper, so the players began to dawdle. I was furious with this, too furious probably, and wrote an article in the *Sydney Morning Herald* condemning the game, the attitude of the players and captains to it and (broadening the argument somewhat) suggested that these games be played for money, winner take all, and that the Ashes be buried under Ayers Rock. This stirred up the traditionalists, and some of the connoisseurs, who considered the game to be full of good cricket. As a bloody-minded professional myself I saw the seven-minute drinks breaks, the deliberately slow over-rates, and the pusillanimous tactics of the two teams and stepped onto the front foot to condemn them. Upon reflection I over-reacted, but it had been a desperately disappointing game, one of those which the players seem to give up before the first ball is bowled.

Cricket can be boring if it is allowed to be. Those thirty hours were very boring, whatever the connoisseurs say. In part this was due to the pitch, in part due to poor bowling, but in part, too, it was a fault of attitude. Twenty-four years ago Sir Frank Worrell and Richie Benaud revived cricket in Australia. A series of magnificent, open games with both teams playing to win, brought thousands through the gate. Kanhai, Hall, Sobers and Hunte, the names echo down the decades. Hundreds lined the streets to say goodbye to this West Indian team and though it lost the series, no-one cared. They had performed a great service. Kids were drawn to them, brought back to the game.

In contrast, lads already tempted by all manner of distractions found in Adelaide a dreary game played by teams who were sparring rather than fighting, as if the audience did not matter. Can anyone seriously expect this sort of cricket to fill grounds? People cannot be expected to pay to attend a game in which the sides take no risks. The dead spirit of Newcastle (on the Hill as 2.30 approached, a lad had said 'they aren't going to make it, Dad' – in his innocence he had not understood the plot unfolding in front of him) had returned to haunt Test cricket.

And worst of all, in my opinion at any rate, the cricketers were playing into the hands of the marketeers and financiers who run the game and want to replace Test matches with more one-day games. Test cricket is bound to be dull from time to time, but it needs not be so by conspiracy. This match was allowed to die as a part of a strategy to win the Ashes. This will not do. Nothing is worth that. Cricket in Australia is in urgent need of a refreshing wind. England, haunted by its own string of defeats, did not provide such a wind here, and is letting down the locals by treating State games disdainfully.

I hope the next two Test matches are played to win, played with imagination, even if England lose them both. The policy of holding onto a one : nil lead must be abandoned.

This was not a good game of cricket, despite the disciplined excellence of some of the players. We are off to Tasmania now, to play the locals up in the hills, hopping onto a plane for the umpteenth time.

THIRD TEST, Adelaide
December 12, 13, 14, 15, 16, 1986

AUSTRALIA

G. R. Marsh	b Edmonds	43	(2) c&b Edmonds	41
D. C. Boon	c Whitaker b Emburey	103	(1) lbw b DeFreitas	0
D. M. Jones	c Richards b Dilley	93	c Lamb b Dilley	2
A. R. Border*	c Richards b Edmonds	70	not out	100
G. M. Ritchie	c Broad b DeFreitas	36	not out	46
G. R. J. Matthews	not out	73		
S. R. Waugh	not out	79		
Extras	(lb 2, nb 15)	17	(b 4, lb 6, nb 2)	12
		—		—
TOTAL	(5 wkts dec)	514	(3 wkts dec)	201

Did not bat: P. R. Sleep, G. C. Dyer†, M. G. Hughes; B. A. Reid.
Fall of wickets: 113, 185, 311, 333, 368.
Second innings: 1, 8, 77.
Bowling: Dilley 32-3-111-1; DeFreitas 32-4-128-1; Emburey 46-11-117-1; Edmonds 52-14-134-2; Gatting 9-1-22-0.
Second innings: Dilley 21-8-38-1; DeFreitas 16-5-36-1; Emburey 22-6-50-0; Edmonds 29-7-63-1; Gatting 2-1-4-0.

ENGLAND

B. C. Broad	c Marsh b Waugh	116	not out	15
C. W. Athey	b Sleep	55	c Dyer b Hughes	12
M. W. Gatting*	c Waugh b Sleep	100	b Matthews	0
A. J. Lamb	c Matthews b Hughes	14	not out	9
D. I. Gower	lbw b Reid	38		
J. E. Emburey	c Dyer b Reid	49		
J. J. Whitaker	c Matthews b Reid	11		
C. J. Richards†	c Jones b Sleep	29		
P. A. J. DeFreitas	not out	4		
P. H. Edmonds	c Border b Sleep	13		
G. R. Dilley	b Reid	0		
Extras	(b 4, lb 14, w 4, nb 4)	26	(b 2, lb 1)	3
		—		—
TOTAL		455	(2 wkts)	39

Fall of wickets: 112, 273, 283, 341, 361, 422, 439, 454.
Second innings: 21, 22.
Bowling: Hughes 30-8-82-1; Reid 28.4-8-64-4; Sleep 47-14-132-4; Matthews 23-1-102-0; Border 1-0-1-0; Waugh 19-4-56-1.
Second innings: Hughes 7-2-16-1; Waugh 3-1-10-0; Matthews 8-4-10-1; Sleep 5-5-0-0.
Toss: Australia.
Man of the match: A. R. Border
Umpires: A. R. Crafter and S. G. Randell.
MATCH DRAWN.

11

Interlude V

BACK TO COURT

Being in Sydney for a couple of days, I popped off to court 8D in the New South Wales supreme court building to catch up with the MI5 case. It appears that the only reason the case is taking place in Sydney is that the British Government imagined Heinemann's central office to be located here. In fact it is in Melbourne. Mr Turnbull was still on his feet, still playing to the gallery and still demolishing the British Government. I caught him in the middle of his final argument. He was in fiery form.

Turnbull said that extracting the truth from Sir Robert was like pulling teeth, you'd heave away and get a bit at a time. His conduct, said Turnbull, was not that of a man who could be trusted. Here was a highly intelligent and articulate man who nevertheless professed to be unable to recollect vital matters to do with this case. If he was vague he'd never have risen so high in the British civil service (this was not universally accepted in court. It was widely doubted if Mr Turnbull understood the workings of the British civil service.) Armstrong's life, barked Turnbull, had been to do with detail yet suddenly he was forgetful. It was beyond belief.

During this blast Theo Scron, the quietly-spoken barrister representing the British Government, rose to interject. His learned friend, he said, was conducting himself in an unprofessional way. Around the court the thought occurred that it was all right to lie, all right to present a rotten case, all right to hold the action of open government in contempt, but not all right to be rude.

Reading from his manuscript, and facing the Judge, Turnbull turned next to the role of the British Attorney-General, Sir Michael Havers, who, he said, had allowed Sir Robert to give evidence which he knew to be false. He had, said Turnbull, allowed another man to lie on his behalf. Turnbull drew a laugh from his audience when, adding sarcasm to his attack, he added

'Presumably Sir Michael knows the importance of telling the truth in court.'

He had, raged Turnbull, connived in an attempt to defraud this court of conscience, and the truth had only emerged because of the sustained questioning of Mrs Thatcher, in Parliament, by Neil Kinnock.

Rarely can any government have been so ferociously condemned in court, particularly in a case which it had initiated. Yet Turnbull's presentation, which lasted for several hours, was unanswerable for it was based on hard facts. The British could only rely on legal technicalities, and could not deny that they had deliberately misled an Australian Court of Equity.

I had lunch with Sandy Grant, the managing director of Heinemann in Australia. We went up to floor 14 of the court building and sat near to Peter Wright, Mrs Wright and Turnbull. They were confident that the case was going well. Turnbull went off for a walk with his wife, who is acting as his solicitor. He'd reappear just before the court was due to resume, to be greeted by a bevy of television cameras. He understood the needs of newspapers and television. In the morning he'd written the headlines, after the lunch interval he made a triumphant re-entry into the court building, recalling Caesar's return to Rome, and throughout the day he barked at the Government of a foreign power which was desperately trying to mislead a court in a strange land.

Wright interrupted our lunch to ask about his expenses, and to suggest they be sent on to Tasmania because he and his wife were heading for home on Sunday. Sandy was confident of victory. Really the British had bungled the entire affair. An old friend introduced himself and said he'd been at school with Sir Robert and he'd been a frightful wet there too. The Judge was not more sympathetic. He said Sir Robert would not lie if a half-truth would suffice.

In England, Peter Wright's family had condemned his conduct as treacherous. The Government has been accused of lying through its Attorney General to a Court of Equity in Australia. Its response is not to answer the charges or to resign. It is to blacken the name of the defendant.

Nor is Heinemann escaping lightly. The office which is in a remote corner of Melbourne's suburban spread, has been attacked by flames and by thieves. Files were destroyed by a fire, though none were important. Peter Wright's manuscript is in the office, as let it be said, is part of this book. Intruders tried to break into the safe too, and failed. In Camberra questions are being asked as to who is responsible for these crimes.

THE WAUGH TWINS

Went off to the Sydney Cricket Ground to see Steve Waugh, and then to Highgrove to see his brother Mark. Robert Marlar primed me about cricket's previous twins, the Bedsers. He recalled that both were medium-pacers until Eric switched to off-spin to distinguish himself from Alec, and never really succeeded after the change. He added that their apparent telepathy (turning up in the same suits and saying the same things) had more to do with the telephone than had been generally realised.

Sydney has had a previous set of sporting twins – the Carter brothers who were rugby players. Apparently one was always held in higher esteem, and was consequently chosen for New South Wales in front of his brother. Apparently the other one turned up and played in one of the State games pretending to be his look alike twin and was man-of-the-match! No-one ever knew but he never was properly selected despite his success!

Alas, the two Waughs do not look alike. In fact they are not even similar as men. Steve is diligent, dedicated and determined. He has a sweetheart and a block of land. Mark is a cheerful, distracted chap who though also dedicated, leaves a lighter impression than his brother.

Steve did not say much, never has said much. He's a star now and has to be careful with every word, which is not difficult for a man who never uses three words when one will suffice. Like Border, he is a fellow who says what you see is what you get. His brother, working in a sports shop owned by Harry Soloman, a Sri Lankan cricketer and sometime friend and employer of both twins, was more talkative, more humorous altogether.

Steve and Mark Waugh, both twenty-one years and four months of age, rose together through the ranks at school, at their club in Bankstown and with various representative teams. I saw them play at Cranbrook School in Sydney as fifteen year olds in the State High School team. Their partnership began with their team on 6/50 and both boys scored hundreds. Their names stuck in the mind because their batting was brilliant and because the other players were in awe of them.

No-one could say which was the better of the two. Steve hit the ball harder, it is true, but Mark was stylish and gifted. If anything Mark was preferred. Unlike Steve he was never dropped by Bankstown's first grade team and it was Mark who first played for the State. But their careers were never far apart. Since the age of eight, when they raced between the wickets like old professionals in short pants, the pair ran neck and neck, as rivals as well as brothers. Their parents arranged for the schoolmaster and the clubs to keep them together, hoping if not to avoid sibling rivalry at least to delay it.

Last week Steve scored seventy-five not out for Australia in Adelaide, and Mark a duck for New South Wales against Western Australia. Tomorrow Steve is playing at the Sydney Cricket Ground and Mark is at the Randwick Oval meeting Randwick's grade team. On Monday Mark will be back at work in the sports shop and Steve will still be at the S.C.G. Steve has played eight times for Australia and Mark seven times for New South Wales. One twin is a Test cricketer, the other is frustrated and bewildered. A kid walked into the shop as Mark talked, pointed to him, and told his friend: 'Hey, there's Steve Waugh's brother.' Mark smiled grimly and said kids said this sort of thing every day. It is not easy to take, when you rose together.

Nor is Mark's state of mind helped by the friends of the family who say that his temporary obscurity was predictable, because of differences in character between the good-looking dasher and the self-contained grafter. Harry Soloman broke off from his sales' talks to tell Mark and his interviewer that Steve was the stronger man of the two. 'It's in his eyes', he said, 'Steve had Border's eyes, burning eyes. Steve is hungry and the wanting is important. All champions have that hard quality, their eyes are cold, as if fixed on their target.' He recalled a family dinner at which cricket had been discussed, Steve, sitting silently, intent upon the debate; Mark jumpy, eager for his food. Listening to the anecdote Mark protested: 'I was hungry.' Soloman smiled, and gently chiding said 'Yes, for food.'

All manner of moral lessons have been drawn from Mark's eclipse. They say he is less single-minded than his brother. Mark denies this, says he never missed a practice session and that Steve hasn't gone on a run in his life. Mark is battling for his future, against the shadow cast by the twin brother he knows to be no more talented than himself. He's fighting, too, against those children who walk into the shop and all those friends who ask what has gone wrong. Probably he's trying too hard, not letting the shots go, in an effort to put an end to this obscurity.

If he could forget about Steve's rise he'd realise that his career was following a well-trodden mile – the long and winding road to the top. He is twenty-one years of age. He is a splendid cricketer in his own right and he fails in comparison with his brother not so much in dedication as in seriousness. He appears flip and can be rude to authorities, talks when he ought to listen. These faults have been exaggerated because their careers have parted so far, a parting that has been as much due to luck as anything. Mark is down in the dumps, rallied occasionally to reject Harry Soloman's teasing comments, and maybe this sense of disappointment will force him to be as determined as his brother, to recognise that talent is not enough. If he can harden his character England will find itself fighting a war on a second front and his friends will no longer call him Afganistan, the forgotten Waugh.

THE MURDOCH TAKEOVER

A headline announced it in *The Melbourne Herald*, the proudest paper in the *Herald* and *Weekly Times* Chain:

'Murdock Herald Bid'

In a move which would make him the most powerful media magnate in Australia Rupert Murdoch made a one point eight billion dollar takeover bid for this old, massive group, a bid which stirred the stockmarket and which was, within hours, accepted by the group's board. If the shareholders follow the board's recommendation Mr Murdoch will have access to one hundred and forty-two newspapers across Australia, with a total circulation of twenty-three million copies. Since Murdoch already owns major newspapers and television channels in America, major newspapers in England, a plethora of satellite television interests and a variety of other computer, magazine and book companies this will make him a considerable force in the western world. In Australia his only rival will be John Fairfax and Co.

Mr Murdoch had always wanted to take control of the Melbourne-based group of which his father, Sir Keith Murdoch, was once managing director. He tried and failed to take it over in 1979.

Today's purchase was a shock and a coup. He flew back from America yesterday, made his offer at 9 a.m., insisted that it was accepted by 5 p.m., met the Prime Minister and the Leader of the Opposition to inform them of his bid 'as a matter of courtesy', and was told at 5 p.m. that his bid had been accepted. The Australian media now waits to see if the other big players – particularly Holmes a'Court – try to outbid Murdoch.

In buying the *Herald* and the *Weekly Times* Mr Murdoch will be the first victim of the new media rules which will force him to sell Channel 7 in Melbourne, Channel 7 in Adelaide and a radio station in Melbourne. He also owns television stations in Sydney and Melbourne. He will be forced to sell Channel 10 in Melbourne if he decides to keep his newspapers there, for he would otherwise be in breach of the new rule that a company cannot own a television station in a city in which it also publishes a daily paper.

Newspapers from the Fairfax empire were critical of Murdoch's purchase. The *Sydney Morning Herald* says it is against the public interest for one man to own so much and added that the paper will become 'an extension to Mr Murdoch's ego' and a very closely managed instrument of his ambition. Mr Murdoch, it continued:

'uses his newspapers, more aggressively than any other major Australian publisher, to influence political events.'

More sanguine, the *Financial Review* observed that

> 'the Australian Labour Government appears to be encouraging the acquisition of a near national monopoly of the popular press – and an absolute monopoly in some places – by an Australian citizen who has a history of using his newspapers to manipulate policies as it suits him.'

Mungo MacCullum, who continues to wander around with the distracted air and lengthy beard of a biblical figure, was more sanguine still. Murdoch had taken over one of his papers and one day had stormed into the office to announce that what the paper had to do was to get rid of all the loony bearded lefties. As he was saying this he stared at MacCullum, who stroked his beard and wondered if it might not be time to move on.

LATER

One of the other media magnates, Robert Holmes à Court, has offered $A13.5 million for the *Herald* and *Weekly Times* shares. At present it is unclear into which hands the vast newspaper empire will fall. Either way the huge, saturated Australian media industry will be run by ruthless barons rather than newspaper men. It is hard to believe that much good will come of this.

12

In Tasmania

UP HILL AND DOWN DALE

Tasmania leads its life at a different pace from the rest of Australia. Sydney is one extreme. It can devour you in the humid fever of its traffic and the glamour of its Americanism. Tasmania is the other. To the fury of the locals it is often forgotten by those who draw the maps of Australia. It is off the main tourist routes, stagnating in its isolation, and parochial and proud. By reputation Tasmanians are strange people with two heads who never marry anyone more remote than their first cousins. They number three hundred and fifty thousand odd – not all odd – a population the size of Somerset's living on an island the size of Ireland. Though it is so small some of the issues fought here send ripples through the rest of the world. Vast tracts of wilderness are threatened by a rapacious electricity commission, and by the timber and woodchip industries. They are defended by the radical 'greenies', who chain themselves to trees and attend burials of trees already chopped for logging.

Dame Nellie Melba sang at the local theatre, and Field-Marshall Montgomery and Errol Flynn were born here, as every local knows. These heroes help bolster up the old rich leaders, the monied fox-chasers, as one unusually impatient local called them; the conservatives who are in charge.

Matthew Engel (who has, by mistake, been given a palatial mansion in our hotel, which is also the local casino, and is situated at the front of Mount Wellington and hard by the mouth of the Derwent) and I decided not to go to the cricket, which is being played half-way up one of the chilly hills in an open ground where spectators and players freeze.

Instead we hired a car and drove inland, through the hills and the forests, past the lakes and the rivers of this unexpectedly beautiful island, and towards the national park area around Hartz Mountain. We'd decided, in short, to go bush.

We had a magnificent time. We clambered up dirt roads in the car, rising as far as we could towards the peaks. We passed through stunning areas of pine and gum forest, through sudden patches full of the skeletons of trees, killed by the cruel winter blizzards, which was like being in the middle of a nuclear winter, except that behind the white trunks there loomed wood and mountains. The silent light of the trees and the mournful blackness of the mountain made us feel eerie, as if this were a twilight zone, a private area into which man ought not to intrude.

We left the car when the road became too rocky, and began to trudge along a wooden path towards some lake till the path was lost in squelchy mud. We continued upwards, through trickling streams and deep mud; where it was too deep we'd walk on the heather and gorse (keeping an eye open for snakes). It was a steady climb, and a quiet one for not even the birds sang. The weather, at first mild and windy, turned treacherously cold. Rain fell, interspersed with sleet and sudden bursts of a milky sun. Engel, wearing sweaters and an anorak, was cold as he rumbled along behind. We'd signed our names in a book at the bottom as trekkers were asked to do. We put the ledger back carefully so that possums, rain, wind and currawongs did not destroy it. The book was full of scribbled messages of departure and return. Most observed that the route had been muddy and cold.

We walked past a monument which remembered Arthur and Sidney Greeves, who returning from a prospecting tour had perished there in a snowstorm on 27 November 1897. Engel commented that we were walking only three weeks later in the year, and his frown deepened. We wondered who'd eat whom first as we continued our journey. We agreed that I could feast on him as he was, in any case, on a diet. Mickey Stewart had told him that he was an athlete gone to seed. He'd given up food, though not alcohol, and wondered, as his middle-aged girth spread, where his youth had gone. We marched on, Engel sometimes falling far behind, moving at his one pace as the sleet cut into our faces. I wore a T-shirt, and a pair of Nike cricket shoes which afforded a good grip on the stones. They were caked in dirt. Occasionally Engel called to ask if it was wise to carry on, not, he said, that he wanted to turn back. He was all for going to the edges of experi- ence, but it was a bit cold and might we not get lost on the return journey? He'd been affected by the monument and had visions of us being lost forever. He didn't want to die as it'd mean missing Botham's oration at my funeral.

We did turn back in the end, with the mountain steep and massive in front of us, its top shrouded in swirling rain clouds. Around us we saw a picture of other moors and mountains, other forests and hills. We contemplated it, awed by it, before turning to begin the search for a long-lost wooden path; enough was enough. The mud was deepening, our bones were freezing. If we'd carried on to the brim of the mountain, we'd have been even more filthy and wet. Moreover the weather was moving in, the clouds lowering, the winds howling, and the sleet biting into our bodies.

We returned down the long trail with Engel crying 'coeee' from time to time lest he lose me in the thickening forest. He was not convinced either that we were going in the right direction or that we'd survive the journey. He said he wanted to go on a proper bush walk one day, not on a freezing trip with a chap in a T-shirt and daps.

Safe in the car we drove down to the Huon River, a wide tongue of water deep in the wooded valleys. Exhausted, Engel had forty winks and then we had a picnic of banana sandwiches and yoghurt. Later we went on a short bush walk in the hills around the wide and splendid Huon River, a walk that would have been a good deal longer had we followed Engel's nose (he considered it to be improbable that the river would flow through the basin of the hills). As night fell we returned to the car and prepared to drive to Hobart.

Tasmania is a stunning island, over which greenies and indus- trialists fight. The environmentalists won the battle of the Franklin River hydro-electric dam project because the Federal Government, realising that there were votes to be had in supporting the greenies, intervened. The dam would have been entirely alien and a boil in a beautiful area, neither of which considerations stopped the local businessmen and politicians trying to build it. Across Australia the fight between preservation and business is being waged. Near Cairns (in tropical North Queensland) the bulldozers are ploughing through the wet rain-forests, building roads for the logging of trees to fuel the woodchip industry (seven hundred and fifty thousand tonnes a year exported). In Perth conservationists are battling to prevent the logging of other areas in this extraordinarily brutal and beautiful land – all of eleven hundred and ten thousand tonnes of woodchip are wanted to be sold to the Japanese. In other States the greenies are trying to stop mining and logging from wrecking the reserves left by nature, and from ruining land belonging, since the birth of man, to the Aborigines.

Tasmania is the woodchipping capital of Australia (it claims to be the apple state too – but apparently most Australian apples are grown in Orange!). It exports two point eight million tonnes a year. The Tasmanian conservation movement says significant and re-presentative areas of natural forest and wilderness in the National Parks must be preserved. The local government, funded by industry and with jobs scarce are reluctant to stop any of the logging. They argue that this is a Tasmanian issue to be decided by Tasmanians. History tells us that the last genuine Tasmanian died in 1876, his people the victims of a deliberate policy of extermination, so the greenies and politicians feel they are trying to discipline the use to which the Tasmanian forests are put.

INTERVIEW WITH STEVE RANDELL

Steven Randell is an interesting man. Still only twenty-nine years of age, he has been a Test umpire for two years already. He is a local hero, and the lads chase his autograph at least as much as they chase David Boon's.

Slumped in his chair, his long body spread-eagled, his white fedora at his feet, he said he was ready for a break. He'd been on the road for ten days, umpiring the Test match in Adelaide and the State game at the T.C.A. To be blunt (and Randell is frequently blunt) he was knackered. He was going to back a few horses, drink a few beers and stay with his family which is very close. His mother died when he was young and his father who is retired now, travels to his games. Sometimes they share a room.

He is not of course a full-time umpire, though he wouldn't mind a season in England. He is, by profession, a school-master. He works now at a school in Zeehan, a tin-mining port on the west coast. The lads are excellent, but the four hour drive every weekend is a nuisance. It's a remote, tiny town which relies upon tin, which they cannot sell at the moment and so are stockpiling. The prospects are grim.

Randell began teaching in Hobart, in charge of ratbags in short pants who'd been turfed out of every other school by the tender age of eleven. He'd learnt to be tough, and this has helped in his career as an umpire. Everyone used to flee when one of these kids put on an act, singing and moaning as if possessed. Randell was not so easily impressed. He'd walk up to the errant child and whisper in his ear 'Cobber, you might have fooled everyone else, but you don't fool me'. One boy had nearly hit him. Under instruction the rest of the class had ignored him as he began to groan, so the lad went berserk, rushing around the room, throwing furniture and screaming. Still no-one moved. The child grabbed a bat and threatened to bash Randell, who continued to read his paper. He brought the bat down to within an inch of Randell's face, and Steve carried on reading. He called the boy's bluff. He broke down and now he's as good as gold. As a matter of fact, Randell had seen him that very afternoon, and he'd waved.

He reckons he can handle a few temperamental cricketers.

These experiences at school have given Randell an understanding of authority. He seeks to win first the respect and then the friendship of the players. He is a convivial soul and would not do the job if he were expected to adjudicate like a robot and then disappear into the night. On the field he chats to the players and chews sweets. He used to take bags of jelly babies onto the field with him, which the West Indians used to eat with particular enthusiasm. Then Rowntree offered to sponsor him if he'd pass minties around instead. He'd agreed, not because of the money which was minimal (though it's right nice) but because it was a chance for an umpire to strike back. Everything else was sponsored so why not an umpire and his sweets? Now he arranges for the Channel 9 crew to catch him passing mints around. They wave, and he passes a mint to the nearest chap. It satisfies the sponsors and anyhow, he likes it and so do the players. Besides which it helps break the barriers.

Randell is a highly respected umpire, one of the best on the international circuit. His eye for the main chance, and his ice--breaking techniques would mean nothing if his decisions were not accurate and his character not firm. In his first one-day international he'd adjudged Jones to be run out, and the replay showed him to be right by a whisker, and everyone else to be wrong. It had made his name. Not that mistakes are not made. He gave Greg Matthews out caught behind in Sydney. As Matthews, whom he considers to be pleasantly troppo, walked off, he'd muttered 'nice one, Steve'. For once Randell watched the replay on the screen, hoping to God Matthews had hit it. He had not. 'He missed it by this much' said Randell, stretching his arms wide, 'it was a bloody awful decision, a shocker'. Randell is straightforward and uses the fruity language of the players. So his occasional errors are forgiven.

He said he'd enjoyed the games with England because the players had been friendly. Randell regards umpiring as fun, a chance to appear on the top grounds and with the best players. He is an impressive man, this Randell, alert and unstuffy. Like Dickie Bird he is a bit of an eccentric, which is an advantage in the job. If you are not a crackpot already you soon will be after a few years in a white coat.

I left Randell a few beers later, thinking that maybe this was how Wooldridge and Keating and the whisky-drinking fraternity get their stories.

A DARK SECRET

One evening in Hobart a gentleman invited me home for a cup of tea. He had a story for me, if I was interested. From a desk this gentleman produced a yellowed document, which, he said, had been given to him by his father. Its contents made him ashamed of being Australian. The front of the manuscript bore the legend

'Commission of Inquiry Concerning the Circumstances Connected with the Attack made by Japanese Aircraft at Darwin on 19th February 1941.'

Mr Justice Lowe had been appointed to lead the inquiry and

this was his report, together with submissions from the army, the navy, the airforce and the Darwin administration.

This particular copy had been offered to an Australian reporter but he'd refused to write about its contents, saying that they were still bound by the Official Secrets Act. He'd end up behind bars if he used it.

I'd heard something about the Darwin business. According to legend a squadron of Japanese bombers had dropped a few bombs on Darwin whereupon the bristling he-men of Australia had jumped into lorries and fled, leaving Darwin to imagined marauding Japs. A secret report on this event might be interesting.

Mr Justice Lowe related that Japanese aircraft, around fifty all told, had begun to bomb Darwin at about 9.58 on 9 February, 1941. No-one knows the time for certain because the three services had not thought to synchronise their watches. This was a confusion symptomatic of the rest of this remarkable day.

This surprise bombing did considerable damage in the docks, where several destroyers (including the *Neptune* and the *Zealander*) were sunk and others were damaged (including the *Barossa*). A few buildings and seventeen aircraft were lost, two hundred and forty-three people were killed and between three and four hundred injured. The bombing was accurate because, apart from the anti-aircraft guns, which were manned by kids undergoing their first experience of battle who nevertheless downed five aircraft, it was unopposed. This was the second confusion. Warnings of the approach of hostile aircraft had been garbled, misinterpreted and lost. Strangely the oil tanks were not damaged, which had a marked effect upon the population once they began to contemplate its significance. Why had the oil tanks been left alone? Had this been deliberate? It occurred to the people of Darwin that the bombing had been pinpoint, and that the oil tanks might have been preserved because the Japanese intended to invade Darwin without delay.

After giving these details to Mr Justice Lowe went on to consider the events after the raid, and it is these events over which the veil of official secrecy has been drawn. At first morale in the town was not noticeably affected by the bombing. People went about their business in good order. Then, slowly, the bombs and the standing oil tanks had their effect. Quite simply the town panicked and the tough, brash, hard-drinking Australians fled south. Almost the entire population of the town went bush, according to this astounding, shaming and in its way, hilarious report. Mr Justice Lowe says that

'there were abandoned drinks left half-consumed in pubs, letters started and not finished, papers strewn about and beds unmade in the bedroom.'

Mr Justice Lowe visited houses and hotels and saw evidence of these hasty exits. By tea-time Darwin resembled the *Mary Celeste*. A few bombs had fallen and hysteria had grown.

By mid-afternoon people were leaving the town by every means available. Word spread that Darwin was being evacuated, and one policeman said martial law had been declared. The report says that

'a long string of vehicles drew up at the petrol stations for the purpose of obtaining petrol for cars about the depart for the south. The administrator, hearing this, forbade the supply of petrol.'

People fled by car, on foot, on bicycles. Even the municipal sanitary carts were pressed into service (later they were located hundreds of miles away). Panic brought opportunism and criminality. Looting broke out, and continued for several days, and was 'indulged in both by civilians and remainder of the military force'. Soldiers broke windows and robbed shops.

Only eleven hundred men stayed in Darwin, the rest upped and ran, most of them to find refuge in the bush. Four days later on 23 February, two hundred and seventy-eight air force men were still AWOL. Mr Justice Lowe called this 'deplorable'. He condemned the lack of leadership in Darwin, and was particularly severe about the Air Station Commander, who'd instructed his men to gather half a mile in the bush to be fed. They were not told to march or to travel in any particular order, simply to report as directed. Of course the orders were distorted by word of mouth, and some men went three miles, others seven miles, and quite a few eleven miles. Most though simply took off into the vast empty middle of Australia. Some were found as far afield as Batchelor, some on the Adelaide River, one was found at Dalleywater and another, 'by an extreme feat, reached Melbourne in thirteen days'.

Thousands of Australians ran at the first dropping of bombs.

TASMANIA v. ENGLAND
December 18 (no play), 19, 20, 21, 1986.

TASMANIA

E. J. Harris	c Athey b Small	14	(2) b Gatting	12
P. D. Bowler	lbw b DeFreitas	7	(1) run out (Foster)	1
K. Bradshaw	c Lamb b Foster	7	c Slack b Foster	4
G. A. Hughes	lbw b Foster	0	lbw b DeFreitas	24
D. C. Boon*	c Broad b Foster	2	(6) c Emburey b Gatting	29
D. J. Buckingham	c Richards b Foster	0	(7) not out	4
R. E. Soule†	c Slack b Small	1	(5) lbw b Gatting	21
R. M. Ellison	c Richards b DeFreitas	13	c Richards b Small	5
T. J.Cooley	c Athey b DeFreitas	16	(10) b DeFreitas	3
R. L. Brown	c Richards b DeFreitas	9	(9) c Lamb b Small	6
S. J. Milosz	not out	0	b Small	1
Extras	(b 1, lb 1, nb 8)	10	(b 4, lb 8, w 4, nb 2)	18
TOTAL		79		167

Fall of wickets: 25, 25, 27, 33, 35, 36, 36, 63, 75, 79.
Second innings: 3, 11, 41, 53, 92, 111, 130, 136, 164, 167.

ENGLAND

B. C. Broad	c Milosz b Cooley	15
W. N. Slack	c Ellison b Brown	89
J. J. Whitaker	c Soule b Ellison	37
A. J. Lamb	c Buckingham b Ellison	19
C. J. Richards†	lbw b Milosz	18
P. A. J. DeFreitas	c Bradshaw b Milosz	3
C. W. J. Athey	not out	30
M. W. Gatting*	b Cooley	30
J. E. Emburey	c Buckingham b Milosz	46
N. A. Foster	c and b Brown	25
G. S. Small	not out	3
Extras	(b 3, lb 5, w 1, nb 18)	27
TOTAL	(9 wickets dec)	342

Fall of wickets: 41, 111, 143, 187, 198, 198, 234, 294, 334.
Toss: England.
Umpires: D. R. Gregg and S. G. Randell.
ENGLAND WON BY AN INNINGS AND 96 RUNS.

They stole trucks and looted shops. The Administrator filled a lorry with his crockery and his wine bottles and sent it towards safety. Those who took to the hills remarked that they did not know how to use arms and were not going to remain to be massacred in the event of a Japanese landing.

This exodus remains one of Australia's dark secrets, though it is forty-five years old. It is not good for the image of this supposedly tough, pioneering nation. It does not sit happily with Chappell, Lillee and Thompson. No wonder it is still being officially hushed up.

Of course Darwin is not typical of Australia. The best fighting men were serving in other arenas of war. Also Darwin, with its hot, humid climate, has the reputation for sending its inhabitants 'troppo' (which is Australian for 'fruity'). A man who stays there too long is reckoned to be suspect. February 19 is a sticky time of year, towards the end of a draining summer in which storm clouds build up every evening to thunder rain upon a steaming people. It is a peculiarly vulnerable town, but even so the degree of the panic and the rashness of the day were extraordinary, possibly unique on the first day of a nation's experience of war. And this was rugged Australia! Mr Hawke and Kim Hughes have cried: (Dame Edna said Hughes' box was too tight). Australia's image of brash masculinity has been dented and bit here and there. It will not be advanced when the report is released.

I closed Mr Justice Lowe's report, finished my third cup of tea and told my host that it was a peculiar story and that I'd contact my paper to see if it was interested. Really this visit to Tasmania had been fascinating and I'd only watched half an hour's cricket!

13
Christmas Diary

2 2 DECEMBER

Flew to Canberra with the team and press corps. Attended a cocktail party at the Lodge, a pleasant, white stone country house in Canberra, which has a swimming pool (added by Gough Whitlam) and a putting green (added by Mr Hawke). Had a chat with the Prime Minister about apartheid, upon which he has firm views, and about Kim Hughes' cricket tour to South Africa. We'd been introduced by Mungo MacCullum, who was an old chum and drinking partner from Mr Hawke's wilder days. Mungo had turned up in his usual bush clothes (everyone else was wearing suits) and he'd greeted the Prime Minister with 'G'day Bob' to which his old mate replied 'G'day Mungo'.

Of course this was not a private party. Channel 9 had been invited. Cameras flitted around the party and as Border and Botham (these, mark you, not Border and Gatting) strode over to meet 'Stork' Hendry, at ninety-one the oldest living Test cricketer, the television men rushed in to record the occasion for the next day's news. Mr Hawke suddenly appeared and the heroic quartet talked for ten minutes as the film whirred.

'Stork' Hendry was lucid and alert, arguing that cricket had lost a generation of cricketers, those reared in this age of World Series cricket. He believed that hope of a cricketing revival lay with the ten-year olds who had not yet been stolen from cricket's true virtues by the flashing lights. Cricket and American commercialism do not mix well, and a game is being ruined. Can the retreat be sounded? Can cricket extricate itself from this unwanted embrace? It has managed to do so, to date, in England. We worry whether it can be wise to leave our game in the hands of Mr Smith and Mr May, yet our cricket is not nearly as avaricious as in Australia. Our changes have been steady, we are prepared to trust cricket to win its public, are prepared to put faith in our game. Australian cricket is in trouble, caught between the inappropriately old and the uncaring new. If only administrators can be found to do battle with P.B.L., not to give them the keys to the castle, perhaps cricket here can return to being the vigorous, healthy occupation it used to be when this was the best-loved game.

Hendry was good on the old days too. He said that Charlie Macartney was the best batsman he has ever seen and Frank Woolley the most graceful. He didn't like Jardine so much. He was fielding at slip once when Jardine was being barracked by the Victoria crowd. To be sympathetic he'd said 'the wolves are out'. Jardine had straightened in his crease, turned and told him that 'all Australians are an uneducated and unruly mob'. 'Well if that's what you think, you can go to buggery', Hendry had told him. We left at 8.30 or so, the introductions made and the photographs taken.

PRIME MINISTER'S XI

The Manuka Oval is one of the prettiest in Australia, a tree-lined and intimate ground, just the venue for this game. An eight-thousand crowd basked in the hot sun, men protecting their heads by stuffing newspapers in their hats, lads sizzling in the heat. Strangely (for we were in the political capital of Australia), a Christmas spirit prevailed, as political sophisticates mixed with people from the bush who'd brought their families for the match of the year. Canberra is implanted inland, two and a half hours from the coast. The dry cowboy towns of the west are not so far away, and Australia remains a farming nation. Canberra is a hybrid and embraces a variety of Australian characteristics.

Some games begin a gin-and-tonic under par and never brighten up; from the start this one was fun, a game played in an old world atmosphere to a back-cloth of white picket fences, poplar trees, pretty dresses, ice creams and a panoply of coloured clothing. Beer and wine were consumed but hardly anyone got drunk. Husbands sat with wives (their own wives that is) and for once they were not disturbed by hideous replays on screens, but could sit and contemplate the score on the old M.C.G. Scoreboard, which is now named after Jack Fingleton. Fingleton used to sit by Sir Robert Menzies in previous Prime Minister's matches, telling him what was happening on the field. After Menzies' retirement the tradition was stopped because none of his successors enjoyed cricket. Mr Hawke revived it upon winning power three years ago because he likes cricket, and because it helps him to present himself to the electorate.

He was right to revive this fixture. Cricket needs more of these gentle occasions, for they amuse and unite people. So much of cricket is tough and cynical; crowds can rarely sit back and enjoy a game without being treated as if they were in a discotheque. Players need these happy occasions too. Teams used to arrive by boat, relaxed, fit and in good spirits after a trip across the ocean. During a tour they could disappear into the bush away from the heat of the cricket and into the heat of the sun. Now they board a jumbo at Heathrow, land twenty-four hours later in Sydney, catch a flight to Brisbane, and plunge immediately into the hurly-burly of posh hotels and solemn cricket. Sport is so frenetic these days, there is rarely time for conversation.

Everyone enjoyed the game, lapping up its mild humour and its sense of tranquillity. Appropriately they applauded the little things that caught the eye – David Gower's flick back to Lamb, who returned flat and hard to the 'keeper, DeFreitas' marvellous throwing, and Veletta's adroit judgement of a run. They cheered for the team representing the Prime Minister (Bob Hope by name, according to DeFretias) but were hospitable towards the English team. Through the tour there has been very little antagonism towards the visitors. Australia's ties with England are so loved, and this land is host to so many different nationalities that the pommie-bashing bit is a tradition rather than an attitude. Instead the spectators barracked anyone who blocked, as if they had declined to answer a question in the Parliament down the road.

No serious conclusion can be drawn from the cricket, though Veletta and Glen Bishop batted well. Veletta was perky and inventive, chipping the ball to leg and darting out for a run. Bishop was firm and upright, moving into his drives as his confidence rose. They found England's faster bowlers to their liking, but the Prime Minister's innings lost its momentum after Bishop edged a leg-side catch to Richards (French is still injured). Ian Botham, returning from injury, slowed things down off what might loosely be called his Somerset run (he used it for the second half of last season and bowled several long spells) and he bowled at around three-quarter pace. It took Allan Border, who was accorded a hero's welcome, to bring life back to his team's innings. He did not find the English bowlers entirely in earnest, though no-one told Brett Henschell this was a friendly and he ran Border ragged between the wickets.

PRIME MINISTER'S XI v. ENGLAND, Canberra
ONE-DAY MATCH (50 overs)

PRIME MINISTER'S XI

G. Bishop	c Richards b Botham	49
M. Veletta	c Lamb b Edmonds	75
T. Moody	c Athey b Botham	17
J. Siddons	run out	12
S. O'Donnell	st Richards b Edmonds	14
A. Border	not out	41
B. Henschell	not out	27
Extras	(lb 4, nb 1)	5
TOTAL	(five wickets)	240

Fall of wickets: 109, 143, 144, 170, 172.
Batting time: 185 mins. Overs: 50.

ENGLAND

C. Broad	c Dimattina b O'Donnell	47
W. Athey	run out	14
D. Gower	b Moody	68
A. Lamb	c Moody b Henschell	9
M. Gatting	c Moody b Tazelaar	30
I. Botham	c Brown b Henschell	43
J. Richards	not out	18
P. DeFreitas	not out	0
Extras	(lb 2, w 4, nb 6)	12
TOTAL	(six wickets)	241

Fall of wickets: 62, 76, 123, 173, 199, 239.
Batting time: 211 mins. Overs: 47.4.
Man of the match: David Gower.
Crowd: 8,102.
ENGLAND WON BY FOUR WICKETS

132

England won easily in the end, hitting the runs off an attack that was unimpressive apart from Whitney, who continues to be the best new ball bowler in Australia. Players, spectators and even reporters enjoyed the day, particularly as the sun shone upon us for the first time in ages. Australia had begun to resemble England, where the sun shines on 23 July.

Stayed at Mungo's for the night to arrange to fly to Melbourne for Christmas and the fourth and perhaps decisive Test match.

CHRISTMAS EVE

Didn't do much. Missed the Pen Party at which John Woodcock arrived as the Master of the Rolls, and presided over court hearings at which various reporters were tried and found guilty of certain offences, and duly fined in order to raise money for the Christmas dinner tomorrow.

CHRISTMAS DAY

Geoff Boycott arrived in Melbourne today. No-one so important can have arrived on this day before. He's lodging in a hotel somewhere, though he will not tell his ghost writer where. Apart from his Yorkshire battles he's been writing his autobiography with journalist Tony Brindle and now he's here to write for the *Daily Mail*.

We had an excellent Christmas Day, beginning with a drinks party in which the British Press entertained the players, and guests from the Australian media. Included in the programme was a pantomime based upon *A Christmas Carol*. Three Ghosts (I can't bat, I can't bowl and I can't field) visited a sleeping Gatting. It was very funny, and wildly applauded. The stars of the show were David Norrie (*News of the World*) who did most of the writing and slept in the bed. As Gatting he promised to make his press conferences less ridden with clichés. He was helped by Martin Johnson, Chris Lander and Paul Weaver. They had written the pantomime during a couple of late nights. Dominic Allan, the London Broadcasting Company radio man, acted as the chorus, intoning his words with an actor's authority. He used to be an actor, as a matter of fact. One of his films was on television last night and he'd rejoiced at the prospect of more royalties. Gower (playing

133

himself) wandered on and off stage with a champagne bottle muttering inaudible (nearly) things about Peter May.

Our drinks party lasted from 11 a.m. till 2 p.m., though the players drifted out earlier to prepare their fancy dresses for their lunch at 1 p.m. Emburey appeared as Rasputin, Gower as a Gestapo officer and Whitaker as a rather sexy number not unlike Marlene Dietrich (in which role he was disturbingly at ease). The Edmonds (cricket's most contrary couple) were fettered by ball and chain and wore striped convict uniforms. 'We thought we'd come as Australians,' said Frances.

For lunch the journalists booked a restaurant not far from the hotel, where we sat around tables sipping wine and chatting with developing hilarity. Apart from the traditional food the purpose of the dinner was to surprise the cricket correspondent of *The Times*, who was on his thirtieth tour and his thirteenth in Australia, with a spoof of *This is Your Life*. A variety of correspondents acted as supposed characters from Mr Woodcock's past, and John greeted them all as if they were indeed long-lost characters from his past. Imitations of E. W. Swanton and John Arlott were provided by Christopher Martin-Jenkins, who has a gift for mimicry. It was hard at times to tell whether Mr Woodock was really enjoying the whole experience. In any event he enjoyed himself enough to make several lengthy speeches, not all of which followed a predictable narrative path. He was presented with a fishing net which, for some time, he appeared to think was a snooker cue. He stamped it to the ground in the course of some of his speeches, till the correspondent from the *London Evening Standard* moved it to a safer place.

Other presentations were made to David Lloyd, who works hard as the reporter for the Press Agency and to Peter Smith, who is the master organiser of the press party.

Afternoon slipped none too quietly into the evening and the correspondent of an English broadsheet rested beside me to say that I was one of the most boring batsmen he'd ever seen and wasn't it odd because I was a witty writer. Didn't I ever feel like just slogging? Christmas spirit prevailed as these observations were repeated fifteen times. My confidant's wife had given birth earlier in the day so we were all in a celebratory mood.

Gradually the party crept back to the hotel, to ring loved ones in England and friends in Australia, and to contemplate that though Christmas is not quite the same in hot, sunny Australia, though it is a mixture of relaxing and hedonism, it can still be a lot of fun. This day has helped to bind players and pressmen together, and to add to the happiness of the tour. For a day, at least, we could pretend to enjoy each other's company, not to be rivals in deed and character.

14

Melbourne: Fourth Test

DAY ONE

A crowd of fifty-eight thousand people gathered at the Melbourne Cricket Ground for this first day of the fourth Test match of the series. There isn't much else to do in Melbourne on Boxing Day (Dame Edna says that the best thing about Melbourne is that it is only twenty-eight hours from somewhere really interesting). Down the road in Kooyong, Sweden was meeting Australia in the Davis Cup final, and these sporting contests provided Australians with two alternatives as they recovered from the excesses of Christmas Day.

Before the game Border had announced that Australia would attack. He said he was prepared to risk losing in order to win this game. This remark dominated the day's play. Gatting won the toss and put Australia in, a move which surprised most critics, including Richie Benaud, who called it an extraordinary decision. Gatting had detected a freshness in the pitch, had noticed that the weather was cloudy and told Benaud that he expected to bowl Australia out for two hundred and twenty. As it turned out he was pessimistic. Australia collapsed abjectly, 7/41, and by the close of play England was in command. Gladstone Small, picked because

Dilley was injured (he'd arrived at the fancy dress party in a wheel-barrow pushed by Gatting), was the best of the bowlers. After an inaccurate opening over he varied his pace and movement, darting the ball away from the batsman. He is top of the bowling averages in Australia, and of late has been bowling better than any of the other seamers. Not for the first time on the tour the effect Hadlee's bowling has had on English cricket was underlined. He trapped Boon and Waugh as they flicked at shortish outswingers, let down by inadequate footwork. He took five wickets for the first time in his Test career and he will not be so strangely neglected in the future.

Ian Botham took five wickets too, to add to his three catches at second slip. He bowled off ten paces or so, about his Sunday League run, and somehow or other five batsmen lost their wickets to him. Batsmen have been losing their wickets to him somehow or other for years. Marsh was the initial wicket. With Australia battling back after the early loss of Boon he dealt with Botham's first few deliveries easily enough, except that he hinted at edginess by rushing down the pitch in search of a single. Then Botham bowled a long hop, a few yards faster. Marsh recklessly pulled at it and Richards jumped high to take a fine catch. This appeared to be a typical Botham wicket. In fact he'd changed his pace suddenly, sharply; he'd detected Marsh's unease, fed him a bumper. He is a subtly psychological bowler, a force on the field. It was, I thought, a good piece of bowling.

Border also fell to Botham, slashing at one too close for so aggressive a stroke, as if determined to carry out his own orders by blazing the way with shots. He and the other Australian batsmen resembled warriors charging down the pitch at machine-gun fire. A wiser strategist might not have attacked without first setting up a base camp. The pitch was good, more bouncy than has been usual of late at the M.C.G., where grasscutters have skittled batsmen for years. Because it was fresh and cloudy, because the bowlers bowled reasonably well and batsmen had to graft for runs, this was not the moment for full-blooded attack, yet Border announced this as his policy from the beginning of the day. There is a want of intelligent strategical thinking in Australian cricket.

Botham's confidence infected the rest of the team, who fielded eagerly. Once Broad chased seventy yards after Gower to collect the ball and return it for him (Gower's arm is still damaged). Jack Richards was a revelation. Before the tour Robin Marlar said that in picking French and Richards as the 'keepers England had chosen one man who couldn't bat and one who couldn't keep. I didn't think much of Richards either, not as a stumper anyhow. Here he added to his hundred in Perth, with catches of Border and Marsh, and a sporty acrobatic catch of Merv Hughes. It has to be said, Australia are a poor team, but the England selectors have not been let down by their team. Not everyone would have brought Broad, Small and Richards on this tour.

The huge, burning crowd had not had much to cheer. They had now, as Merv Hughes strode to the crease. Merv is a game 'un and he marched in purposefully as if the career record of three innings and no runs was one of those perverse twists of fate which simply defies belief. The crowd raised the roof as he drove Small through the covers for his first two runs in Test cricket.

They followed the tennis too, as the organisers put the score on the screen every four overs. Mightly applause greeted Cash's victory over Edberg, a victory which coincided with and delayed the beginning of the English innings, which appears certain to give Gatting and his men the Ashes.

In the press-box Boycott sat and chatted, talking to me for an hour about the Somerset business. He could see how it had happened, and sympathised with both sides. He is an extraordinary man. He sat firmly in his chair on the edge of the press-box and wouldn't tell his ghost his thoughts, saying they were secret until near the end of the day when the pair had themselves to themselves in a private corner. I advised Boycott to save his best stuff for his autobiography.

Gladstone Small returned to the hotel tonight to say that people in the restaurant where he'd dined had stood to applaud as he walked in. He'd been cheered on by the crowd in the notorious Bay 13 too, and had been surprised by the friendliness of the spectators.

DAY TWO

In the morning Broad and Gatting piled on the agony, collecting runs easily despite the accurate bowling of Peter Sleep. Australia were woefully incompetent in the field, but did not bowl as badly as in Brisbane and Perth. Catches were dropped – by Border at slip, by Waugh in the gully and by Sleep off his own bowling – and a straightforward run out was missed through a series of schoolboy howlers. Broad cut to Boon at backward point and for obscure reasons, ran. Gatting was slow out of the blocks and had given up his chase half-way down the pitch. Boon picked up the ball, from twenty yards away, threw it wide of Zoehrer and at his toes. Zoehrer slipped on the ball but removed the bails with his gloves, with Gatting not present in a photo-finish. Meanwhile the ball, which had in fact eluded Zoehrer's gloves, meandered towards the square leg boundary. At slip Border stared and chewed, his expression unchanging.

Gatting was not fluent, grafting for his runs as Broad, ever more impressive, a pillar rather than a foundation stone, moved serenely towards his third century, which he duly completed with a simple off-drive between Sleep's cover fieldsmen. Broad has now scored centuries in three successive Test matches against Australia, a feat previously achieved only by Hobbs, Sutcliffe and Hammond. He has been unruffled and distinguished, the man of the series.

Australia tightened its game after lunch, with the bowlers never flagging and the fieldsmen at last giving them some support. Gatting fell to the first ball after lunch, hooking Reid to Hughes at long leg (Merv continues to be the hero of the M.C.G.). Broad flashed and edged to the 'keeper, Gower battled to keep Sleep, who was bowling into the footholds, at bay and then slogged him to deep mid-off. Lamb clipped useful runs, and Botham put his head down for an hour before, to his immense disgust, slashing at McDermott and edging to the 'keeper. From 3/219 England collapsed to 8/289, and briefly Australia was back in the match. McDermott was, by now, thundering in, his red hair flowing and his face twisted into the fury of a roused warrior. At every wicket he snarled and pounded the air, not so much in joy, as in exultation as if his bowling at the English tail vindicated his recall. McDermott, like Lawson before him, appears to feel obliged to be the nasty fast bowler in the Lillee tradition. Yet Lillee looked wicked – all moustache and glare – while McDermott simply appears silly; while his antics are not those of the aggressive man but of the petulant youth.

McDermott spoiled and soured the day. Between them Gower, Gatting and Border have returned to Ashes cricket a lot of the dignity and decency that were lost when Chappell and his cronies were in charge. There has scarcely been a moment's unpleasantness in this series, or in the previous one in England in 1985. The teams have shown that Test cricket, however tense the battle, need not lose its manners and its respect for the opposing player. In achieving this they have done cricket a great service, and it is to be hoped that someone lands a foot squarely on McDermott's backside for his immaturity today.

England's tail, stirred by McDermott, added another sixty runs, with Edmonds and Emburey staunch and practical, and Gladstone Small flamboyant in his strokes. With these extra runs the game was put beyond the grasp of the Australians, who lose the match either tomorrow or on Monday.

Only twenty-six thousand people turned up today, and they followed the tennis on the screen no less assiduously than the cricket. They cheered wildly as Australia took a two:one lead in the Davis Cup, with Cash and Fitzgerald beating Jarryd and Edberg. They like to win in Melbourne, yet have not been in the least impolite. This is an open country and people do not hide their emotions. Australia is not nearly so brazen or vulgar a country as prudish and ill-informed people imagine. The Ocker is no more Australia than the pin-striped bowler-hatted man carrying a *Financial Times* is England.

28 DECEMBER

England has won the Ashes. Australia has won the Davis Cup.

At 4.39 this afternoon, big Merv Hughes, of the big bristling moustache, swept Edmonds to Small at deep square leg, whither he had been moved two balls earlier. Small took the catch and then hurled the ball into the air, forgetting it in his eruption of joy to keep as a memento. Gatting had led his team to victory, and to an unassailable two:nil lead. Nineteen England captains had put the opposition in, Gatting was only the third to win the game. It was a marvellous achievement but, oh, how poorly the Australians played.

Two men ran themselves out. Boon did not move his feet, Border flashed at one a little too wide, and the tail crumpled to the

English spinners, who'd worked hard throughout for little reward. It was appropriate that Emburey and Edmonds took the final wickets, because they'd been used in long containing spells which had taken the pressure off the seamers and enabled Gatting to use Botham as an occasional bowler. Whenever Edmonds and Emburey bowled England was in charge of the game (a few hours in Adelaide apart) yet they've taken very few wickets in the series.

It was appropriate, too, that Gladstone Small was made man of the match. He has sat patiently, sometimes unjustly, on the sidelines and finally his chance came. He bowled very well, and everyone was pleased that things had worked out well for so nice a chap.

Rarely can an Australian team have offered so little resistance. After Marsh's run out (the result of confusion with Waugh) they lost six wickets for forty-one runs in nineteen overs, most of them through failures of technique. Once Border was gone the team had no substance. Border must be depressed, for there is so little hope of revival. His men simply have not learned from their experiences, and their cricketing judgement is immature. Maybe this is because they are brought up to play unthinkingly, whereas the English are brought up to play as well as they can. This team, unable to win, had no *nous*, no idea of surviving or making do. They tried to show the arrogance of winners – witness McDermott's violence upon taking a wicket, and Zoehrer's petulance in the field. (As Edmonds came in to bat he said 'here's Frances' husband'. He fumbled the next ball and Edmonds replied, 'Ah, Mr Zoehrer fumbles, not for the first time I understand'). Unable to be in charge they floundered, throwing their wickets away in a desperate imitation of aggression.

At the end of the fourth Test match has anything been learnt? At his press conference, at which he was grave and dignified, Border could not find much hope. He said he'd simply soldier on, and that he intended to see this thing through. There is no one else, whatever his critics say. Border is destined to end up with the worst record of any Australian captain in history. Yet really he has never had a chance. He is a simple man who has no unusual grasp of tactics, who finds it difficult to talk to his players. He'd happily relinquish the captaincy if any other candidate had the credentials. No-one has, because the State captains are not convincing except for Wellham, and he has so far been unacceptable because of his connection with the South African renegades (the current players regard their conduct as a betrayal of Australian cricket). Wood cannot be considered for the same reason and Hookes, who might have succeeded Kim Hughes, is on the point of retiring. This leaves Boon, Bright and Border and of these Border is the only man who can be confident of a place in the team. Australian cricket is still in a fearful mess.

England have gained much from this series. Gatting's success as a leader (Brearley did not win the Ashes so easily against a full-strength Australia) is important because it will help to break up the old guard, who'd been in charge since 1981.

Ever since he strode out to bat at first wicket down in Brisbane, Mike Gatting has been in charge of the England team. It was a bold move. Another man, a less cocky leader, might have told Lamb or Gower to pad up. Gatting had been having trouble with his team, who had been carousing till late at night. He was determined to impose hard and professional attitudes upon them, determined to instil pride, and he was finding it difficult to do this with one or two of the older, distinguished players who had been around too long to be easily manipulated.

Gatting has stuck to his guns, and although there is still much to do he has brought back an honesty to English cricket, returned a standard to our touring team. For this he is to be congratulated. The series was decided on that first morning, as Gatting swished away without losing his wicket, as Australia bowled badly and England batted well, a pattern that has not changed.

Yet Gatting is getting very little credit for his triumph. Neither Botham's revival nor England's remarkable improvement since last summer has been associated with him. The truth is he doesn't look like a good captain. He has a beer barrel for a body and a disturbingly innocent face. He doesn't sound lucid or intelligent either, not like Benaud, Brearley and the other obviously astute captains who treated the press (as might any other skilled public relations officers) with trust and respect, as if they knew something about the game. At press conferences Gatting tuts and clucks. He is neither fit nor articulate, and can be rude and abrupt. He is not, consequently, taken seriously as a good captain. His record though (with Middlesex and with England) is beyond reproach.

Gatting has led this team very well, that is the fact of the matter. He is just what they needed, a sergeant-major type to bully them out of their pleasant, careless repose. He has been tactically good too, using Edmonds and Emburey as his stock bowlers, resting his fast men without losing command of the game. He has bowled Botham only when the force was with him, rather than when Botham wanted to bowl (for the first time since Brearley, Botham is the servant and not the master of his captain. The friction between Gatting and Botham has worked well). His field placements and his selection have also worked well. He refused to drop a spinner on a grassy pitch here, and he was right. He asked Australia to bat first and that was right. He picked Broad and Richards and that was right. Of course it has helped that Australia has been so weak. England has climbed the north face of a sand castle. Nevertheless Gatting has led England admirably.

His senior colleagues are not tumbling over each other to sing his praises, though Gower's warm handshake on the field this afternoon was the mark of a man. (Gatting is not the only outsider who owes much to Gower's humanity. Edmonds' career only revived when Gower took over from Willis.) Some of the others still dislike Gatting's rumbustious ambition and bluff personality, still resent his simple, no-nonsense and disturbingly innocent approach.

It will be interesting to see if he can sustain the disciplined approach for the rest of the tour. Even the Indian trip of happy memory (for once teamwork and camaraderie were to the fore) ended badly with England falling apart on the unwanted trip to Australia which followed. Gatting has corrected some of the things wrong in English cricket, and now he must carry on the good work.

His team deserves the Ashes. They pass into myth as befits men who have played dedicated and intelligent cricket in Test matches (a veil can, for today, be drawn over the occasionally irresponsible efforts in the State games) and England has been by far the best side.

FOURTH TEST, Melbourne
December 26, 27, 28, 1986

AUSTRALIA

G. R. Marsh	c Richards b Botham	17	(2) run out	60
D. C. Boon	c Botham b Small	7	(1) c Gatting b Small	8
D. M. Jones	c Gower b Small	59	c Gatting b DeFreitas	21
A. R. Border*	c Richards b Botham	15	c Emburey b Small	34
S. R. Waugh	c Botham b Small	10	b Edmonds	49
G. R. J. Matthews	c Botham b Small	14	b Emburey	0
P. R. Sleep	c Richards b Small	0	run out	6
T. J. Zoehrer †	b Botham	5	c Athey b Edmonds	1
C. J. McDermott	c Richards b Botham	0	b Emburey	1
M. G. Hughes	c Richards b Botham	2	c Small b Edmonds	8
B. A. Reid	not out	2	not out	0
Extras	(b 1, lb 1, w 1, nb 7)	10	(lb 3, w 1, nb 2)	6
TOTAL		141		194

Fall of wickets: 16, 44, 80, 108, 118, 118, 129, 133, 137.
Second innings: 13, 48, 113, 153, 153, 179, 180, 189, 189.
Bowling: Small 22.4-7-48-5; DeFreitas 11-1-30-0; Emburey 4-0-16-0; Botham 16-4-41-5; Gatting 1-0-4-0.
Second innings: DeFreitas 12-1-44-1; Small 15-3-40-2; Botham 7-1-19-0; Edmonds 19.4-5-45-3; Emburey 20-5-43-2.

ENGLAND

B. C. Broad	c Zoehrer b Hughes	112
C. W. J. Athey	lbw b Reid	21
M. W. Gatting*	c Hughes b Reid	40
A. J. Lamb	c Zoehrer b Reid	43
D. I. Gower	c Matthews b Sleep	7
I. T. Botham	c Zoehrer b McDermott	29
C. J. Richards †	c Marsh b Reid	3
P. A. J. DeFreitas	c Matthews b McDermott	7
J. E. Emburey	c & b McDermott	22
P. H. Edmonds	lbw b McDermott	19
G. C. Small	not out	21
Extras	(b 6, lb 7, w 1, nb 11)	25
TOTAL		349

Fall of wickets: 58, 163, 198, 219, 251, 273, 277, 289, 319.
Bowling: McDermott 26.5-4-83-4; Hughes 30-3-94-1; Reid 28-5-78-4; Waugh 8-4-16-0; Sleep 28-4-65-1.
Toss: England.
Man of the match: G. C. Small.
Umpires: A. R. Crafter and R. A. French.
ENGLAND WON BY AN INNINGS AND 14 RUNS.

15

Interlude VI

THE ABORIGINES

The European invasion of Australia in 1788, led by Governor Phillip, was a disaster for the Aboriginal people. A great many perished and the rest had their culture severely disrupted and their freedom taken away.

There were only three hundred thousand Aborigines in 1788 in a country which their ancestors had populated for nearly forty thousand years, first around the lakes in New South Wales and later all around Australia. Governor Phillip's arrival in Sydney Cove began a history of conflict against them which includes atrocities, massacre and wholesale slaughter, particularly in Tasmania where the last full-blooded Aborigine died in 1876. A quarter of a million Aborigines disappeared within a generation.

The British Government failed to realise the land rights of the Aborigines. Efforts to convert them to Christianity failed, and the missionaries, having concluded that these people were beyond redemption, removed children from their parents so that with a proper education, they could fit into white society. From 1909–1930 more than one-third of Aboriginal children were taken from their parents and sent into virtual domestic slavery. Violet Shea was one such. She was snatched from her mother at the age of three, brought up on a reserve and with next to no education sent into service at the age of twelve. The body responsible for the deed was called the Aboriginal Protection Board. On the reserve she was fed with flour, sugar, tea and baking powder – nothing else. If the Aborigines ventured into the nearby town of Maclean they'd be treated with contempt. In cinemas they'd be told to sit with the other 'Koons' at the front while all the whites gathered at the back. This was not very long ago.

None of it worked. As far back as 1840 Mr C. G. Teckleman assessed that

'Nobody can give them a taste for that for which they have none.'

The Aborigines endured apalling attitudes and privations and somehow survived. In the 1950s they were a non-people. Australia had a whites-only immigration policy which was used to exclude coloureds – not officially, on the grounds of the colour of their skin, but because they could not pass the literacy tests at the airport. These tests were given in Estonian, Eskimo and French, and if a coloured did by some freak pass the test he was presented with a second in, say, Welsh. One Minister, justifying the deportation of a Chinese man who'd hoped to be allowed to stay because he'd married an Australian girl, told Parliament 'two Wongs don't make a white'.

Aborigines were banned from the swimming pools in most inland towns – 'who'd want to use the pool after an Abo?' – and from most parks. When a census was taken the counting was limited to the 'non-Aboriginal population'. They could not vote, nor own property, and if they were allowed to take a job their wages were paid to the local 'protector' of Aborigines. Efforts were made to destroy farms and tribal structures, to destroy the clusters of culture and Aboriginal life.

Incredibly, despite nearly two hundred years of prejudice and neglect (of course there have been good and noble dissenters from these prevailing attitudes), the Aboriginal communities have survived. The cost has been great. In outback towns and in some inner-city areas groups of Aborigines drink and fight, lost between the white world and their own tribes. Some whites regard them as lazy, violent and drunken people, and imagine that they are typical of Aboriginal culture, justifying its destruction. Yet most Aborigines are teetotal. As Philip Knightly observed 'those who do drink tend to do so on benders with long periods of abstinence in between. Moreover when the time comes to attend a ritual, the Aborigine sobers up as if he'd been thrown into a cold lake.'

Nevertheless old attitudes persist. In some places the police still carry air-guns 'to shoot at koons'. Aborigines have demanded that a Royal Commission be held into the deaths of six Aborigines in police custody over the last few years, deaths which they allege were the result of beating by police and prison warders. The most notorious case is that of John Pat, a sixteen year old, who died in 1983 after a brawl with police in the remote outback town of Roebourne, eight hundred miles north of Perth. We studied this case at the school where I taught in Sydney, and I want to record the history of it.

Pat went to the aid of a friend who was fighting with five off-duty policemen who'd been drinking in the same pub. For his trouble he was thrown into a police van, taken to the station and dragged to a cell where he was found dead a short time later. The police said he hit his head when he fell on the road, but witnesses at the subsequent trial of the five policemen on charges of man-slaughter said they saw the police kick Pat in the head. One Abor-iginal woman, Julie Tucker, said that she'd seen a constable kick an apparently unconscious youth in the face:

'I looked away when I heard the boot connect with the face. It made me feel sick.'

She'd seen the policeman leaving the pub and shouting to one of the Aborigines: 'Come on, have a go! . . . what are you, girls?' An earlier witness, Nicholas Guinness, testified that he saw John Pat trying to break up the fight. Min Park, a white barmaid, de-scribed the policemen's conduct as being drunken and violent.

A series of witnesses testified that the policemen had punched and kicked this sixteen year old Aborigine boy. Peter Copper told the court that he'd seen Pat thrown on to the concrete surface of the police-station, where

'He fell on his face and they started pounding and kicking him and banging his head on the concrete. He never moved at all.'

These policemen were acquitted by an all-white jury. At the burial Mr Keith Whitney, a white Roebourne businessman and a lay preacher, abandoned the traditional service and said

'The grog got him . . . People in this town are angry . . . Their hearts are full of hate . . . I think most people would say if this young man had kept off the guy he would be alive today.'

Reporters said that some mourners appeared to be shocked and angry at this departure from the traditional burial service. John Pat's father, deeply distressed, said

'Bad men kill my son.'

He'd taken a lock of his dead son's hair before his body was buried and would keep this hair 'to be near my boy's spirit'. The old man said he had not eaten kangaroo – his favourite food – since his son had died. Kangaroo was his son's totem, he explained, and fasting was a sign of respect.

In a year's time Australia celebrates the two-hundredth anniversary of the invasion of the Aborigines home by the white man. Understandably different tribes, different Aborigines, have mixed feelings about this bi-centenary.

However, all is not lost. In the last twenty years efforts have been made to educate whites in the ways of the Aboriginal tribes, and to find ways in which the two cultures can live in harmony. As Neville Bonner, the only Aborigine to win a seat in Parliament, has said:

'I'm very optimistic about the future. A happy coincidence of Aborigines prepared for a bigger slice of Australia's riches with that of a major change in the attitude of white Australia convinces me that my optimism is well-founded.'

There are now nearly as many Aborigines as there were in 1788. Their culture has not died, though for two hundred years it went underground, with its beautiful drawings and ritual dances. Now that white attitudes are changing, their traditions are returning.

Land is of vital importance to the Aborigines. Xavier Herbert wrote in 1979 that until the black man was given back his land with no strings attached, Australia would be 'not a nation but a community of thieves'. Their relationship with land is private and complicated; the land is called Kunappi, the earth mother, the beginning and end of life itself. Our view of land as a commodity is reprehensible to the Aborigine, who regards mining as a penetration of the earth, a particularly traumatic experience. There are rich uranium deposits on land claimed by the Aborigines. It will be interesting to see how this battle between culture and humanity on the one hand and industry on the other is resolved.

So large is Australia that occasionally Aborigines turn up who have not yet encountered what we are pleased to call civilization. In October a group was found in the outback who had been isolated from the outside world for twenty years. Apparently they had been reluctant to join even so rudimentary a settlement as an outstation (which usually consists only of a bore hole and a few huts), preferring a nomadic existence in one of the world's harshest environments, dependent for survival on killing kangaroos, rabbits and other wild creatures. It is believed that somewhere in the vast outback there are still many Aboriginal communities, surviving without contact with the white invader. In two hundred years the white man has confined himself almost exclusively to the coastline, with its beaches and its milk-shake parlours. (It is thought, by anthropologists, that these latter were not present before the white man arrived.)

I include here a poem written by Kevin Albert, one of the most talented of the Aboriginal writers. It is an attack on Evonne Cawley (née Goollagong) who had not used her victory at Wimbledon to draw attention to the plight of her people in her native land.

'I wonder, Evonne, when you're playing straight sets
And you "haste" your opponent so well,
Do you ever look back at your grandmother, black,
And catch glimpses of her in her hell?
Do you ever see past the net on the court
To the horrors that make you scream "Fault"?
Do you open your eyes when the whites victimise
Your family? You never scream "Halt!"

'Remember, Evonne, the song of the swan
I sang you in Griffith's heat daze;

149

Wheeling your pram thru' the dust past the dam
To the tent shanties we lived in so long.
Remember old tin, broken flagons, the din
The people so poor and oppressed,
Scratching for crusts of damper and meat
Day after day without rest.
Remember my aunt; your grandmother, "Doll",
Our cousins, our blood kept in chains?
Remember the hate, the mortality rate
The tumble-down shacks, the rains?

'Win your games Love, may they all be straight sets
But "I accuse" for our people again;
Go on and win with your calm easy grin
And when sycophants raise wines to "toast",
Say a few words so the truth can be heard
About victims with no chance to win.'

A STATE GAME

One hot day I went to the Sydney Cricket Ground to watch New South Wales play South Australia.

The S.C.G. was a sorry sight. The Hill was empty. A gardener wandered to and fro around its base and at 11.45 began to work with a rake and a bucket. He went off to fetch a hosepipe and for the rest of the day the Hill was being watered as a State game took place in the middle. Other stands were empty too, the Brewongle, the Bradman and the Walters'. They hadn't even bothered to open the kiosks selling flavoured milk. The cricket was superb, the most enjoyable day of the tour. I watched under blue skies as Glenn Bishop, a brutal and simple batsman, who strikes from a short backlift like a snake biting at its prey, hit the bowlers all around the oval. His footwork was imprecise and though he is not always judicious, he hits hard and is quicker onto the short ball than most tall men. Apparently he has hit the ball for a straight six at the Adelaide Oval, one of the few men to achieve this feat. He scored one hundred and thirty-five clean runs under the scrutiny of a Test selector.

His partner was Andrew Hilditch, recalled to the State team with one last chance to resume his career. He'd been on the radio in Adelaide when Border set two long legs for Athey. 'He'll never fall for that' said Hilditch. He scored, too; well-made, tremendous runs by a batsman better than his crabby stance predicts.

Theirs was a lovely, forceful partnership on a slow, brown pitch against New South Wales' spin attack. Actually Holland and Bennett bowled badly. As Hilditch blocked Bennett one barracker called 'C'mon Hilditch, you're making them look good'. Bennett spins the ball at the front of his fingers, which prevents him getting it to dip, a skill which demands wrapping the fingers over the top of the ball. In the sun-blessed seats, John Inverarity recalled Prasanna's oriental ability to dip the ball, as apparent half-volleys died on a length, as if the ball had been poisoned by an arrow. He said that Prasanna used to stand at the end of his run staring at the batsman, the huge whites of his eyes bright and mischievous. At times Inverarity felt like holding up his hand to ask the bowler to stop fixing him with those eyes, so that he could watch the ball.

Only the Indians can dip the ball in this way. Edmonds and Emburey cannot, for their finger and wrist movements are too restricted.

Greg Matthews hardly bowled at all, being brought on with South Australia's score standing at 0/153. Another barracker called out 'Give Matthews a bowl. He's supposed to be a Test bowler'; to which Matthews shouted back 'I'm an all-rounder'. Of course he is scarcely a State bowler really, just a good cricketer thrown into Test cricket and expected to bowl before his education is complete.

New South Wales' best bowler was Michael Whitney, the reformed surfer, who swung the ball late and yet again appeared to be the most dangerous new ball bowler in Australia.

The barrackers' voices carried across the ground. With so few people at the game rowdy spectators can carry on a conversation with men two hundred yards away. One bloke called 'c'mon South Australia, 'ave a go', whereupon a voice from the side of the ground shouted 'they're going all right. Leave them alone'. Even the players' words can be heard. Matthews shouted 'well bowled Max (Bennett) good loop' and Wellham encouraging his men with 'c'mon lads, work hard'. Just the ordinary comments that sprinkle around a day's cricket, but interesting for their insight into the group dynamics.

This was a day for the connoisseur, a day to sit and chat and enjoy the gentleness and poetry of cricket. Only the brazen voice of the man on the microphone, uttering his banalities as if the crowd were as ill informed as those who go to the hamburger cricket, and the crass advertisements for the one-day series on the huge screen behind the Hill, broke the reverie of a happy day's play. The old scoreboard, unused and unwanted, stood forlornly behind the Hill, a relic of more dignified times.

No-one was there. Manufacturers say that bat sales are in a trough. Hardly any kids attended this game, which is not included in the P.B.L. advertising campaign. Hardly anyone knows it is taking place. It has not been mentioned in television or newspaper advertisements. Yet two cricketing heroes, Waugh and Mathews, and a variety of past, present and future Test cricketers were on the field. Twenty years ago an ordinary grade game would have attracted a similar number of spectators.

On the empty seats, under a blazing sun and with the cricket flowing in front of us, John Inverarity and I discussed the demise of Shield cricket. It is hard to say whether it has been caused by World Series cricket, or whether W.S.C. was a reaction to a change in society. Inverarity took the view that fewer people in Australia have a deep-rooted love of cricket than in England, where village, school and club cricket thrives. People here enjoy the outdoor life, follow a variety of sports and hope Australia does well. Few watch cricket for its own sake, as a study of men, techniques and beauty. They demand famous men and exciting contests. Cricket's following is shallow. So, with basketball and baseball and American football appropriately jazzed up and on television every day, cricket, proper cricket, has fallen into decline. Sport's new, aggressive and selfish audience demands action, is not interested in subtle changes of fortune. Packer recognised this change and has marketed his product without sentiment. No effort has been made to promote State cricket because people are not interested in going to watch it. Lots of New South Welshmen follow the State's scores in the paper but few go to a match. Even the Shield final between New South Wales and Queensland, which turned out to be a great game, drew only four thousand spectators.

Australians are playing sports more, and more are watching them on television. They only go to a live game if something big and bright – night cricket for example – drags them to the ground.

Individual sports like surfing, wind-surfing and skate-boarding are replacing the old team games, which are supposed to breed fellowship and unselfishness. These new spectators do not want to give to the game, they want to take from it.

This trend is exaggerated by the power of the media in Australia, which seizes upon heroes and turns them into superstars. A man near the top of his profession is used to sell the game, so that gradually the attention of the supporter is focused upon the individual. Pop stars are treated in much the same way, with hype and money. Eventually, though, they fall by the wayside if their music is not good enough. P.B.L. has driven cricket, one-day cricket at least, up the pop charts, just like Adam and the Ants, but the new-fangled game is not good enough. One-day cricket is shallow. It might bring in the dollar, but it doesn't create a large number of people who hold cricket, as opposed to entertainment, closest to their hearts. In cashing in on the hollowness of it, P.B.L. has done the game a disservice. If only it had tried to educate the public, to present Shield cricket to them as something worthwhile, then this day at the S.C.G. might not have been so bleak. Cricket is raking in the bucks as it digs its own grave.

We had a lovely day at the match. One man sat reading a Russian novel and a few lads, just the uncorrupted few, collected autographs and had their bats ready for a game. Shield cricket is in a far worse position than county cricket. It is being allowed to die, as if it were an old man with cancer rather than an intelligent adult with 'flu.

NEW SOUTH WALES *v.* S. AUSTRALIA: DAYS 2 & 3, Sydney December 19, 20 1986

S. AUSTRALIA, FIRST INNINGS, RESUMED at 3/327

D. O'Connor	lbw b Whitney	120
W. Phillips	c Taylor b Whitney	35
P. Sleep	b Bennett	26
S. Wundke	c Small b Bennett	8
N. Plummer	b Bennett	0
T. May	c Bennett b Matthews	4
A. Zesers	run out	3
T. Birchall	not out	2
Extras	(b 10, lb 10, nb 8, w 1)	29
TOTAL		493

Fall of wickets: 269, 280, 280, 350, 400, 418, 426, 449, 465, 493.
Bowling: Gilbert 24-2-70-0 (w 1, nb 1); Whitney 30-3-97-5 (nb 7); Holland 37-8-111-0; Waugh 9-1-28-0; Bennett 41-15-86-3; Matthews 20-6-56-1; O'Neill 5-0-25-0.
Batting time: 595 minutes. Overs: 166.

NEW SOUTH WALES

S. Small	lbw b Sleep	52	run out	5
M. Taylor	c and b Sleep	26	b Zesers	186
D. Wellham	c Bishop b May	48	b Sleep	119
S. Waugh	b Zesers	14	c Barchall b Sleep	10
M. O'Neill	lbw b Plummer	3	not out	5
G. Matthews	b Plummer	0	not out	3
G. Dyer	c and b May	1	lbw b May	
M. Bennett	c Sleep b Zesers	39		
D. Gilbert	c Plummer b Wundke	6		
R. Holland	not out	11		
M. Whitney	c Hilditch b Sleep	8		
Extras	(lb 3, nb 7)	10	(b 6, lb 5, nb 3)	14
TOTAL		218	(5 wkts)	342

Fall of wickets: 81, 84, 121, 126, 126, 137, 169, 193, 199, 218.
Second innings: 9, 270, 306, 307, 336.
Bowling: Zesers 20-6-36-2; Hookes 6-1-18-0; Wundke 10-3-16-1 (nb 4); May 36-13-74-2; Sleep 31-6-48-3 (nb 3); Plummer 18-3-23-2.
Second innings: Zesers 14-3-36-1; Wundke 7-0-30-0 nb 3); May 35-12-59-1; Sleep 39-11-96-2; Plummer 26-7-67-0; Hookes 12-0-43-0.
Batting time: 395 minutes. Overs: 121.
Second innings: 425 minutes. Overs: 133. Crowd: 1169.
SOUTH AUSTRALIA WON ON FIRST INNINGS
Points: SA 2, NSW 0.

THE DAVIS CUP FINAL

At the request of the noble Murdoch newspaper *The Sunday Times* I went to the Davis Cup final at Kooyong. In the press tent, I found journalists from all over the world, including a lady from Thailand with whom I had lunch, and a gentleman from Yugoslavia who poured hot chocolate down my trousers. Sport is big business, and tennis is a much bigger sport than cricket. The German newspaper *Bild* ran stories on consecutive days about Becker's triumphs in the American Masters and about a huge political scandal. Sales of *Bild* rose fifteen per cent whenever Becker was on the front page. In Thailand sales of the sports papers trebled during the World Cup, in France *L'Equipe* rose rapidly at the same time.

Tennis players earn millions of pounds. According to David Miller of *The Times* a week's tennis at Wembley costs Benson & Hedges around five times as much as the entire Benson & Hedges cricket competition. Botham earns next to nothing compared to the top six Swedish players. Wilander, Edberg, Nystrom, Jarryd, Carlsson and Pernfers are paid tens of thousands of pounds for one night of exhibition tennis. Nor are they overpaid, for the promoters make plenty of money too. They are paid the market rate.

In English cricket the reporters earn as much as the cricketers (£25–30,000 a year plus expenses). Cricket is a pip-squeak of a game, compared to tennis. It is played in a handful of countries, several of them poor. Money is only made in England and Australia, which is why the players are keen to return to Australia so often. In these countries a man like Botham is a huge star, yet in Europe and elsewhere no-one has heard of him. Neither of the television sets in the press tent are tuned to the cricket, both were showing horse-races. This morning I shared a sauna with an American who had never heard of cricket, though he'd noticed how many lovely young ladies hang around the players' hotel.

Australia won the doubles easily, and can now only lose the cup if the redoubtable Pernfers beats Cash and Edberg awakens himself to defeat MacNamee. Cash and Fitzgerald were aggressive, scurrying around the court, hurrying the Swedes into mistakes. They were a yard faster, a second sharper and a lot hungrier than the Swedes who never did find their rhythm.

Jarryd and Edberg were out of sorts, particularly Edberg who did not seem capable of carrying the burden of his team. He is ranked four in the world yet lost in straight sets to Cash on Friday and, despite the urgings of his manager, Hans Ollson and of his tenacious partner, did not raise his game today. Maybe he is not ready yet to take his country to a Davis Cup victory as Becker, McEnroe and Wilander have done, and as Cash appears to be doing for the second time. It is hard to believe that Wilander, a doughty fighter, would have lost his two games so easily. Edberg appeared to be a gifted player but out of sorts, a man relying on his extraordinary ability to such a degree that, when it cheats him, he does not know what to do. Jarryd was more alert, had a brightness and a wit about him, and I felt sorry that his partner was playing so abjectly.

In the press tent after the game, Jarryd, his face betraying a deep disappointment, was still alert and intelligent. He did not say much in English. He'd already played a game in a foreign land and on a foreign surface. No doubt he did not feel inclined to speak his heart in a foreign tongue. Later, surrounded by Swedish reporters, he opened up. I did not understand a word of it, yet found him to be impressive and likeable. Edberg sat, tired and depressed, a man who had been lifted by the occasion, a man who plays the tennis circuit as a routine and found nothing left in the locker for this cup-tie. He did not say much; trying to answer the questions his pale face had hollow, deeply set eyes and again I felt sorry for Swedes.

Cash and Fitzgerald won the first two sets 6–3, 6–4, twice breaking Jarryd, the natural leader of the Swedish pair, though not a good enough player to carry his partner. Edberg was erratic, drilling his ground strokes into the net and serving nine double faults in the match. Sweden fought back almost by accident in the third set when Edberg, at 0–40 and 4–4 suddenly served aces to take the game. Just as suddenly – this is a game of suddenlies – Fitzgerald lost his serve and Sweden had taken a set. A revival by the dominant Nordic pair appeared to be imminent. If only they could seize this game they could still win. Fitzgerald and Cash were hitting hard, playing old-fashioned serve and volley grass tennis. Cash was particularly inspired, his overhead shots flawless and his serving powerful and accurate. He scarcely made a mistake from first to last. Really, he hasn't made a mistake since thumping a photographer on Tuesday. He has lots of Botham's competitive courage, and a lot of his audacity too. At the press conference he wore an earring.

Sweden did not revive. Instead Edberg lost his first service game, serving two doubles faults, a feat which was repeated later to give Australia the game at 6–1. The Kooyong crowd cheered loudly without ever being rude, and for a second time the Melbournians displayed Australia's reputation for brash naturalness. Cash and Fitzgerald waved to the crowd and pounded the air as Jarryd and Edberg left the court disappointedly. It had taken two hours and ten minutes, and now Sweden had to rely upon Pernfers and Edberg to win the reverse singles. Suddenly I am an authority upon the game! Tennis too, I found to be simple, as I sat on the press benches.

16
Perth: One-day Series

VICTORY IN PERTH

The captain of the 'plane taking us to the one-day tournament in Perth reported upon progress in the game between Pakistan and the West Indies, the first of the series. Incredibly as they crossed the Nullabor plain and the Simpson desert the English players began to realise that a West Indian victory was not inevitable. By the time the 'plane landed they'd heard that the Pakistanis had won. The mighty West Indians had collapsed to the unconsidered bowling of Mudassar Nazar, who bowls tiny away-swingers of the sort with which Madan Lal and Mohinder Amarnath beat the West Indies in the last World Cup.

The result cheered the English players immensely. Suddenly they were flying to Perth not to face harsh reality but to measure themselves against powerful but by no means invincible opponents.

Can it be that this formidable West Indian team is in decline? A month ago they could only draw a Test series in Pakistan, and now they have lost the opening game of this 'special America's Cup' competition so that their place in the final is in peril. Suddenly England is travelling if not with expectation at least with hope.

The team does not appear as doom-laden as the one which went to the Caribbean a year ago.

Is this West Indian defeat a temporary lapse, or a sign of a great team in decline? No team is invincible in fifty-over cricket, because these games are too short to determine the merits of the teams. Moreover this vibrant Pakistan team, led by the magnificent Imran Khan, is bubbling with eager if obscure youngsters (on no previous occasion had I heard of Manzoor Elahi, Asif Mujtaba or Salim Jaffer). This defeat is not conclusive evidence that Viv Richard's team will not dominate the next decade as it has dominated the last one, a juggernaut storming down a hill, demolishing everything in its path. No shame, and not much significance, in losing in such circumstances.

Nevertheless the top West Indian cricketers are ageing. In the past ten years the West Indies' greatest cricketers have been Viv Richards, Gordon Greenidge, Joel Garner, Michael Holding, Clive Lloyd and Malcolm Marshall. Of these only the astonishingly fit Marshall is still at his peak. Lloyd has retired and the others are over thirty-two years of age. They are still magnificent cricketers but time is an unsympathetic enemy. Greenidge is thirty-five, Richards thirty-four, Holding thirty-two and Garner thirty-four. Batsmen's reactions slow as they age, and the eyes are less reliable. Bowlers find it more difficult to bowl long spells, and harder still to get those creaking bones going for a second burst later in the day. It'd not be surprising if the West Indies did fall a shade below the high standard they've kept up since 1976.

Batting is a particular problem. Besides the ageing titans, Haynes and Dujon are thirty and Gomes is thirty-three. Only Richardson (twenty-four) is in the first flush of youth. Is there a single young batsman of authority in the West Indies to challenge Greenidge? Do any young men in the Caribbean have the brilliance, the audacity and the character to rival Viv Richards? This distinguished willow quintet has been representing the West Indies in its years of supremacy; if supremacy is to be maintained men just as good must be found to replace them. Maybe the wills of the young men have been broken by the barrage unleashed upon them at home. It cannot be much fun facing great fast bowlers on club and Shield pitches. Even Viv Richards averages only twenty-one in his games against Barbados in Bridgetown. Every youngster on those diverse islands so brilliantly united by Lloyd must yearn to be a fast bowler, to be the giver of punishment, not the taker.

But do not toll the bells for this West Indies team just yet. They are still very, very good, and the physical durability of their older cricketers is remarkable (and a tribute to Denis Waight, their rugged Australian trainer). There are two reserves for Holding and Garner, who rested during the tour of Pakistan and are rusty: Winston Benjamin, twenty-one, and Courtney Walsh, twenty-three. Tony Gray and Roger Harper are also twenty-three. This is a powerful and astute quartet, to which Marshall can be added to form a bowling team not much less ferocious than the great attackers of the past.

Walsh and Gray are not yet quite as skilful as their distinguished elders, but they are bright and humble and can be expected to improve quickly. In a year or two Garner, a gentle giant will probably step aside in their favour as has Holding already. Significantly Patrick Patterson has not been brought on this tour. Apparently he is much slower than the others over a hundred yard sprint (Dennis Waight measures these men in every detail) and this is regarded as evidence that his potential is not as great as that of Walsh and Gray. Part of the reason for West Indian dominance has been their extreme professionalism.

One final, vital reason for the West Indies eclipse in this series is the new rule outlawing the bumper. Any delivery which passes above the shoulder of the batsman is to be called as a no-ball. This rule denies the West Indian bowlers their most brutal weapon. Fear is to play no part in this backwater tournament, so games against Richards' team will be untypical. Only when this rule is taken away will cricket be able to judge whether the balance of power is beginning, at last, to shift.

England's first match is to be against the Australians, who have included in their squad several one-day specialists, including Simon Davis, an accurate medium-pacer from Victoria, Simon O'Donnell, a handsome, forthright all-rounder from Melbourne, and Ken MacLeay, who specialises in bowling his out-swinger into the sea breeze, in Perth, following the tradition of Alderman, Malone and Massie. MacLeay can also hit the ball hard, and is a splendid, composed cricketer who has been ignored for several years despite his evident control over the ball. Ritchie has been dropped because he cannot field and Hughes because he is not a defensive bowler, besides which he appears to be carrying a beer-belly.

England, forced to pick fourteen cricketers, omitted the unfortunate French and Slack (who have not played since Tasmania and who might not play again until the tour ends in the middle of February). With the surprising defeat of the West Indies, England have a chance of keeping up their good work, rather than returning slowly to the cynicism of previous tours.

PAKISTAN v. WEST INDIES: FIRST MATCH, Perth December 30 1986.

PAKISTAN

Shoaib Mohammad	c Richards b Benjamin	34
Qasim Omar	run out	30
Rameez Raja	c Richardson b Gray	42
Javed Miandad	c Richards b Walsh	53
Imran Khan*	c Benjamin b Gray	16
Manzoor Elahi	c Richardson b Gray	4
Ijaz Ahmed	c sub (H. A. Gomes) b Gray	2
Wasim Akram	c Harper b Walsh	9
Salim Yousuf†	not out	2
Mudassar Nazar		
Salim Jaffer		
Extras	(lb 3, w 3, nb 1)	7
		___
TOTAL	(50 overs, 8 wkts)	199

Fall of wickets: 51, 72, 163. 166, 177, 188, 188, 199
Bowling: Gray 10-1-45-4; Walsh 10-0-48-2; Holding 10-0-30-0; Benjamin 10-2-35-1; Harper 10-0-38-0.

WEST INDIES

C. G. Greenidge	b Akram	22
D. L. Haynes	c Yousuf b Mudassar	25
R. B. Richardson	run out	38
I. V. A. Richards*	lbw b Mudassar	10
A. L. Logie	c Yousuf b Mudassar	7
P. J. L. Dujon†	c Shoaib b Jaffer	13
R. A. Harper	not out	20
W. K. M. Benjamin	c Jaffer b Shoaib	3
M. A. Holding	b Shoaib	5
A. H. Gray	c Imran b Jaffer	3
C. A. Walsh	b Akram	2
Extras	(lb 16, nb 1)	17
		___
TOTAL	(46.2 overs)	165

Fall of wickets: 40, 71, 105, 106, 123, 128, 139, 150, 155, 165
Bowling: Imran Khan 7-2-18-0; Salim Jaffer 10-2-29-2; Wasim Akram 7.2-2-13-2; Manzoor Elahi 2-0-10-0; Mudassar Nazar 10-0-36-3; Shoaib Mohammed 10-0-43-2.
Toss: West Indies.
Man of the Match: Mudassar Nazar
Umpires: S. G. Randell and P. J. McConnell
PAKISTAN WON BY 34 RUNS.

GAME 2: AUSTRALIA *v*. ENGLAND

Under spectacular lights and in front of a vibrant crowd England confirmed its supremacy over Australia with a thirty-seven run victory. Three Englishmen played distinguished innings as the Australians toiled. Broad, easing into his drives, an ever more impressive figure upon the field, gave England a good start against Davis and Whitney, Australia's new one-day opening attack. Lamb, who'd had a wretched Test score so far, enjoyed the greater freedom the fifty-over game, enjoyed the ball rising quickly on to the bat on this Perth pitch. Botham struck out massively, incredibly and yet typically in a devastating assault that mixed calculated belligerence with swashbuckling spirit. Botham's innings was awesome in its brutality. He had never readily succeeded in Australia as a batsman until that forceful innings in Brisbane two months ago, and Australians were still under the impression that his triumphs were flukes. In Brisbane they'd seen him play a proper innings, as he has done for years in England, and today they witnessed one of his Sunday League efforts, carrying the ball over cover, stepping back to strike it to the off, slogging it hugely over deep mid-wicket. Botham murdered the bowlers, who tried yorkers which came out as full-tosses, and good length balls which he caught on the rise.

Australia were incredibly incompetent in the field, conceding overthrows, bowling wides and no-balls, dropping catches. They played like a badly coached school rugby team, all gung-ho and no direction. Their supporters were shocked by their ineptitude, cheering whenever a fieldsman stopped the ball cleanly, applauding whenever a bowler was on target with a delivery. Australians, even in their good years, do not appear happy in one-day cricket. They are reared to bowl people out, and to hit fours. They do not have the skill or the wit to work the ball into gaps, to drop their pace to concentrate upon accuracy. The English are much better at the conservative, restrictive tactics required in this cricket, angling the ball onto the pads or running hell-for-leather. Of course English county players have much more experience in the arts of surviving in one-day cricket than their brethren in Australia; they are versed in street wisdom, understand how to manage within the confines of this cricket.

Really the Australians ought to be learning, particularly the younger players. Men like Waugh and Jones played plenty of

AUSTRALIA v. ENGLAND: SECOND MATCH, Perth
January 1, 1987

ENGLAND

B. C. Broad	run out	76
C. W. J. Athey	c Zoehrer b O'Donnell	34
D. I. Gower	c Zoehrer b Whitney	6
A. J. Lamb	c Zoehrer b Reid	66
I. T. Botham	c Zoehrer b Waugh	68
M. W. Gatting*	not out	5
C. J. Richards†	c Border b Reid	4
P. A. J. DeFreitas	not out	0
J. E. Emburey		
G. R. Dilley		
G. C. Small		
Extras	(b 2, lb 6, w 4, nb 1)	13
TOTAL	(49 overs, 6 wkts)	272

Fall of wickets: 86, 95, 150, 256, 262, 271.
Bowling: Davis 8-1-48-0; Whitney 10-0-56-1; MacLeay 9-0-51-0; Reid 10-1-46-2; O'Donnell 7-0-39-1; Waugh 5-0-24-1.

AUSTRALIA

G. R. Marsh	b Botham	28
D. C. Boon	c Emburey b DeFreitas	1
D. M. Jones	c Gower b Dilley	104
A. R. Border*	b Emburey	26
S. R. Waugh	c Richards b Small	16
S. P. O'Donnell	run out	0
K. H. MacLeay	c Emburey b Dilley	21
T. J. Zoehrer†	c Botham b DeFreitas	1
M. R. Whitney	run out	6
B. A. Reid	b DeFreitas	10
S. P. Davis	not out	1
Extras	(lb 7, w 10, nb 4)	21
TOTAL	(48.2 overs)	235

Fall of wickets: 7, 50, 125, 149, 158, 210, 214, 217, 233, 235.
Bowling: DeFreitas 9.2-0-42-3; Dilley 10-1-31-2; Botham 10-0-52-1; Small 9-0-62-1; Emburey 10-0-41-1.
Toss: England.
Man of the match: I. T. Botham.
Umpires: R. A. French and P. J. McConnell.
ENGLAND WON BY 37 RUNS.

defensive, stifling cricket in their early days, unlike their elders, who were raised on two-day grade games with each side batting once (if the other let it). They ought also to find one-day games easier to understand than Test matches. Several times – twice in Melbourne – Waugh has been uncertain what tactic to adopt. In the first innings he took guard with Australia's score at 3/82. This certainly advised caution, but he'd read Border's comments in the papers about Australia's determination to attack. He lost his wicket forcing half-heartedly. In the second innings he was left with the tail; nothing in his twenty-one years had prepared him for this eventuality, and he was uncertain whether to keep the bowling or to trust his partners. He was being educated not *for* Test cricket, but by it.

One-day games are much simpler than Test matches. They dictate to the players, which is why they are also much less interesting. In Test matches a cricketer has choices to make, and his career and the game depend upon the wisdom of those choices. In limited-over games he simply has to whack the ball, field like a demon and bowl straight.

Australia pursued their target with aggressive batting, after the portly Boon had lost his wicket to another vague stroke. Jones, Marsh and Border hit hard and ran hard, briefly threatening England's command. But it was not to be, as Jones slowed, approaching his hundred, and the Englishmen kept their heads. A chance on this scale can be stopped by the fielding team with a couple of good overs, a quick wicket or a sudden run-out. Australia could not score at five point five runs an over without taking the risks for which, in the end, they paid.

England's victory was decisive and bodes well for the rest of the competition. Evidently they do not intend to rest upon their laurels.

GAME 3: AUSTRALIA *v.* PAKISTAN

Till the last few overs the Australians appeared certain to record their first victory of the summer. Dean Jones had struck a second splendid century, and Steve Waugh had cracked eighty-two.

Chasing a big total, batting second in a night game, Pakistan slipped to 6/128, with only the inexperienced tail left to pursue a daunting total. Yet they won, with one wicket and one ball to spare, the last two wickets adding fifty runs. It was as if Australia was destined never to win a match. They snatched defeat from the very jaws of victory, fielding badly and bowling without maturity. They left the field tired and woebegone, scarcely believing that this match was not theirs. Border walked off slowly, and one felt deeply sorry for him. He appeared to be in shock, and reporters wondered if this might be the end. It was not so. At the press-conference, though haggard, he observed that things could only improve.

Apart from the brash inaccuracy of the Australians in the field (too much of the bowling was too little considered) the highlight of the game was the play of the young Pakistanis, play proving that the strength of Pakistan cricket does not end with the professionals (of whom Abdul Quadir and Salim Malik were absent through injury). These youngsters, notably the nineteen-year-old Asif Mujtaba, showed the vigour of youth and the judgement of age. Perhaps we have been too soft on the young men in the Aus-

AUSTRALIA v. PAKISTAN: THIRD MATCH, Perth
January 2, 1987.

AUSTRALIA

G. R. Marsh	run out	28
G. A. Bishop	c Jaffer b Imran	6
D. M. Jones	b Akram	121
A. R. Border*	b Mudassar	14
S. R. Waugh	b Imran	82
G. R. J. Matthews	b Akram	3
S. P. O'Donnell	not out	9
K. H. MacLeay	not out	1
T. J. Zoehrer†		
M. R. Whitney		
B. A. Reid		
Extras	(b 2, lb 1, w 5, nb 1)	9
TOTAL	(50 overs, 6 wkts)	273

Fall of wickets: 26, 49, 70, 243, 254, 271.
Bowling: Imran Khan 10-0-43-2; Wasim Akram 10-1-58-2; Salim Jaffer 10-2-43-0; Mudassar Nazar 10-1-56-1; Asif Mujtaba 5-0-32-0; Shoaib Mohammad 3-0-22-0; Manzoor Elahi 2-0-16-0.

PAKISTAN

Qasim Omar	c Border b Waugh	67
Shoaib Nohammad	lbw b MacLeay	9
Ramiz Raja	c Bishop b MacLeay	0
Javed Miandad	b Reid	7
Mudassar Nazar	lbw b Reid	7
Imran Khan*	c Zoehrer b Waugh	20
Manzoor Elahi	c and b Whitney	48
Asif Mujtaba	not out	60
Salim Yousuf†	c O'Donnell b Whitney	31
Wasim Akram	c Whitney b Waugh	5
Salim Jaffer	not out	3
Extras	(lb 15, w 1, nb 1)	17
TOTAL	(49.5 overs, 9 wkts)	274

Fall of wickets: 34, 40, 73, 93, 96, 128, 181, 224, 267.
Bowling: MacLeay 10-0-36-2; Whitney 10-0-48-2; Reid 10-1-61-1; Waugh 9.5-0-58-4; O'Donnell 10-0-56-0.
Toss: Australia.
Man of the match: D. M. Jones
Umpires: A. R. Crafter and S. G. Randell.
PAKISTAN WON BY ONE WICKET.

tralian team. They are older than Asif and his team mates (Rameez Raja is twenty-four, Manzoor Elahi twenty-three, Wasim Akram twenty). Maybe the Australians are simply slow learners. Maybe they lack cricketing intelligence, the wit to sense the moment and to seize it.

GAME 4: ENGLAND v. WEST INDIES

England's cricketing revival, led by Gatting and his management team of Lush and Stewart, reached a fresh peak in this game, when a fine team effort enabled them to defeat the mighty West Indies by nineteen runs, to ensure not only their appearance in the final of this challenge cup competition, but also the eliminatuion of their most feared opponent.

In an old-fashioned rush of blood at the end, the West Indies lost their last six wickets in seven overs, and the game finished when Courtney Walsh swept at Emburey, missed and was adjudged LBW. At once the England players jumped, hugged and shook hands (there are still a couple of traditionalists in the team). Incredibly they had won on their merits, incredibly a winter of hard work had borne fruit. Till this game England had not known if their success had been an illusion or a reality. They had passed a few months beating the Australians. Here they met a strong team, urgently seeking victory, and they did not withdraw; rather they passed the test with flying colours.

At last we can be certain that England has a cricket team which plays with discipline, purpose and intelligence. At last the parts are not greater than the whole. A disjointed outfit has been turned into a crack troop, rather as Lee Marvin did in *The Dirty Dozen*, and more recently, Clint Eastwood in *Heartbreak Ridge*.

Gatting's team did not catch the West Indians on a bad day, nor was it unduly lucky. All was fair and square and on the day, England were the stronger team. Under Gower in the Caribbean a year earlier, just one one-day game was won, that owed much to a belligerent innings by Graham Gooch. This victory was an all-round effort.

England began badly, with Broad fending Marshall to gully, and Garner (who bowled ten no-balls between some fiery deliveries) having a tentative Athey taken at second slip. Gower flashed wantonly, and it was Gatting who first brought some fight to the innings. Then he edged Walsh to slip. Botham put his head down till he top-edged Harper to square-leg, whereupon England's score, after twenty-five overs at the crease, stood at 5/98, a familiar and sorry position. A year ago, a doleful year ago under different management, England would have cracked and collapsed. They had begun the game today as if they already feared the worst, and the early batsmen had sunk into habits conquered so far in Tests. A year ago no-one would have marched out, as did Jack Richards here, with an air of confidence and determination, as if he had never been told about West Indian invinicibility. He walked out like a child walking in the forest who had never heard of dragons or ghosts. No-one had told him, apparently, that these fierce opponents had demolished England in each of the last ten Test match meetings.

I would not have picked Richards for this tour. He'd appeared to be a chirpy cricketer who could bat well, but whose 'keeping, particularly standing back, was wayward. He is still not a top-class 'keeper, especially in his failure to anticipate deflections and angles of delivery when he is twenty yards back from the stumps, but he has served England extremely well on this tour and proved my judgement to be wrong. His innings in Perth can now be seen not as a fluke but as the work of a competitive cricketer who overcame a nervous start in Brisbane with a splendid determination to prove himself to his critics.

With Allan Lamb, Richards took England towards a decent score. I'd bumped into Lamb in the streets the previous evening. He was returning home with his wife from a vegetarian restaurant (I was hunting, despairingly, for an Indian takeaway still open late at night) and heard with joy about Pakistan's incredible victory over Australia. He was looking forward to the game with the West Indies, saw it as a chance to avenge past defeats and to prove this resurgence to be genuine. He batted splendidly, scoring seventy-one runs in a hundred and thirty-three minutes with seven boundaries, most of them carving crashes over point, off shortish bowling outside the off-stump. He deserved this return to form, not least because of his forthright approach.

This pair added sixty runs, a partnership full of alert running and intelligent placement. They were only stopped when Harper, the greatest fieldsman of the era (he'd made a stunning run, scoop, step and throw at Wellingborough a few months earlier, turning a Botham drive into a single) rose feet into the air to catch a fierce cut. It was one of the most extraordinary catches I've even seen.

During this period of England recovery the West Indian tactics were curiously unflexible. After Lamb's departure no pressure was put upon Jack Richards, no effort was made to bowl him out or to deny him singles. Instead Harper bowled with five men on the boundary, giving Richards an easy run to long-off, helping him to pass the strike to Lamb to build the score steadily in this time of rebuilding.

With Richards being helped by Emburey, Edmonds and Small, England ended its innings with two hundred and twenty-eight runs, the product of spirit and a belief in the possibility of victory. Now the West Indies had to chase and pass a dangerous score if they were to reach the final. Suddenly the pressure was on their batsmen.

History indicates that the West Indians are more dangerous when taking first innings, because this gives their batsmen the freedom to go for their shots, and forces their rivals to score at an increasing rate against an attack that does not weaken from first to last. Moreover the evidence suggests that the ball begins to swing here under the lights at around 6.50 p.m., the very time when the chasing team begins its innings. All the night matches so far have been won by the team batting first, and students of the game are gradually concluding that this is not a coincidence. Surprisingly, Viv Richards asked England to bat first, and surprisingly Gatting, had he won the toss, would have done the same.

In the field England were at once impressive. In the stands Vic Marks observed that this was a strong team, words not uttered by professional cricketers about England's national team for years. Dilley and Small were more dangerous with the new ball than Marshall and Garner. This will scarcely be believed in England, yet there it was in front of our eyes. Small, every muscle under control, in stark contrast to his wild earlier days, jagged the ball back off the pitch to beat the illustrious Haynes and Greenidge. Richardson fell to Botham, who operated at medium-pace, demanding respect with his inswing and building pressure upon Richards and Logie, the diminutive and busy number five who had replaced the calm Gomes. Gradually the required rate mounted, (Richards surviving a half-chance to Athey) until, finally, Gatting introduced his ace, Emburey, to twist the knife.

167

Emburey is a superb one-day bowler, hard to get after because he can fire the ball down, hard to milk because he can cramp the batsman by bowling short of a length and into his pads. On the other hand he loses confidence when attacked, a weakness ruthlessly exploited by Viv Richards a year earlier. Already Richards had forced Edmonds from the attack by punching boundaries which threatened to reduce England's control of the match; facing Emburey he hinted at mastery, and then swept. Richard is a devastating batsman, but his touch shots are poor. He can lose his wicket to delicate late cuts and to careful sweeps, because his powerful body is rigid, his muscle function so strong that he can lose the feel for the ball. Here he swept, top-edged and Broad took the catch on the boundary, staring into setting sun.

All was not yet won, though a dangerous batsman had been laid to rest. Logie was joined by Dujon, and in one of those drastic changes that colour this game, the West Indies were suddenly on top. This pair added seventy-four quick runs and the game was within their grasp. Gatting, as he does with Middlesex, was bowling Emburey and Edmonds towards the end of the innings. He had only a few overs of Dilley in hand.

Then, just as suddenly, the West Indies began to panic. Dujon and Logie had an hilarious escape when one of them (God knows which) lobbed a catch to deep mid-on which Edmonds was slow to judge. The batsman – it was Dujon, I think – rushed to the bowler's end where a certain commotion began. Logie was awaiting the catch, Edmonds was diving and Gower was interfering. Dujon's arrival was greeted with surprise which rapidly turned into consternation. By now Edmonds was on the ground and Gower, who had picked up the ball, was wondering what to do with it. A serious assessment of the situation was needed but who, apart from Rudyard Kipling's man, can be serious at these times? Dujon turned and tried to complete a second length, whereupon the ball began an indirect course towards the wicket-keeper, who was screaming for it. Gower passed to Dilley, who hurled inaccurately towards Richards, who could not beat Dujon to the stumps though he did not fail by much. A measure of pandemonium had been fitted into a moment. An opportunity, perhaps the last opportunity (we pondered glumly in the press-box) had been missed.

It was not so; Dujon slogged massively at Dilley's next ball and was bowled. By now Dilley was bowling fast, swinging the ball away from the bat in the most impressive spell of the match. Next Athey dived heroically to stop a Logie drive and to run out Harper, a brilliant interception by the determined Yorkshireman. At once Logie edged Dilley, to be caught by Richards, and seven wickets were down for one hundred and ninety-seven. Holding and Marshall ran well till Holding, who had struck Edmonds for a huge six, swung at Dilley to be caught at mid-on. Dilley, working up his head of steam, bowled Marshall, which left Garner and Walsh to

ENGLAND v WEST INDIES: FOURTH MATCH, Perth. January 3, 1987.

ENGLAND

B. C. Broad	c Garner b Marshall	0
C. W. J. Athey	c Richardson b Garner	1
D. I. Gower	c Dujon b Garner	11
A. J. Lamb	c Harper b Marshall	71
M. W. Gatting*	c Garner b Walsh	15
I. T. Botham	c Greenidge b Harper	11
C. J. Richards†	c Dujon b Garner	50
J. E. Emburey	c Harper b Garner	18
P. H. Edmonds	not out	16
G. R. Dilley	c and b Garner	1
G. C. Small	not out	8
Extras	(lb 10, w 8, nb 8)	26
		—
TOTAL	(50 overs, 9 wkts)	228

Fall of wickets: 3, 10, 35, 67, 96, 156, 194, 209, 211.
Bowling: Marshall 10-1-30-2; Garner 10-0-47-5; Holding 10-0-33-0; Walsh 9-0-40-1; Harper 10-0-63-1; Richards 1-0-5-0.

WEST INDIES

C. G. Greenidge	b Small	20
D. L. Haynes	lbw b Small	4
R. B. Richardson	c Gatting b Botham	12
I. V. A. Richards*	c Broad b Emburey	45
A. L. Logie	c Richards b Dilley	51
P. J. L. Dujon †	b Dilley	36
R. A. Harper	run out	4
M. D. Marshall	b Dilley	7
M. A. Holding	c Edmonds b Dilley	7
J. Garner	not out	4
C. A. Walsh	lbw b Emburey	0
Extras	(b 4, lb 9, w 4, nb 2)	19
		—
TOTAL	(48.2 overs)	209

Fall of wickets: 9, 39, 51, 104, 178, 187, 187, 201, 208, 209.
Bowling: Dilley 10-0-48-4; Small 10-1-37-2; Botham 10-1-29-1; Edmonds 9-1-53-0-2; Emburey 9.2-0-31-2.
Toss: West Indies.
Man of the match: G. R. Dilley.
Umpires: R. A. French and P. J. McConnell.
ENGLAND WON BY 19 RUNS.

score twenty-one runs for victory. They managed only one (which is not to say that their partnership did not include several hair-raising examples of fast bowlers running between the wickets) till Walsh, heaving in the heat of the moment, was beaten by Emburey to decide the match.

England had not only triumphed over the West Indies, they had beaten themselves, a more difficult task. This could not have happened even three months ago, when a feeling of *Déjà vu* would have spread through the dressing-room once those early wickets fell, and like a pack of cards England would have collapsed. Two or three of the players began this game with their past doubts renewed. By the end, to a man, they realised that they were good enough to bear the responsibility of carrying on the work of taking England up the international cricketing ladder.

GAME 5: AUSTRALIA *v*. WEST INDIES

Unfortunately for the organisers, the last two qualifying games were, in tennis parlance, dead rubbers. Neither of the teams could qualify for the final. The only interest was to see whether the West Indies could end their poor run by asserting their authority. They did so in no uncertain terms.

First, with Greenidge to the fore and Australia's thicker-skinned support bowlers still far too inaccurate, the West Indies plundered two hundred and fifty-five runs. Greenidge scored a century and Michael Holding, crucially dropped by Steve Waugh at long-off, hit fifty-one quick runs to take the West Indies from 7/203 to a respectable total.

In the field this was a different West Indies team altogether. Garner, Gray and Holding roared into their work, thundering the ball in short of a length, causing it to rise past the batsmen's chins. They didn't so much ignore the bouncer rule as by-pass it, causing the ball to rear at the top order batsmen who quickly conceded second best. This was a vengeful, aggressive effort by the West Indians, an effort that sent down shudders down the spines of those who might be forced to face the still vigorous giant in the next couple of years. Those defeats had hurt their pride, sparked their ambition, and the Australian batsmen paid the penalty.

Only Waugh resisted for long as the Australians hopped and skipped for their lives. This was a comprehensive victory, which showed the futility of the rule excluding bumpers from these games. It is too vague a rule, and umpires will not create trouble for themselves by applying it too hastily. Ever since the Bodyline series we have needed a rule rendering illegal all deliveries pitching in the bowlers' half of the wicket. Instead the rule-makers changed the laws governing field placements behind square leg, reacting to the line of the ball when the true danger is from its length.

AUSTRALIA v. WEST INDIES: FIFTH MATCH, Perth.
January 4, 1987.

WEST INDIES

C. G. Geeenidge	b Waugh	100
D. L. Haynes	c Zoehrer b MacLeay	18
H. A. Gomes	b O'Donnell	18
I. V. A. Richards*	lbw b O'Donnell	13
A. L. Logie	b Reid	13
P. J. L. Dujon †	c Zoehrer b O'Donnell	9
R. A. Harper	c Zoehrer b O'Donnell	2
M. A. Holding	not out	53
J. Garner	lbw b McDermott	1
A. H. Gray	not out	10
C. A. Walsh		
Extras	(lb 13, w 3, nb 2)	18
TOTAL	(50 overs, 8 wkts)	255

Fall of wickets: 46, 95, 127, 176, 176, 180, 203, 210.
Bowling: Reid 10-2-40-1; MacLeay 10-1-29-1; McDermott 10-0-67-1; Waugh 0-0-41-1; O'Donnell 10-0-65-4.

AUSTRALIA

D. C. Boon	b Garner	2
G. R. Marsh	c Richards b Gray	5
D. M. Jones	c Harper b Garner	2
A. R. Border*	c Greenidge b Holding	9
G. A. Bishop	c Dujon b Holding	7
S. R. Waugh	b Harper	29
S. P. O'Donnell	lbw b Harper	8
K. H. MacLeay	c Logie b Holding	5
T. J. Zoehrer †	lbw b Gray	4
C. J. McDermott	c Gomes b Gray	7
B. A. Reid	not out	1
Extras	(lb 5, w 2, nb 5)	12
TOTAL	(35.4 overs)	91

Fall of wickets: 4, 12, 16, 25, 36, 66, 78, 78, 89, 91.
Bowling: Garner 6-2-10-2; Gray 7.4-0-9-3; Walsh 6-1-11-0; Holding 10-1-32-3; Harper 6-1-24-2.
Toss: Australia.
Man of the match: C. G. Greenidge.
Umpires: A. R. Crafter and S. G. Randell.
WEST INDIES WON BY 164 RUNS.

GAME 6: ENGLAND v. PAKISTAN

England won this irrelevant game to give them a third victory in succession. Not so long ago, hats would have been thrown in the air about beating Pakistan in any sort of a game. As it is England is in the final, and her supporters almost blasé about it. This wasn't much of a game, nor was there much of a crowd. England won batting second (this was a day-time match), choosing to do so

**ENGLAND v. PAKISTAN: SIXTH MATCH, Perth.
January 5, 1987.**

PAKISTAN

Qasim Omar	b Botham	32
Shoaib Mohammad	c DeFreitas b Emburey	66
Rameez Raja	run out	15
Javed Miandad	c Athey b Emburey	59
Imran Khan*	c Gower b DeFreitas	23
Manzoor Elahi	not out	9
Wasim Akram	not out	1
Mudassar Nazar		
Asif Mujtaba		
Salim Yousuf†		
Salim Jaffer		
Extras	(lb 15, w 1, nb 8)	24
TOTAL	(50 overs, 5 wkts)	229

Fall of wickets: 61, 98, 156, 198, 225
Bowling: DeFreitas 9-1-24-1; Small 10-1-41-0; Foster 4-0-23-0; Botham 10-1-37-1; Gatting 7-0-24-0; Emburey 10-1-65-2.

ENGLAND

B. C. Broad	c Yousuf b Imran	97
C. W. J. Athey	b Manzoor	42
D. I. Gower	c Shoaib b Mudassar	2
A. J. Lamb	c Miandad b Shoaib	32
I. T. Botham	c Rameez b Akram	10
M. W. Gatting*	run out	7
C. J. Richards†	run out	0
P. A. J. DeFreitas	not out	13
J. E. Emburey	not out	11
N. A. Foster		
G. C. Small		
Extras	(b 1, lb 13, w 3, nb 1)	18
TOTAL	(49.4 overs, 7 wkts)	232

Fall of wickets: 104, 108, 156, 184, 199, 204, 208.
Bowling: Wasim Akram 9.4-1-28-1; Salim Jaffer 10-2-43-0; Imran Khan 9-0-41-1; Mudassar Nazar 10-0-39-1; Asif Mujtaba 3-0-19-0; Manzoor Elahi 3-0-24-1; Shoaib Mohammad 5-0-24-1.
Toss: Pakistan.
Man of the match: B. C. Broad.
Umpires: A. R. Crafter and R. A. French.
ENGLAND WON BY 3 WICKETS.

because the Pakistanis tend to bat too cautiously at first, an approach in part due to each batsman's desire to build a big total for himself.

CUP FINAL: ENGLAND *v*. PAKISTAN

On a fresh pitch, enlivened by a watering on the rest day, Gatting won the toss and invited Pakistan to bat first. Six hours later England, after two early alarms, had coasted to a comfortable victory. They were, on the day, much too professional, experienced and mature for the Pakistan team. This might be hard to believe, but has been the case throughout this tournament, which we'd all expected to be such a nuisance but which has in fact run smoothly and been full of interest.

England were again effective in the field, with all the seamers working hard, bowling as a team. DeFreitas had replaced Edmonds, and appeared to be bouncier than earlier in the tour, bounding in to bowl with the zip he'd lost over the Christmas period. Even Gatting took a wicket, Imran edging as he tried to cut a short delivery on this lively pitch. Pakistan batted to 5/127, and nearly overcame the disadvantage to losing the toss. Then, unexpectedly, they lost four wickets for four runs, in a couple of overs, to Small and Emburey. These wickets were lost to lolly-popped catches from balls that bounced surprisingly quickly. This left the inventive Javed to manufacture as many runs as he could in partnership with Salim Jaffer, a tailender who if not exactly inept is not exactly ept either.

Javed is a brilliant player in these games, deflecting twos which he scoops like one of Fagin's gang.

He moves his feet to place the ball where he wants it, and occasionally launches into a blistering drive between boundary fieldsmen. He is an astounding player, not classical in technique, more a product of the modern game. Chest-on and his wits about him, he is ever searching for a gap. These two added thirty-five runs in the final few overs, and Jaffer hardly faced a ball (and so did not lose his wicket to a 'jaffa').

With the pitch drying in the lunch interval Pakistan did not really have a chance. They did snare Athey (who is beginning to look less solid as an opening batsmen) and Broad, who was mistakenly given caught behind after missing the ball by some distance. Broad has a habit of walking from the crease after an appeal, a habit that makes him appear guilty when he is not. He'd be well advised to put his head down, scratch his crease and ignore the appeals until the umpire has made his judgement.

Broad had looked weary in the field. It is harder, these days, for a player to sustain his effort on tour because there are so many internationals. He has to prepare himself mentally and physically not for ten major innings but for twenty-five. Apart from the Tests every innings he plays will take on the importance of an international match; fifteen innings or so on the trot that are important to his future and to his national team's hopes. This is not entirely healthy.

England hit off the runs easily enough, with Gower, Gatting and the resurgent Lamb seeing off Imran and Wasim and then tucking into Pakistan's less serious bowlers. The game was over with ten overs to spare, and afterwards the large and somewhat drunken English contingent on the Hill ran across the pitch towards the man-of-the-match ceremony. They were stopped en route by hefty policemen, who interrupted their flight with some thudding rugby tackles. An ugly fracas developed as the unruly mob, which has been accompanying England throughout this tour, fought with the formidable policemen from these parts. Sadly, England has been followed around by Union Jack-waving cavaliers whose conduct has been much worse than anything managed by the locals. It is not clear if they are emigrants, sailors in town or over on holiday. Whichever they are they are a damned nuisance, and deserved their thick ears after this performance. Later, one was sentenced to six months' imprisonment.

Javed was man-of-the-match and England were left to celebrate an auspicious victory, one of their first in a one-day tournament. Once again Gatting was outstanding as a captain, and once again a suspicion lingers that not everyone is absolutely delighted about this. Team spirits were as high at the end as at the beginning, and Gatting, who led on sufferance at first, is emerging as the man in charge.

Ian Botham, apart from his colossal innings against Australia, was throughout strangely muted in the field. I did not notice this until friends pointed it out. He looked a bit sad, a bit lonely, rather burdened. Maybe he has some private grief. In this mood he is a sympathetic character. These troubles did not affect his game, but in the field he existed on the edge of the team, and his happiness at the fall of wickets was not as spontaneous as that of his mates. Perhaps he is simply tired. I do not know because, apart from a couple of pleasant conversations, we have not met on this trip.

If the management is as firm and as sensitive next year, if it continues to treat players with respect rather than contempt, with honesty rather than fear, there is no reason why English cricket should not emerge from the darkness of the past five years. It was nice, at any rate, to win something, nice to add this odd challenge cup to the Ashes.

ENGLAND *v.* PAKISTAN: FINAL, Perth.
January 7, 1987.

PAKISTAN

Qasim Omar	c Broad b Botham	21
Shoaib Mohammed	b Dilley	0
Rameez Raja	c Athey b Botham	22
Javed Miandad	not out	77
Asif Mujtaba	c Gower b Botham	7
Imran Khan*	c Richards b Gatting	5
Manzoor Elahi	c Gower b Small	20
Salim Yousuf†	c Athey b Small	0
Mudassar Nazar	c Gower b Emburey	0
Wasim Akram	c Gatting b Small	2
Salim Jaffer	not out	3
Extras	(lb 5, w 1, nb 3)	9
TOTAL	(50 overs, 9 wkts)	166

Fall of wickets: 2, 36, 58, 76, 89, 127, 127, 128, 131.
Bowling: DeFreitas 10-1-33-0; Dilley 10-0-23-1; Botham 10-2-29-3; Small 10-0-28-3; Emburey 8-0-34-1; Gatting 2-0-14-1.

ENGLAND

B. C. Broad	c Yousuf b Akram	0
C. W. J. Athey	c Yousuf b Imran	1
D. I. Gower	c Shoaib b Imran	31
A. J. Lamb	c Yousuf b Akram	47
M. W. Gatting*	b Akram	49
I. T. Botham	not out	23
C. J. Richards†	not out	7
P. A. J. DeFreitas		
J. E. Emburey		
G. R. Dilley		
G. C. Small		
Extras	(lb 8, w 1)	9
TOTAL	(40.1 overs, 5 wkts)	167

Fall of wickets: 1, 7, 47, 136, 145
Bowling: Imran Khan 8-2-30-2; Wasim Akram 10-2-27-3; Salim Jaffer 10-1-43-0; Mudassar Nazar 5.1-0-22-0; Shoaib Mohammad 2-0-11-0; Manzoor Elahi 5-0-26-0.
Toss: England.
Man of the match: Javed Miandad.
Umpires: A. R. Crafter and R. A. French.
ENGLAND WON BY FIVE WICKETS

17

Interlude VII

ENGEL AT THE YACHTING

No mention has been made in this book of the America's Cup yachting tournament taking place in Fremantle, a pleasant town full of interesting clothes' shops and cafés which is just down the road from Perth. Since this race between yachts owned by millionaires (don't bother to enter unless you have forty million dollars or more to spend) has dominated the sports' pages for months, some reference ought to be made to it. Rather than go to Freemantle to offer my own ill-informed, unhelpful and no doubt inaccurate observations on the matter I decided, with the author's permission, to borrow a piece written by Matthew Engel which is, in any case, much better than anything I could have managed. I offer no apology for this, and pause only to remind readers that otherwise they might have missed it. Lead on, Macduff.

'First, a personal statement. I have, in my time in this business, acquired some expertise in the matter of naff sporting events. I have been to Wellingborough Town FC in a blizzard: I have done a Test match in Faisalabad: I have reported the Pro All-in Karate circuit. I reckon I deserve to be under blue skies in

Fremantle in a Lacoste shirt and soft shoes with all these underdressed blondes about.

'The great thing about Wellingborough Town, however, is that the stand, under normal circumstances, stays where it was when the game started. The Tasmanian Devil, the 30ft catamaran which serves as one of the main vantage points for the America's Cup, does not.

'It moves about vaguely in the direction of the competing yachts. It also goes up. And it goes down. And it repeats the procedure at unpleasantly frequent intervals. When I went on it, the sky was not even very blue: it was a sort of grey-blue which went with the grey-brown of the sea and the grey-green of my countenance. Conditions were officially described as "moderate".

'There are moments at least occasionally in most people's lives when the world starts shifting around and you suddenly realise you're pissed. I spend five hours like that, and I'd only had a cup of tea. A lot of beer gets drunk each night in Fremantle: I don't think it's relaxation so much as acclimatisation.

'From a distance, this was probably the most thrilling day so far in the Great Australian Sailathon, the day the New Zealanders beat Stars and Stripes. Yet even for the privileged spectators in the flotilla off the coast, very little of the thrill managed to convey itself.

'Dozens of boats were out there, including the Aga Khan's huge second-best yacht ("my other car's a Porsche") as well as several helicopters. I rather hoped one of those might be Air-Sea Rescue and winch me up. Among the regulars on the Devil there was some discussion about the racing tactics. Among us grockles there was rather more discussion about sea-sickness. One Aussie suggested an infallible cure: "go and sit under a tree."

'In the evening Alan Bond, the ex-signwriter from Ealing who brought the cup to Australia, appeared at a press conference, which he is likely to do more often as his current boat, Australia IV, approaches the moment of truth. Lately, he has been devoting more time to running his businesses and Australia, which he appears to do in a syndicate including Messrs Murdoch, Packer, John Elliott the Foster's brewer, Holmes a'Court and occasionally Bob Hawke.

'The manoeuvres on the water constitute less of a spectator sport, which is the main reason Western Australia has had to halve its original estimate of a million visitors, and why a lot of people here may go bust even if Australia retains the trophy, rising to an awful lot if it goes elsewhere.

'But now that so many countries can compete with the Americans, this thing is bound to find a place among the world's major sporting events.

'It all seems very far-fetched, but if White Crusader were to win, Torbay would probably be turned into the next Fremantle. I remember the Fremantle of just four years back, a run-down port whose main claim to sporting fame had ceased in 1960 when English cricket teams stopped arriving by boat.

'Now it is all boutiques and pedestrian malls and poncey restaurants and pavement cafes with names like Lombardo's and Papa Luigi's. It would be nice to come back in February and report on a British triumph. If that happens, I propose to cover it from under a parasol at Papa Luigi's. Alternatively, under a tree'

THE ART OF CRICKET

It was odd to be asked, by the *Sydney Morning Herald* to write about the art of cricket on a day when black men dressed in red clothes and white men dressed in blue clothes were doing battle for a silver cup on a green pitch with floodlights blazing and sight screens blackened so that the white ball could be seen by batsmen wearing cages on their head. A subdued sport of green and white has erupted into a wildness of brilliant colour. A game of sheltered upbringing has exploded into the bright lights and sinuous temptations of the modern world.

The art of cricket? What could this mean? Had the paper taken leave of its senses? Then, dimly through the mists of time, remembrance returned, a remembrance of Sobers and Graveney, of Greg Chappell and Graeme Pollock, mesmeric cricketers one and all. And a remembrance, too, of words catching the grace of Hobbs and Kippax, and the kindness of Oldsfield and Ranjitsinghi.

Yes, cricket is artistic, the most artistic of all games. Oh, it is played by dullards at times and, occasionally, reading about it, you'd think it was as artistic as a nest of cockroaches eating their supper, but Cardus, Ray Robinson, Arlott, Pinter and Betjeman and so many other men of sensitivity have understood it, sympathised with its victims and written about it. So many men have found a peculiar satisfaction in the game.

However it might seem, sitting glumly in a press box, surrounded by the clacking of word processors and contemplating the compulsory excitement of a one-day game, cricket is a loved and beautiful game. Has this art survived the move into the marketplace? Can a game in the hands of hard-headed financiers nevertheless be called artistic? It can.

The essence of the game has not changed. A rose is a rose for all that. Cricket is a difficult, frustrating and frequently witless game, but though the rules have been changed it has not lost its smattering of breathtaking moments nor its occasional geniuses who, scarcely realising it, follow a tradition and give immense pleasure to their audience not so much by their achievements as by their methods.

No other sport rivals cricket's instinctive art. Others are more spinetingling, rugged, fascinating, disciplined, fast and tense. In comparison, cricket is a route march which occasionally passes through leafy lanes and majestic forests. As a competition between teams it is frequently disappointing, can be spoilt by rain, and ruined by the players. It can last five days and still end without resolution, for it is a ridiculous game, absurdly long and ludicrously indecisive.

It survives because of the enduring appeal of its vignettes, because of the singular way in which character and beauty find expression within its confines. No moderately sane person could consider it satisfactory as a whole. It is a deceitful, hypnotic, treacherous game which has appalling faults and extraordinary qualities.

All-in wrestling might be more fun, but it is not poetic. Rugby is an invigorating game, but it does not inspire paintings. Musicians are not moved to compose as a golfer strikes a ball on to the green.

Bodies thudding to the floor to be trapped in arm locks, a prop forward driving to the line and a chip creeping to the flag – these are tense, telling moments which are cheered by spectators caught in the drama of the competition. They are skilful and courageous reactions to tension and the players deserve the applause for their temporary triumphs. But wrestling, rugby and golf crowds do not blink at the beauty of their sports; they do not contemplate them in this way. They are not games of wonder; rather they are contests between rivals.

Cricket is the most beautiful of games, which is why it is celebrated in verse, on canvas and in music. On the field, some of the players are able to move as if in a ballet without losing their effectiveness. Players dressed in white (well, usually anyhow) move into neat gymnastic positions against a back-cloth of grass and a kaleidoscope of colour and cacophony of noise blaring behind the fence. It is a bizarre medieval scene, a mixture of ritual, entertainment, sport and art. And it has not lost its appeal, will never do so, for it is intrinsic and beyond the everchanging laws.

Nothing is more graceful in this or any other game than an off drive played by David Gower. A rhythmic drift towards the ball is followed by a smooth sweep through a straight line which sends the ball scorching across the turf. A Gower drive is a mixture of delicate, unobtrusive footwork and a fluent swing which ends in a comforting thump as wood and leather meet.

This game is satifying because it is a game of straight lines. Cricket demands them of its players and those who defy it risk failure. Ugly angles and jagged lines are rejected by the classical technique required in those without genius. As if by accident, cricket pleases the eye as well as the mathematical and aesthetic mind.

Nor are the graceful and classical movements on the field the only ingredients in cricket's appeal. Is anything in sport more tantalising than a duel between a spinner and a batsman prepared to use his feet? When Edmonds bowls to Dean Jones, then occurs an enthralling battle of wits, one man stepping forward boldly, ready to strike and determined to dictate to his rival, who, full of cunning, is using flight and guile in an effort to sneak one past the bat.

These exchanges are secret, private to the cognoscenti who alone can understand the peculiar duel. Cricketers and spectators are in constant conversation as the movement of the players reveals to the audience their plans, worries, hopes and fears. The uninformed will not grasp the significance of these strange events, will not understand what Edmonds is endeavouring to do nor why Jones is dancing with such vigour as the cat and mouse do battle.

And, because the game stops and starts so often, because a day's play consists of 540 separate and yet dependent incidents, students can swap opinions, comment upon the action to their friends, and predict the course of events to follow.

Cricket is a game that asks much of its followers; it expects them to join in. A good crowd recognises mastery and beauty and applauds them irrespective of whether a run has been scored, a wicket taken or the game advanced in any way. Cricket catches the eye and satisfies the wit. And at best it is full of pleasing movements and ideas.

But this not a nice game. It is a temptress, a Cleopatra of a game. Here in lies its greatest appeal. Its art is elusive. Cricket cannot be mastered. Like a seductress it moves away, cocking a finger, asking you to follow and yet warning you as to the consequences. On the field tragedy follows hard upon triumph, ease and discomfort sit side by side.

Cricket is dangerous and not to be trusted. One minute it is enticing, rhythmic and charming and the next it betrays you. This is a fragile game which treats its players unkindly. So many cricketers are insecure, lured by taste occasionally experienced and then let down by it. This game gives its players hope in a moment and then chastises them, throwing them back onto the heap. For a moment it is in our grasp and then it has escaped. Hardly anyone who has played the game has not, even if only once, done something artistic, something upon which Trumper and Bedi could scarcely improve. A late cut dashes to the boundary and at once the batsman realises he has got it right, his body fulfilling the idea in his mind. This illusion, these sweet moments, are part of the game's trap; the dreadfulness usually follows.

This is why the poets and the writers came to the game. They recognised its wickedness and its bloodymindedness as well as its beauty. So many cricketers, their careers behind them, have committed suicide. Bored by ordinariness, unable to find a new refuge or simply despairing of the future, they choose their moment and put an end to it all.

A long list could be drawn of cricketers who have taken their lives. It is not a coincidence but a terrible revelation about cricket and cricketers. The game does not break them, rather they are drawn by temperament to it, finding in it an expression of their precarious characters. They play the game, try to master it and occasionally succeed, joining a fraternity of men no less frustrated and no less in search of a reliable method. They try to find an answer where there is none. Try to find a stone where there is only sand.

Cricket is a game played on the edges of nerves. It requires men of stoical and stout temperament yet attracts players with artistic yearnings who hover around it as a moth hovers around a flame. Spectators sense this vulnerability. A man who scored 100 yesterday falls for a duck, and a cricketer invincible one year fails the next. They sense that cricket is a prickly game which hurls misfortune and joy at its players without warning and expects them to bear each with fortitude. Spectators understand too that some men of artistic temperament are peculiarly tempted towards the game and yet are uniquely unsuited to its changes.

These are the arts and the attractions of cricket, some of them obvious to a casual follower, some of them hidden and apparent only to those who have tried themselves. Tomorrow's match at the S.C.G. is not merely a competition between two international teams. It is an occasion on which men will be stretched and tested, it is a game of sudden movements, and a game of a beauty that endures despite the odd things done to it.

BOTHAM DEPARTS

Ian Botham has left Somerset and signed for Worcestershire, one hundred miles up the M5. He expects lots of Somerset supporters to drive those one hundred miles, or so at any rate he says.

I did not attend the signing, which was held on a Saturday night in Sydney, a time chosen after some fearful bickering between the B.B.C. and *The Sun*, an argument won by the B.B.C. Brian Rose, Derek Taylor and Nick Pringle, players present, past and future were at the Chateau Commodore and they saw Ian, reported that the champagne had flowed freely and that Duncan Fearnley, Worcestershire's cricket committee chairman and Ian's bat-maker and chum, had said he was 'over the moon' to bring such a player to his club.

Botham's departure from Somerset was no surprise. In

November reporters said that I was flying to Australia to see Botham, and hoped to persuade him to stay on at Somerset. It was never quite like that. At the press conference after the Somerset members meeting at Shepton Mallet on 8 November I was asked about my plans, and replied that I was off to Australia to work for *The Sunday Times* and *The Sydney Morning Herald* . . .

'Will you see Ian over there?'
'Er . . . yes . . . I suppose so.'
'Will you be talking to him, man to man?'
'Er . . . yes . . . I expect so.'

On this slender evidence it was announced that I was off to meet Ian in Australia, which seemed rather a long way to go to see him. Ian, meanwhile, called a press conference of his own and said that I'd be a lot safer if I stayed in Somerset. Next after-noon, at Heathrow Airport, a television crew filmed me as I checked-in for my flight, and asked for a reaction to Botham's statement. I said no-one could tell a fellow where he might and might not go safely.

There never was much chance of Ian staying at Somerset. He'd entered the dispute about the sacking of Richards and Garner from the start, ignoring the advice of close friends who'd told him to keep out of it, on the grounds that any threat by him would appear to be counter productive. Botham believed he could swing the ordinary people behind him, as he had done on his celebrated sponsored walk, as he had done by contesting subsequent charges levelled at him. He believed he could carry the day against the county committee, and was worried only that he had not been born in Somerset which, he thought, would weaken his case. In fact, members realised he was not the issue, and his stance was scarcely mentioned on 8 November. He had, in any case, been absent most of the season, having been banned from first-class cricket for two months for writing an article admitting he'd smoked cannabis in his youth. He had, in the previous few years, lost some of his following at Somerset. Members cared very much about Joel Garner and Viv Richards and the arguments raged about their departure, not about Ian's threats.

I had not thought that Botham would leave Somerset. He could, of course, be expected to fight, and to fight ardently, but I did not at first expect him to leave. As the debate grew in passion it became obvious that he had no other choice. Nor was his conduct during the debate satisfactory. He put up a poster by my place in the dressing-room, upon which was writ large the word Judas. By chance the local paper had arranged to borrow the ground at Taunton a few days later, and a photographer and journalist saw the sign and wrote the story. This attack forced me into the debate, forced me to articulate the case for the decision, and made it appear as if I was not only the spokesman but also the manipulator, an historical inaccuracy. In fact by this time I was already disillusioned with Ian, who had called a players' meeting during which he spoke of me as 'Judas' to every player, young and old, on the staff. Also he'd tried a variety of somewhat crude tactics to persuade other players to join him in his crusade again Somerset's decision. Very few of them were having any of it, at least in part because the younger ones had never seen him at his best at Somerset – as a man, that is.

And so Botham was bound to leave. We met twice during this tour. In Adelaide he called me into the England dressing-room to say that he'd heard a Somerset player was very sick, and the club neglecting him. I was shocked, rang the club that night, and found that Botham had been misinformed, a sign no doubt that passions were still running high in Taunton. Nevertheless our chat had been friendly enough. In Canberra we found ourselves at the Prime Minister's house, the Lodge, drinking a few cocktails. Again we chatted, this time with Michael Whitney in our party, and again we avoided the prickly topic and our conversation was friendly. (I have not seen Joel or Viv since their arrival in Australia, though I did find myself closeted on the next table to Viv at the fish restaurant in Perth – I was writing *The Art of Cricket* at the time, and had just been joined by two friends from the bush. I hoped to speak to him but this was not possible.)

Upon reflection it is no surprise either that Botham has left Somerset or that he has joined Worcestershire (not that any other county made a concrete offer for him, a curious reflection both on English cricket and on Botham). Ever since 1974 this extraordinary cricketer, this hot-spirited genius from Yeovil, an unremarkable town in the south of the county, has played for Somerset in the summer and for England in the winter. A man who loves mateship above all else, a man who seeks to be a hero and yet who fears loneliness (as opposed to solitude), he began to hate life on tour, finding it claustrophobic, finding himself penned into his hotel room, watching videos and talking to colleagues. On this tour he has spent most of his evenings, many of his nights, in the presidential suite hired by Elton John.

He has survived this decade of touring by surrounding himself with a close coterie of fellow-travellers, men of similar spirit who probably do not realise how precious they are to Ian. On this tour his mates have been Lamb, DeFreitas and Dilley (and in this light the news that Dilley has joined Worcestershire is no surprise). He speaks of them as being 'great lads' who are 'crackers', a word Botham invests with immense prestige. These players share his sense of fun and he feels at home with them. It is significant that because Botham has behaved so well on this tour, because he has been at his best as a man, his influence upon these colleagues has been almost entirely healthy. DeFreitas has followed Botham everywhere, has been his shadow, as if he were were a long-lost son. He has played with Botham's children in hotel swimming pools, has sat beside Ian in aircraft and at every other opportunity. Botham is giving to him things he has not given to young cricketers for years.

Even so Botham dreaded life on tour, and his first decision – to leave it and to join Queensland – was predictible. He wanted to leave the touring merry-go-round and to play regularly in Australia, where he hopes to feel less hemmed in.

He had not, though, planned to leave Somerset. He expected to play full-time for the county for several years after retiring from Test cricket. Despite his image, Botham plans his career years in advance. His move to Queensland and his slow retreat from the Test arena were not ideas suddenly hatched but plans carefully laid. Botham is more astute and powerful than he would have his public believe.

His decision to leave Somerset is in part protest and in part a painful recognition of a process that began years ago, before the first salvos were fired. Botham did not feel at home in the club, did not feel loved, did not feel wanted. More than anything else he fears isolation, yearns for companionship. At Somerset, because he was away so often on tour or at Test matches, because of his ban and his boredom with county cricket, and because of his different, higher lifestyle, he could find little companionship. He was close to

Richard Ollis, but Ollis hadn't made it (not that Botham ever gives up – last year when Somerset were struggling for runs he told me that Ollis was getting stacks for Keynsham), and to Trevor Gard, an amiable, loyal man. He could tease these two, feel an empathy with them. He had other friends from his earlier, easier days – notably Jennings, Breakwell and Denning – but one by one they'd left, the victims of time, leaving Botham almost deserted. By September he was nearly alone.

Irrespective of his genuine anger at Somerset's decision to re-lease Viv Richards and Joel Garner, Botham could not have stayed forever, could not have continued in a place where he was be-ginning to feel like an alien. In leaving Somerset Botham believes he is going from the cold to the warmth.

He was hardly likely to join a big club, where he'd feel regi-mented and ill at ease. He could not have joined Lancashire, Leicestershire or Middlesex, for example. In the end he had a choice between Warwickshire, where he is close to Bob Willis, David Brown, Norman Gifford and Andy Lloyd, and Worcester-shire. Warwickshire did not offer him a contract, the committee being split between those who wanted Botham the cricketer and those who did not want Botham the man. Worcester did not, could not, back down. Botham has plenty of friends at New Road and they would not let him down.

At Worcester he will join Duncan Fearnley, bat manufacturer, cheery host and chairman of the cricket committee. He is a friend with whom Botham can be happily vulgar. Mike Jones, chairman of the club, is an unusual companion too, and Botham recognises him as a chum, calls him by a nickname, a certain sign of affec-tion.

He'll not find so many friends in the team, though he likes Paul Pridgeon, a long-suffering seam bowler and surprisingly accurate tipster. Typically, because of their friendship, Botham holds Pridgeon's bowling in high esteem. He invariably has a high opinion of the cricketing merits of his mates. He is man of loyalty rather than intellect, a man of blood rather than water. He's joined Queensland (a hot, empty and ferociously conservative state) be-cause there he will find Alan Border, and Jeff Thompson, fisher-man, fast bowler, larrikin, raconteur and man of rude words, who – to Botham's vast amusement – is doing well as a landscape gardener. He will be aware, too, that Queensland has never won the Sheffield Shield, aware of another chance to be a hero, another chance to go down in history.

Botham did not join Worcester because he has changed his ways, did not leave the England touring circuit because he yearns for a quiet life. He has moved his tent, pitching camp in a friendly place where he will have enough fellow-travellers around to keep him happy. This is the conduct of a cricketing genius, born into the body of a lad who grew up in a small town of Somerset and who fears, beyond all else, being left out and being left alone. Good luck to him.

18

Sydney: Fifth and Final Test

Australia has taken 'the gamble of the century', as *The Age* called it, by including Peter Taylor in its team to meet England tomorrow. Taylor, a tall, fair-haired off-spinner of thirty summers, has played only six first-class matches for New South Wales, two of them in Zimbabwe last March. He's bowled ninety-nine overs in Sheffield Shield cricket, taking eight wickets at an average of thirty-five. He has played only one Sheffield Shield game this season – against Tasmania last week – taking one wicket, that of an obscure Tasmanian opening batsman of whom no one has heard, called Neville Jellich, at the cost of fifty-eight runs. For the rest of the season, while May, Bright, Holland and Bennett were in the Shield teams, Taylor was bowling for the northern district grade team in the Sydney competition.

This is a remarkable selection, but it is not as implausible as it appears. Taylor did bowl in the Shield final against Queensland last year (taking 5/109 in thirty-eight overs), a grand game of cricket won by N.S.W.'s final pair. He bowled well enough to show that he had maturity, a grooved run, a new high action and a hard-earned mastery of flight and guile. Also, obviously, he is a cricketer of temperament.

At first Taylor assumed his selection to be a joke. He imagined that the selectors had meant to pick Michael Taylor, New South Wales' opening batsman. This, too, was a plausible tale believed by many – not least Peter McFarlane and John Woodcock. Had there been a confusion? David Boon had been omitted, and no opening batsman had been chosen in his place. On the other hand Wellham was in the squad, and an extra batsman hardly made sense. On balance the selectors probably did mean Peter Taylor rather than his more illustrious namesake.

Taylor, an economics graduate who runs a family investment business and has plenty of money, reacted to his selection with dignity, saying he was happy and recognising that 'there are a lot of very good players who go through their careers without getting this opportunity, and some get the opportunity and don't deserve it. Maybe I'm one of those people. I hope to show I'm not.' With that he went off to the golf course before moving on to the State's nets. He has suddenly displaced Greg Matthews in the Test team, though he has not yet been able to do so in the State eleven. It has been quite a year for Mr Matthews. If Taylor succeeds, can Matthews get his place back in the N.S.W. side?

Bill O'Reilly alone of the critics considered Taylor's selection to be inspired. He said it reminded him of Henry Lawson's lines:

> 'Who's, who's coming to join us?
> Who wants to join the push
> God strike me dead, it's Mulga Head
> The nameless from the bush.'

He added that when Taylor's name had been 'dragged out of the hat' last year it had taken an 'enterprising media sleuth' to find him 'somewhere up in the North-west, near Moree', which is a long way away, and where he was engaged in the wool trade. He said that Taylor would 'do for him' if he took it easy, and concluded:

'He runs much farther than the accustomed tweaker, who generally waddles in from somewhere within conversational distance of the umpire.'

This incredible choice will, if nothing else, provide interest in the Final Test match. There is nothing like a mystery man, not to mention a local mystery man, to fill the grounds. Some cricketers argued that Taylor's selection was an insult to all those who had grafted for years for a Test place. This is nonsense. If Taylor is the best off-spinner, as Greg Chappell (who saw last year's Shield final) and Dick Grey (who managed the tour to Zimbabwe on which Taylor took seven for ninety-one and six for eighty-one) believe, the selectors were right to choose him. And if he is the best, the real question will by why N.S.W. have neglected him for so long.

The selection of Taylor rather overshadowed what was, to me at any rate, a more disconcerting choice. Wellham has replaced Boon, who has been out of form and overweight. Wellham was one of the men who turned their backs on Border and Australian cricket to go to South Africa, a decision which he reversed when he was offered a job by Kerry Packer's P.B.L. He is also being paid by the Australian Cricket Board but has, he says never received a penny, indirectly or directly, from the South African Cricket Association. He intends to stand as a Liberal (i.e. right wing) candidate in the Carlingford constituency at the next general election, and is a man of ambition. He has scored lots of runs this summer (five hundred and ninety-two runs at fifty-three point eight) but has played only six Test matches since that promising debut in 1981, and these have mostly been in the final Test of a series. He is not reputed to be close to Border, who remains a popular captain with his team.

If the choice of Wellham as a batsman was not altogether surprising (though he has never opened in first-class cricket, so presumably poor old Greg Ritchie will be promoted) it was alarming to hear that the selectors wanted Wellham to be the team vice-captain. If ever a blatant threat was made to an incumbent captain, this was it. Wellham is an astute leader with the knack of appearing in command on the field, whereas Border usually appears flummoxed. He is not a brilliant captain, nor a brilliant batsman, merely a diligent and effective cricketer. It'd be hard on Border to replace him with someone who has done so little in Test cricket, someone who lacks Brearley's sagacity, and someone who has managed to face in so many different directions.

Luckily the A.C.B. refused to accept the selectors' recommendation, and instead appointed the simple, durable Geoff Marsh as vice-captain. There is no-one yet to replace Border as Captain. Until an outstanding leader appears he may as well carry on. I've said this often enough, and still people search for prophets in the desert.

DAY ONE

A cricket game, a cricketer's career, can turn on a couple of vital moments. I can remember my first success in 1975. I'd been playing dreadfully, and had grown intense and irritable. In the first innings of our game in Swansea, I scored thirty-three before hitting a tame catch. That evening I went to the Mumbles to stare at the sea. After a few hours contemplation I decided to stop pratting around and to start attacking. Next day I recorded my first hundred in first-class cricket (one hundred and forty-eight not out) and a couple of days later hit one hundred and fifty-six in the Varsity match. In that innings I was dropped on nineteen. I can remember it still. A clip to leg, a favoured shot in those days, followed by an agonised wait as Pathmanathan, a genial Sri Lankan, chased back from short leg, reached the ball and promptly dropped it. No-one would have been interested if I'd fallen for that nineteen.

About Australia were lucky today, when Dean Jones glanced Small off the full face of the bat to be caught down the leg-side by Jack Richards. England appealed confidently, but umpire Randell shook his head. Jones had scored five runs at the time and Australia was already in trouble at 1/27. The English team were furious that Jones had not walked, though it is hard to see any justification for this. Walking is not the fashion, and several England batsmen await the umpire's verdict, as is their right. At least Jones is not hypocritical, walking magnanimously when it suits him, standing at the crease when it does not.

About three hundred and thirty minutes later Jones left the field to a warm ovation, his score resting on one hundred and nineteen, the product of deft footwork to the spinners, and fierce drives. An on-drive against Small was the most vivid stroke of the day. This was an accomplished innings by a man who has matured quickly during the year. We'll never know what would have happened if he'd been given out on five – either to Jones or to Australia.

A few hours later, tea having been taken with the score a solid if sedate 3/184, with Australia at last building a secure total, the game, as guided by lady luck, took a turn in the opposite direction.

Gladstone Small's nineteenth over, the seventy-first of the innings, began with no promise of dramatic events. Botham had crept close to the bat at third slip, indicating his opinion of the pitch, and parts of the crowd had begun to slow hand-clap the batsmen, though most were content to sit in the sun and watch the Australians carefully accumulate a winning score on this oddly straw-coloured pitch which, they say, will not last. Then, suddenly, unexpectedly, two wickets fell. First Dirk Wellham, who had been collecting runs busily, cutting the ball with his dominant right hand and chipping to leg and darting off for a single, unluckily tickled one down the leg-side to the 'keeper, who held the ball aloft as Wellham walked off. The score was 4/184 and the game in the balance. Steve Waugh's first ball from the worthy Small also careered down the leg-side, a rare lapse from this bowler. On its way through to Richards it flicked either Waugh's ribs or his gloves. England, still smarting from Jones' escape, appealed long and loud, Richards shaking his hands in exultation, for he had dived far to his left to catch the ball. Waugh was given out, wrongly in my opinion, but correctly in the opinion of the England players and some of the reporters (later, rumours had it that Waugh admitted to gloving the ball). In any case within the space of two innocuous deliveries Australia had collapsed to 5/184, a vulnerable position from which they clawed their way back through the excellence of Jones and the grafting of Sleep and Zoehrer. In three balls, a game and three careers, those of Wellham, Waugh and Jones, had changed.

These events served to remind students of the game that cricket can never be taken for granted. A collapse is never more than five minutes away. Nor is any situation beyond redemption.

This was a good, hard day's cricket, with both teams vying for supremacy. It contrasted starkly with the tame offering in Adelaide, where the scoring was slightly quicker and yet the cricket much less purposeful. This was a proper Test match, whereas Adelaide was a charade and Melbourne a disaster.

Unfortunately the peace of the day was spoilt not so much by the moments of controversy but by their repetition on the electronic screen that dominates the ground. When England's appeal against Jones was turned down the players stood, hands on hips, waiting for the replay. For seconds all eyes, save those of the poor umpire, were turned towards the screen. Umpire Randell simply stared at the ground, waiting for the game to resume, wondering if the screen was making a fool of a Solomon. Umpires might as well peruse the screens themselves, because they can quickly tell, from the reaction of the players and the jeers of the crowd, whether or not the replay is embarrassing.

This is intolerable. Cricketers are brought up to respect the umpire's word as final, yet here the players understandably waited to consider the replays, to see if their eyes had deceived them. The umpiring has been good in the series, and these replays serve only to undermine the authority and the confidence of the adjudicators. Surprisingly, umpires object only to slow-motion replays. After the boos from the yahoos of Sydney they might object with more conviction.

By coincidence a message roared across from the showground next door. Presumably a religious meeting was taking place, though since the message was also there yesterday, it must have been a long meeting (the Catholic services of my upbringing only seemed to last twenty-four hours). Up on the screen were written these words:

> 'The first virtue is to restrain the tongue; he approaches nearest to the gods who knows how to be silent even when he is in the right.'

The profundity of this observation was slightly reduced by the message placed above it, which said 'Anyhow have a Winfield 25?'

DAY TWO

By the close of the second day Australia had the edge, and for the first time in the series a chance of winning a Test match. England had hicupped to 5/132 in reply to Australia's three hundred and forty-three, a total almost entirely due to Dean Jones innings of five hundred and forty minutes. He did bat uncommonly well, as Woodcock would say, using his feet to the spinners, driving them hard and straight, and then picking up the singles.

Jones is twenty-five years of age; he came of age as a cricketer last September, in the Chidanbaran Stadium in Madras, where he scored two hundred and ten while suffering from acute gastro-enteritis. He ended up in India with three hundred and seventy-one runs at ninety-two point seven five, and has scored four hundred and eighty-one at sixty-eight point seven one in this Ashes series. He needs only eighty-three more runs to take him to a thousand Test runs in nineteen innings. Only Bradman (thirteen), Harvey (fourteen), and Sid Barnes (seventeen), Herbie Collins and Davy Walters (each eighteen) have accomplished this feat in fewer innings.

Jones' partnership with Hughes was the most significant of the innings. They added sixty-seven runs, after Taylor (who'd added thirty-nine runs with Jones) had lost his wicket to an indiscreet heave. Throughout this series the Australians have not used their brains to collect valuable runs. Hughes cannot bat, but he held his end up, and the significance of his effort will be seen at the end of the match. Nothing is more disheartening to a team than the swift demise of its tail, and nothing is more irritating to a fielding team than stout resistance from the men down the order.

Taking the field in good spirits, the Australians at once dismissed Athey, failing to take his glove away from a bouncer, Broad, inadvisably padding-up to a straight ball, and Gatting, unluckily adjudged LBW to Reid. Merv Hughes took two of the wickets, his beer-belly wobbling. He might lend a few pounds to Reid, who lost a stone in India, though from where no-one can tell. (Tony Hancock was once appalled to hear he was expected to give a full pint of blood, complaining that he had only eight.)

Gower swished around, which is his way of playing himself in, and then began to middle the ball sweetly. Lamb punched some drives away and finally the great moment arrived: Border brought Taylor on to bowl.

His first delivery was on a good length outside the off-stump. Lamb cut at it, and bottom edged it away from the stumps. Taylor was not to be denied; a few minutes later Lamb again edged a cut, to be caught behind the wicket. Taylor, an alert bowler, jumped and punched the air as if he had scored a goal in a cup final. Remarkably he has shown no sign of nerves at finding himself playing in a huge stadium in front of nearly twenty-four thousand people. Maybe he has simply not had time to worry about it. Maybe he is simply a sane, balanced character of the sort scarcely to be found in this hurly-burly world of international cricket (though Derek Underwood was here today).

Nor did Taylor stop there. His first two balls to Botham were short and wide, and Botham cracked them to the boundary. Aha, we scribes thought, Lamb had been beginner's luck. That was the end of the over. Botham, evidently deciding to hit this whipper-snapper out of Test cricket forever, smashed his next delivery to Reid at deep mid-off, almost breaking his shins. Then he carted him over long-on to the boundary. Wellham offered some advice, presumably instructing him to persevere and not on any account to panic. In any event Taylor got his man. He did not try to bowl any faster, was not intimidated by these gigantic blows. He rolled down another off-break, Botham, on the rampage, tried to chip it to mid-wicket, misjudged the length as the ball dipped, and saw his chipped stroke end in the stomach of Marsh at forward short leg, who jubilantly clung on to it. Well, guv, you could have knocked me down with a feather. Taylor had dismissed Botham and Lamb, two men determined to strike him into the never-never. A fairy-tale had come true. The thirty-year-old man from Moree had dismissed Botham, the greatest genius in modern cricket.

Richards and Gower stroked England to the close, but everyone eagerly awaits tomorrow.

DAY THREE

Incredibly, unbelievably, the gamble worked. Peter Taylor, the unheralded off-spinner, whose selection had been greeted with headlines saying 'Peter who?' has bowled England out.

Taylor took six wickets for seventy-eight runs, including those of Lamb, Gower, Botham and Emburey. In part this was a fluke. Taylor was bowling on a turning pitch, a rare luxury in Test cricket these days, and all his wickets were taken when the batsmen played erratic shots, a second unusual event in Test cricket. Nevertheless this was a splendid piece of bowling by Taylor, who with his high arm was able to flight and bounce the ball. At the end of the day spectators were again asking why it was that this man, in a time of limited spin resources, had only played six games for New South Wales. They might also, had they known, have wondered why Steve Whitfield, Taylor's spinning partner at the Northern Districts club in Sydney, had not played at all. Taylor says that Whitfield is the best spin bowler in Australia, and having batted against him, I can support his opinion. Yet Whitfield is thirty-six, and though he has been in the Shield squad, he has not played in a single Shield game.

Probably England did take Taylor too lightly. Botham had tried to hit him off his length yesterday and had failed. Taylor is inexperienced at this level, but he is not young in the craft of spin bowling. This morning he dismissed Gower, who played one of those dreamy off-drives that signify he is content to be a minor batting genius, happy enough to tootle along in his sports car, sipping champagne, like some latter-day Percy Fender. The ball to Gower did dip, falling short of his foot as he moved in to drive, but it was a careless stroke.

At this point England had sunk to 6/232, and were in peril of giving a handsome lead to Australia. Then Emburey joined Richards, and the two hard-headed men of London (actually Richards was born in Cornwall, but he has some cockney characteristics) began to repair England's innings. Richards, a twittering, nervous wreck in Brisbane, has been one of the revelations of this remarkable winter, 'keeping splendidly in Melbourne and batting with astonishing fortitude in Perth. Here he was resolute, defiantly cracking boundaries through the covers whenever Taylor dropped short and wide. Emburey, England's vice-captain, chose the right shots to play; awkward as ever, he collected some runs. He says he loses his wicket when he goes beyond his frugal range of strokes (a sweep, a block, an off-drive and a second sweep) and so he rejects ventures into the unknown. He is by no means a copy-book player, unless the copy-book was written in some rude fish market in the back streets of London.

These two practical fellows added seventy-one runs, to Australia's immense frustration. Sleep, Border's second amateur spin bowler, still on leave from his council job in Adelaide, did not pitch his leg-spinners accurately enough to trouble the batsmen, as they rebuilt England's reply, and there was nothing much in the pitch for the faster men. England lost another wicket only when Richards drove to Wellham, who had been positioned square of the wicket to cut off Richard's favourite shot. This was good captaincy by Border, who has begun to be aware of batsmen's strengths and weaknesses, has begun to realise the need to winkle batsmen out when he is otherwise stuck.

After that England lost wickets regularly, as batsmen struck out at Taylor. Edmonds edged to square leg, Small played some exotic shots, in partnership with Emburey, and then missed a heave, and finally Emburey's alert resistance ended when he hit across the line and was bowled. Taylor left the field in front of his colleagues, near to tears. His career, his years in obscurity, his years without much hope or ambition, had taken an unexpected turn. It was all difficult to adjust to, even for so sane a man.

Curiously Taylor did bring a sense of maturity to this Australian eleven. In Melbourne and Perth spectators had to endure silly antics from McDermott and Zoehrer. Upon taking a wicket McDermott grimaced, punched the air, pointed to the pavillion and appeared to shout like some Sioux Indian at a war dance. Zoehrer was foolish in Melbourne (greeting Edmonds with vulgar remarks) and petulant in Perth, where he exchanged words with Pakistan's Qasim Omar on the subject of a drink of water being sipped by a Pakistani tail-ender. Unnecessary deeds such as these had marked Australian cricket ten years earlier, and Border has done much (as have Gower and Gatting for England) to discourage them. Players had kicked one another, men had been run out for backing up too far, and slowly the lie had been perpetuated that success on the field demanded arrogance and vitriol. Despite the many impressive heroes which sports have bestowed upon us, excuses had been offered whenever a crude, adolescent sportsman had a tantrum. Border has done cricket a great service by not spitting or snarling, by not railing about umpires or shrieking about bad luck. He has blamed no-one but himself and his colleagues for losing this series. His conduct on the field has not suffered, and he had brought no indignity upon the game. Marsh, Waugh and Reid are others who have played cricket with fierce spirit and in disciplined manner. They seem to have managed perfectly well.

This Australian team is not hyped up, is not as subversively aggressive as some of its predecessors. Taylor fits into this new pattern. He appears composed and intelligent on the field, as if he is blessed with an astute cricket brain. He is a responsible cricketer, a reliable elder, a man to whom Border can turn. For once, Border is not surrounded by hysterical young men but by mature adults.

In the field he can take advice from Marsh and Wellham. If Border can merge these thoughtful cricketers with his lean and hungry men (Jones is of the type feared by Julius Caesar) he can form a team that is tougher than those of 1985 and 1986. Slowly, this summer, he has lost his portly cricketers, soft in belly and in mind, and slowly he must lose his more immature players, as they decline. He could include Veletta, Dyer and MacLeay to give Australia, at last, a team capable of thinking and playing hard, rather than impersonating an idle masculinity posing as aggression.

Australia quickly lost Ritchie and Marsh in its second innings. Marsh has failed in the last two Test matches, unsurprisingly so after the reserves of concentration he drew upon in the first three. Border marched to the crease with the score standing at 2/31 and his team wobbling. He began aggressively, tackling Dilley, carrying on a personal battle that began in Adelaide. He smashed him to cover, pulled him square and cut him to the fence. After each blow he chided him, stirring him up, urging him to bowl faster. Dilley responded with a bouncer, and Border contemptuously rounded on him, saying faster please, faster.

He hit Dilley out of the attack, and the spearhead left the field in some distress, with Border still teasing him. This was the stuff of Test cricket, fierce duels, one man trying to goad, to upset, to destroy his rival. Border ended with thirty-eight vivid runs, scored off fifty-eight balls.

Dean Jones' second innings was, in its way, no less impressive than his first effort. Runs did not come easily to him, so he was prepared to defend his wicket, to support his captain rather than to try and outshine him. He scored only six runs in seventy-nine minutes, a humble effort after so brilliant an innings on Saturday, and in doing so showed that the had reached a fresh maturity. He did not play yesterday's innings today, but fought for his team, proving his right to be regarded as a responsible cricketer.

DAY FOUR

A tenacious partnership by Waugh and Peter Taylor (oh yes, he can bat too) gave Australia a wonderful chance of ending the series on a high note. England has to score three hundred and twenty runs to win, a feat she has achieved only once before in six hundred and thirty-three Test matches (at Melbourne in 1929).

After Border had been beaten by Edmonds, lying back to cut and being surprised by the spin (a rare failure to pick the correct stroke by Australia's master batsman) Australia collapsed, losing wickets and losing the momentum gained by a bright start to the morning's cricket. Jones was caught behind, cutting at a ball too close to him, trying too hard to press for runs. Wellham was given out caught at silly point, a decision with which neither he nor the cameras entirely agreed. Sitting in the sun a hundred yards away I thought he had hit the ball. Television replays and batsmen's reactions are not to be relied upon (nor are my eyes infallible). Moreover some batsmen are better than others at creating the impression of bad luck, without actually doing anything so bold as dissenting from a decision.

Zoehrer was caught on the back foot by Emburey, which left Australia, their first innings advantage thrown away, at 7/145. Waugh had already been missed by Richards, a stumping chance off Edmonds, and it was he, with Taylor as his partner, who gave Australia its chance. Waugh used his feet to the spinners, forcing Edmonds and Emburey to send a man back on to the straight boundary, rather prematurely I thought because this gave Waugh the opportunity to pick up singles at will.

Taylor adopted some good old-fashioned techniques to deal with the turning ball, thrusting his front foot down the pitch and using his bat only when absolutely necessary. He hit only one boundary in one hundred and sixty minutes of resistance, collecting his runs in hurried singles or from occasional, uncomplicated thumps off the back foot, and sweeps to backward square leg.

England toiled in the field, on a blisteringly hot day which reduced the vigour of the bowlers. Edmonds bowled thirty-two overs and Emburey thirty-nine, wrapping their fingers around the ball, trying to get it to bite from the pitch. Emburey has not been at his best since Brisbane, but he returned to form here.

His action recovered its smoothness as he wheeled away, as if the sun were oiling his joints and the heat jolting his memory. He's worked hard throughout the tour to amend his faults, re-examining his game, and here he received his reward.

Edmonds has bowled well from the start. He is far more content these days to graft for his wickets rather than to imagine himself wearing a turban and, imperiously, dismissing batsmen with deceptive, devious deliveries. Apparently he talked to a sports psychologist a year ago, who told him to examine his game critically, to assess its strengths and its weaknesses, and to stop pandering to his image of himself as a haughty genius. He has followed this advice, realising that he was hit too often in certain directions, and he's bowled much better ever since. He did not take many wickets here, but he kept the pressure on and helped Emburey diddle the batsmen out, both before and after the game's latest magnificent late-order partnership.

Emburey did indeed diddle out the tail, giving him a career best 7/78 to add to his effective innings yesterday. These efforts were the more remarkable because he has been hobbling thoughout the last two days, having pinched a nerve in his groin. He was practically immobile in the field and yet bowled his overs, did not desert the ship.

At the close England has lost the tiring Broad (he, too, may be running out of steam) to a soft catch to the bowler Sleep (nickname Sounda), at which Gower joined Athey. Presumably he was promoted in the order because of his dislike for spinners, and his gift for dominating the fast bowlers.

These two held firm till the close, leaving a splendid cricket match evenly balanced. The game has restored faith in Test cricket, after the banalities of Adelaide, and Australia's foolhardiness in Melbourne. It has turned this way and that, defying prediction. Whatever happens tomorrow a lot of good will come of this game.

It'd probably be best if Australia were victorious. They won the Davis Cup, Greg Norman is going like a tornado, and the yachtsmen are going like the wind. Australian cricket could do with a victory or two in the second half of this season.

Australia does in fact usually win in Sydney. Two years ago they beat the West Indians here, with Murray Bennett and Bob Holland bowling them to victory, whereupon hats were thrown in the air and hasty talk of revival began (Australia's opening batsmen in that game were Wessels and Hilditch). A year ago New Zealand were beaten here, as David Hookes and Simon O'Donnell hit the winning runs. A month later the Indians were held to a draw. Both these misleading results were treated as signs of imminent revival, cheering followers through a winter of grunts and groans, giving them hope. Unfortunately they were false hopes, and by the beginning of the following season the Australian selectors were once again thrashing around like salmon on the end of a hook (how clever of Greg Chappell to find Peter Taylor swimming in his pool).

For despite those victories Australia was still in the dumps at the start of the 1986–7 season, still battling for the wooden spoon with the men from Sri Lanka, all of whom appear to be called De Silva (and all of whom are nicknamed 'Lock-up'). If Australia win tomorrow there will be more talk of a revival. This one may be built upon more solid foundations; Waugh, Reid, Jones, Marsh and Taylor will improve, whereas Hookes and Holland were past their best even as they trooped victoriously from the field.

Tomorrow's cricket, the last of this series, might be the most avidly contested of the season. This is the delight of Test cricket. Spectators can watch the rejuvenation of one team and the gradual reformation of the other.

DAY FIVE

This match will go down in the record book, quite rightly, as Taylor's match. For all eternity Wisden will record that on his Test debut Taylor, almost unkown a week ago, took eight wickets for one hundred and fifty-four, and scored fifty-three runs, to give Australia a rare victory. It is lovely that such things can still happen.

In fact he did not bowl particularly well today, a point he made in his press conference afterwards. The conference was a touching occasion, as Taylor hugged a variety of ladies ('they can't all be his wife' said one hard-bitten journalist) who turned out to be his sisters. He was near to tears, and said that his entire family had been present at the game throughout, and that they numbered about ten all told. There are still, in this world, corners of romance.

It was a wonderful day's cricket, which see-sawed till the final ball of the penultimate over. It began with Athey and Gower defending stoutly as Reid (unlucky as on so many previous occasions) and Taylor fought for a break-through. They survived nearly till lunch, taking England carefully to 1/91, a platform from which an assault could be launched. In desperation, with Taylor, his arm lowering, not used to the wear and tear of five-day cricket, let alone its drain of the emotions, and Sleep unable to pitch his leg-

201

break reliably, Border brought himself on to bowl. Almost at once Gower lost his wicket, negligently turning an innocuous delivery into the hands of short-leg; 2/91. Next Athey swept at Sleep, failed to cover the line of the ball with his pads and was bowled leg-stump; 3/91. In a couple of overs the game had turned another way. Lunch was taken with Lamb and Gatting at the crease.

Soon after, with the spinners on, England lost two further wickets. Lamb was caught at silly point off Taylor and once again it was hard, from the boundary's edge, to know if he'd hit the ball or not; 4/101. In marched Botham to play his last overseas Test innings for three years, perhaps his last ever. He swung his arms hugely, intent upon fulfilling his prophecy that he'd go out blasting. He took guard and surveyed the field, studying the deep as if the men around him were of no consequence. Taylor, the novice from the north of Sydney, ran in to bowl with his springy, bubbly stride. His first ball was short; Botham shaped to turn it to mid-wicket for a single. It bounced and hurried on to him, deviating to his hip. Instead of guiding it he chipped it – into the air, the ball striking the leading edge of his bat. For a moment it hung in the air, and time appeared to stop. Then Wellham, the sharpest of the fieldsmen, darted forward, dived, thrust his hands under the ball and caught it. At once the Australians chased towards him. Botham stood transfixed, not so much uncertain of the catch, as stunned by his dismissal. The umpire raised his figure, and Botham trudged from the Test match arena. As he passed Gatting, his rival, captain, and colleague, he shrugged as if to say 'oh well, that's the way it goes'. I'd fixed Botham in my binoculars, interested in his reactions; he left the field still in a state of shock, as if he'd been dismissed, yet nothing had really happened; as if the whole transaction had been unreal.

In the dressing room he muttered that he should have hit the ruddy long-hop down the road to Bondi Beach. He doesn't change. He passed a similar remark after stroking a gentle catch in his first innings in county cricket.

England were now 5/102 and apparently doomed. The next wicket did not fall for three hours, during which time Gatting and Richards added a hundred and thirty-one, taking England to within eighty-seven runs of a remarkable victory. Gatting had fallen for a duck in the first innings. Here he set about the spinners, pulling Sleep and showing for Taylor the contempt he reserves for off-spinners in general. Richards was trenchant and busy, and in the press-box Jack Bannister was beginning to take bets on an England victory. Entering the last twenty overs, ninety odd runs were needed, and Australia had to take five wickets to record its first victory in fourteen Test matches, an apparently hopeless task.

Gatting and Richards coasted to two overs and then Border, in desperation, threw the ball to Waugh, his first good move in a tense hour's cricket. At once Waugh caught and bowled Gatting, whose innings deserved a century. He left the field nonplussed, disappointed at his failure to lead his team to victory.

Back, in the game, Australia battled on. Border called up Sleep, who had been bowling with increasing accuracy during the day. England crept to two hundred and fifty-seven, falling behind the run-rate. Then, suddenly, Richards was fooled by a rare googly from Sleep. He played outside the ball, got an inside edge and was bowled between bat and pad. Nor did Edmonds long detain the Australians. He missed a full toss and was hit on the foot. Maybe he was a trifle unlucky to be adjudged leg before. This was a difficult game for the umpires, and neither McConnell nor Randell had a particularly good match. Neither captain complained, both accepted this as the rub of the green.

Small held on for twelve overs, restraining his flamboyant strokes until, with two wickets to take in only three overs and his desperation returning, Border tossed the ball to Reid. (There'd been a committee meeting on the field, when Border had discovered that he had rather more vice-captains then he'd imagined.) This was a good move, because the spinners were not looking dangerous, particularly against Emburey, who was playing Sleep off the back foot. Reid bowled a good over, in the course of which Small edged a catch to slip. His wicket depended on whether Border squeezed his hands under the ball, or whether it brushed the grass. No-one on the ground questioned the call, and the issue was raised only by Border, in the post-match conference. The catch looked fair to me.

One wicket to take, and now there were only two overs left. Should Sleep bowl again? A second huddle took place on the square as Emburey lent on his bat, apparently unflustered. I thought Border might throw the ball to Waugh, backing the youngster's talent and temperament. He gave it to Sleep, whose first four balls included an attempted bouncer (a bright idea badly executed), and three ordinary deliveries which did not disturb Emburey. Sleep's fifth delivery was a good leg-break, which Emburey carefully smothered. For his final ball of this penultimate over Sleep decided to bank upon a flat leg-break, which might hurry Emburey. It left his hand flat, and appeared certain to drop short, allowing Emburey to stay on the back foot, as he prefers. Oddly the ball did not dive into the pitch, rather it slid sinuously forward, like a train surging into a tunnel, and then darted downward. After bouncing it jumped forwards, shooting low to the ground like a fighter in an air battle. Emburey, sensing danger, realising he'd misjudged the ball, jabbed his bat down on it, but too late. The ball had already eluded him. Appearing to speed off the pitch, it careered into the bottom of the leg-stump, whereupon a roar of released tension erupted across the ground. Players hugged and dived upon each other, Taylor and Zoehrer grabbed stumps, and the Australians led a merry dance as Emburey and Dilley walked disconsolately from the field.

It had been an excellent match, a splendid end to an interesting if not brilliant series. Both sides had improved, and maybe this time the improvement would not be deceptive, but England had won the Ashes.

Could it be only two months ago that pundits were forecasting an Australian victory in this twenty-seventh Ashes series? Those predictions were based – then – on facts. An Australian victory? It subsequently seemed far-fetched, at least till today, yet had sounded perfectly feasible eight weeks earlier. England had arrived in Australia having lost series to New Zealand and India. England had played badly in those first few State matches, while Australia had drawn in India. Yet within a couple of hours of the series beginning it was obvious that England were the better side. We imagined this was because the Australians were so weak and immature, wasting the new ball in Brisbane and in Perth. Then, a week ago, in Perth, we could see the full extent of England's achievement – of the achievement of Gatting, Peter Lush and Mickey Stewart. What is more, England beat Pakistan and the West Indies too. It was all enough to make followers wonder what on earth had been going on in English cricket these last five years.

Obviously some players had improved – notably Small – but only DeFreitas was new.

Perhaps the clue to this series, as to so many others, lay in the relationship between Botham and his captain. Gatting demanded that Botham work hard in the nets from the start of the tour. He treated him like any other player, and this time Botham's genius was incorporated into the team effort, rather than living independ-

FIFTH TEST, Sydney.
January 10, 11, 12, 14, 15, 1987.

AUSTRALIA

G. R. Marsh	c Gatting b Small	24	(2) c Emburey b Dilley	14	
G. M. Ritchie	lbw b Dilley	6	(1) c Botham b Edmonds	13	
D. M. Jones	not out	184	c Richards b Emburey	30	
A. R. Border*	c Botham b Edmonds	34	b Edmonds	49	
D. M. Wellham	c Richards b Small	17	c Lamb b Emburey	1	
S. R. Waugh	c Richards b Small	0	c Athey b Emburey	73	
P. R. Sleep	c Richards b Small	9	c Lamb b Emburey	10	
T. J. Zoehrer†	c Gatting b Small	12	lbw b Emburey	1	
P. L. Taylor	c Emburey b Edmonds	11	c Lamb b Emburey	42	
M. G. Hughes	c Botham b Edmonds	16	b Emburey	5	
B. A. Reid	b Dilley	4	not out	1	
Extras	(b 12, lb 4, w 2, nb 8)	26	(b 5, lb 7)	12	
TOTAL		343		251	

Fall of wickets: 8, 58, 149, 184, 200, 232, 271, 338.
Second innings: 29, 31, 106, 110, 115, 141, 145.
Bowling: Dilley 23.5-5-67-2; Small 33-11-75-5; Botham 23-10-42-0; Emburey 30-4-62-0; Edmonds 34-5-79-3; Gatting 1-0-2-0.
Second innings: Dilley 15-4-48-1; Small 8-2-17-0; Edmonds 43-16-79-2; Emburey 46-15-78-7; Botham 3-0-17-0; Gatting 2-2-0-0.

ENGLAND

B. C. Broad	lbw b Hughes	6	c and b Sleep	17	
C. W. J. Athey	c Zoehrer b Hughes	5	b Sleep	31	
M. W. Gatting*	lbw b Reid	0	(5) c and b Waugh	96	
A. J. Lamb	c Zoehrer b Taylor	24	c Waugh b Taylor	3	
D. I. Gower	c Wellham b Taylor	72	(3) c Marsh b Border	37	
I. T. Botham	c Marsh b Taylor	16	c Wellham b Taylor	0	
C. J. Richards†	c Wellham b Reid	46	b Sleep	38	
J. E. Emburey	b Taylor	69	b Sleep	22	
P. H. Edmonds	c Marsh b Taylor	3	lbw b Sleep	0	
G. C. Small	b Taylor	14	c Border b Reid	0	
G. R. Dilley	not out	4	not out	2	
Extras	(b 9, lb 3, w 2, nb 2)	16	(b 8, lb 6, w 1, nb 3)	18	
TOTAL		275		264	

Fall of wickets: 16, 17, 17, 89, 119, 142, 213, 219, 270.
Second innings: 24, 91, 91, 102, 102, 233, 257, 257, 262.
Bowling: Hughes 16-3-58-2; Reid 25-7-74-2; Waugh 6-4-6-0; Taylor 26-7-78-6; Sleep 21-6-47-0.
Second innings: Hughes 12-3-32-0; Reid 19-8-32-1; Taylor 29-10-76-2; Sleep 35-14-72-5; Border 13-6-25-1; Waugh 6-2-13-1.
Toss: Australia.
Man of the Match: P. L. Taylor.
Umpires: P. J. McConnell and S. G. Randell.
AUSTRALIA WON BY 55 RUNS.

ently of it. If this is correct then Gatting deserves the congratulations of every English cricketer, for having handled Botham better than any other previous tour captain. That he could do this was probably because of the unspoken, scarcely acknowledged friction between these two men who rose together, as the hopes of English cricket, in 1977. Maybe, at last, it is not Botham and Gatting, but Gatting and Botham.

Appendix

AUSTRALIA v. ENGLAND 1986–87 TEST AVERAGES

Compiled by Richard Lockwood of **The Cricketer.**

E N G L A N D

Batting and Fielding

	M	I	NO	R	HS	A	100	50	ct	st
B. C .Broad	5	9	2	487	162	69.57	3	—	5	—
D. I. Gower	5	8	1	404	136	57.71	1	2	1	—
M. W. Gatting	5	9	0	393	100	43.66	1	3	5	—
C. J. Richards	5	7	0	264	133	37.71	1	—	15	1
J. E. Emburey	5	7	2	179	69	35.80	—	1	3	—
C. W. J. Athey	5	9	0	303	96	33.66	—	3	3	—
I. T. Botham	4	6	0	189	138	31.50	1	—	10	—
P. A. J. DeFreitas	4	5	1	77	40	19.25	—	—	1	—
A. J. Lamb	5	9	1	144	43	18.00	—	—	6	—
G. C. Small	2	3	1	35	21*	17.50	—	—	1	—
P. H. Edmonds	5	5	1	44	19	11.00	—	—	2	—
J. J. Whitaker	1	1	0	11	11	11.00	—	—	1	—
G. R. Dilley	4	4	2	6	4*	3.00	—	—	1	—

Bowling

	O	M	R	W	A	BB	5I	10M
G. C. Small	78.4	23	180	12	15.00	5-48	2	—
G. R. Dilley	176.1	38	511	16	31.93	5-68	1	—
I. T. Botham	106.2	24	296	9	32.88	5-41	1	—
P. H. Edmonds	261.4	78	538	15	35.86	3-45	—	—
J. E. Emburey	315.5	86	663	18	36.83	7-78	2	—
P. A. J. DeFreitas	141.4	24	446	9	49.55	3-62	—	—
M. W .Gatting	23	7	39	0	—	—	—	—
A. J. Lamb	1	1	0	0	—	—	—	—

207

AUSTRALIA

Batting and Fielding

	M	I	NO	R	HS	A	100	50	ct	st
D. M. Jones	5	10	1	511	184*	56.77	1	3	1	—
G. R. J. Matthews	4	7	3	215	73*	53.75	—	2	6	—
A. R. Border	5	10	1	473	125	52.55	2	1	4	—
S. R. Waugh	5	8	1	310	79*	44.28	—	3	8	—
G. R. Marsh	5	10	0	429	110	42.90	1	2	5	—
G. M. Ritchie	4	8	2	244	46*	40.66	—	—	1	—
P. L. Taylor	1	2	0	53	42	26.50	—	—	—	—
D. C. Boon	4	8	0	144	103	18.00	1	—	1	—
T. J. Zoehrer	4	7	1	102	38	17.00	—	—	10	—
G. F. Lawson	1	1	0	13	13	13.00	—	—	1	—
D. M. Wellham	1	2	0	18	17	9.00	—	—	3	—
C. D. Matthews	2	3	0	21	11	7.00	—	—	1	—
P. R. Sleep	3	4	0	25	10	6.25	—	—	1	—
M. G. Hughes	4	6	0	31	16	5.16	—	—	2	—
B. A. Reid	5	7	4	14	4	4.66	—	—	—	—
C. J. McDermott	1	2	0	1	1	0.50	—	—	1	—
G. C. Dyer	1	—	—	—	—	—	—	—	2	—

Bowling

	O	M	R	W	A	BB	5I	10M
P. L. Taylor	55	17	154	8	19.25	6-78	1	—
C. J. McDermott	26.5	4	83	4	20.75	4-83	—	—
B. A. Reid	198.4	44	527	20	26.35	4-64	—	—
P. R. Sleep	136	43	316	10	31.60	5-72	1	—
A. R. Border	16	6	32	1	32.00	1-25	—	—
S. R. Waugh	108.3	26	336	10	33.60	5-69	1	—
C. D. Matthews	70.1	14	233	6	38.83	3-95	—	—
M. G. Hughes	136.3	26	444	10	44.40	3-134	—	—
G. R. J. Matthews	83	11	295	2	147.50	1-10	—	—
G. F. Lawson	50	9	170	0	—	—	—	—

FINAL TOUR AVERAGES

Batting and Fielding

	M	I	NO	R	HS	A	100	50	ct	st
N. A. Foster	4	6	2	172	74*	43.00	—	1	4	—
B. C. Broad	10	18	2	679	162	42.43	3	1	7	—
I. T. Botham	8	14	2	481	138	40.08	1	2	11	—
B. N. French	3	5	2	113	58	37.66	—	1	9	1
D. I. Gower	9	16	2	508	136	36.28	1	2	4	—
A. J. Lamb	10	18	1	534	105	31.41	1	3	11	—
J. J. Whitaker	5	7	0	214	108	30.57	1	—	2	—
M. W. Gatting	10	18	0	520	100	28.88	1	3	11	—
C. W. J. Athey	9	16	1	422	96	28.13	—	4	7	—
C. J. Richards	9	14	1	335	133	25.76	1	—	25	3
J. E. Emburey	9	14	3	279	69	25.36	—	1	6	—
W. N. Slack	5	9	0	184	89	20.44	—	1	5	—
P. A. J. DeFreitas	7	10	2	130	40	16.25	—	—	1	—
G. R. Dilley	6	6	3	39	32	13.00	—	—	1	—
G. C. Small	8	11	3	100	26	12.50	—	—	4	—
P. H. Edmonds	9	10	2	95	27	11.87	—	—	7	—

Bowling

	O	M	R	W	A	BB	5I	10M
G. C. Small	258.4	72	626	33	18.96	5-48	3	—
M. W. Gatting	92	27	195	9	21.66	4-31	—	—
N. A. Foster	149	40	352	16	22.00	4-20	—	—
I. T. Botham	182.1	41	496	18	27.55	5-41	1	—
G. R. Dilley	231.1	44	685	21	32.61	5-68	1	—
J. E. Emburey	463.5	131	1 023	31	33.00	7-78	3	—
P. A. J. DeFreitas	239	43	754	22	34.27	4-44	—	—
P. H. Edmonds	428.4	122	929	25	37.16	3-37	—	—
C. W. J. Athey	4	0	25	0	—	—	—	—
A. J. Lamb	1	1	0	0	—	—	—	—

STATE MATCHES

England XI 135 and 339 lost to *Queensland* 311 for 7 dec and 164 for 5 by five wickets.
South Australia 305 for 8 and 269 lost to *England XI* 407 and 169 for 5 by five wickets.
Western Australia 275 and 207 for 8 dec drew with *England XI* 152 and 153 for 6.
England XI 197 and 82 lost to *New South Wales* 181 and 99 for 2 by eight wickets.
Victoria 101 and 345 lost to *England XI* 263 and 184 for 5 by five wickets.
Tasmania 79 and 167 lost to *England XI* 342 for 9 dec by an innings and 96 runs.

BEST PERFORMANCES ON TOUR

Hundreds (9)

3	B. C. Broad	162 v Australia (2nd Test) at Perth
		116 v Australia (3rd Test) at Adelaide
		112 v Australia (4th Test) at Melbourne
1	I. T. Botham	138 v Australia (1st Test) at Brisbane
	M. W. Gatting	100 v Australia (3rd Test) at Adelaide
	D. I. Gower	136 v Australia (2nd Test) at Perth
	A. J. Lamb	105 v South Australia at Adelaide
	C. J. Richards	133 v Australia (2nd Test) at Perth
	J. J. Whitaker	108 v South Australia at Adelaide

Five or more wickets in an innings (8)

3	J. E. Emburey	6-102 v South Australia at Adelaide
		5-80 v Australia (1st Test) at Brisbane
		7-78 v Australia (5th Test) at Sydney
	G. C. Small	5-81 v Victoria at Melbourne
		5-48 v Australia (4th Test) at Melbourne
		5-75 v Australia (5th Test) at Sydney
1	I. T. Botham	5-41 v Australia (4th Test) at Melbourne
	G. R. Dilley	5-68 v Australia (1st Test) at Brisbane